MULTISYSTEMIC THERAPY
AND NEIGHBORHOOD PARTNERSHIPS

MULTISYSTEMIC THERAPY AND NEIGHBORHOOD PARTNERSHIPS

Reducing Adolescent Violence and Substance Abuse

Cynthia Cupit Swenson
Scott W. Henggeler
Ida S. Taylor
Oliver W. Addison

Foreword by Patricia Chamberlain

THE GUILFORD PRESS
New York   London

© 2005 The Guilford Press
A Division of Guilford Publications, Inc.
72 Spring Street, New York, NY 10012
www.guilford.com

Printed in the United States of America

This book is printed on acid-free paper.

Last digit is print number: 9 8 7 6 5 4 3 2 1

Library of Congress Cataloging-in-Publication Data

Multisystemic therapy and neighborhood partnerships: reducing adolescent
violence and substance abuse / Cynthia Cupit Swenson . . . [et al.].
    p. cm.
  Includes bibliographical references and index.
  ISBN 1-59385-109-X (hardcover: alk. paper)
  1. Juvenile delinquents—Mental health services—United States. 2. Juvenile
delinquency—Treatment—United States. 3. Conduct disorders in adolescence—
Treatment—United States. 4. Violence in adolescence—United States—
Prevention. 5. Teenagers—Drug use—United States—Prevention. 6. Youth—
Drug use—United States—Prevention. 7. Adolescent psychotherapy—Parent
participation—United States. 8. Combined modality therapy—United
States. 9. Community development—United States. I. Swenson, Cynthia
Cupit.
  RJ506.J88M84 2005
  362.2'0425'083—dc22

                                                              2004022183

This book is dedicated to the memory of O. Roscoe "Mitch" Mitchell—the man, the husband, the father, the grandfather, the politician, and the community advocate. Roscoe believed that anything is possible; if you want something to happen, you can make it work. This is why the Union Heights community was able to achieve the level of respect that it currently holds. Roscoe never asked for anything for himself. He only wanted to ensure that the people of the community were provided for. Anyone who needed help would seek out Roscoe, and he would find a way to help—no matter what time, day or night. Roscoe was a friend to anyone who needed or wanted a friend. He was the mentor and guide of the Neighborhood Solutions Project, and he taught more than can ever be learned from any book. Although we lost him way too early, his "Roscoeisms," infectious laugh, and life teachings continue on in our hearts and minds.

About the Authors

Cynthia Cupit Swenson received her PhD in clinical psychology from Florida State University in 1991 and completed a postdoctoral fellowship in child clinical and pediatric psychology at the Medical University of South Carolina (MUSC). Dr. Swenson is Associate Professor and Associate Director of the Family Services Research Center in the Department of Psychiatry and Behavioral Sciences at MUSC. She has conducted extensive clinical work with children and families over the past 24 years and is Principal Investigator on a randomized clinical trial, funded by the National Institute of Mental Health, comparing parent training to multisystemic therapy with physically abused adolescents and their families. Dr. Swenson has published many journal articles and book chapters and a recent book on treatment of physically abused children and their families. She is currently on the board of the American Professional Society on the Abuse of Children.

Scott W. Henggeler received his PhD in clinical psychology from the University of Virginia in 1977. He is Professor of Psychiatry and Behavioral Sciences at the Medical University of South Carolina and Director of the Family Services Research Center (FSRC). The mission of the FSRC is to develop, validate, and study the dissemination of clinically effective and cost-effective mental health and substance abuse services for children presenting serious clinical problems and their families. FSRC projects include numerous community-based randomized trials with challenging clinical populations (e.g., violent and chronic juvenile offenders, youth presenting psychiatric emergencies, substance-abusing juvenile offenders, maltreating families) and dissemination studies for multisystemic therapy and other evidence-based treatments being conducted in multiple states and nations. The FSRC has received the Annie E. Casey Families Count Award and the

Points of Light Foundation President's Award. Dr. Henggeler is on the editorial boards of nine journals; has published more than 200 journal articles, book chapters, and books; and is the recipient of numerous grants.

Ida S. Taylor completed an associate's degree in commercial graphics at Trident Technical College in Charleston, South Carolina. She is currently employed by the North Charleston Recreation Department and serves as Director of Gethsemani Community Center located in the Union Heights community. A leader in Union Heights for over 20 years, Mrs. Taylor is a member of Noah's Ark Baptist Church and serves on the Usher Board. She is involved in community service through participation on a Weed and Seed Steering Committee and is a 4-H volunteer coordinator. She received a community service award from the Medical University of South Carolina for her work in bringing a health clinic to the Union Heights community and developing programs for youth. The Girl Scouts of America recently recognized Mrs. Taylor as a member of the select group of Women of Distinction.

Oliver W. Addison attended Palmer College and Trident Technical College in Charleston and studied accounting, industrial health and safety, and automobile mechanics. He worked for Norfolk Southern Railroad for a total of 28 years, 12 of them as a switchman and conductor and 16 as General Yard Master. He was awarded for having the safest terminal on the railroad in its size category and received accolades for on-time service for the industry. Mr. Addison has been a leader in Union Heights for 38 years and served on the Community Council for over 20 years. He recently received a commendation from the Medical University of South Carolina for his work in bringing a health clinic to the Union Heights community and developing programs for youth. Mr. Addison served on the Charleston County School Board for 8 years and was the board's chair for 1995–1996 and 2001–2002. For his work on the school board, he received a high-profile award from the *Post and Courier* newspaper.

Foreword

A key question these days is whether evidence-based treatment models for youth and families can make a difference in "real" communities. Evidence-based interventions have typically been developed within the context of carefully controlled research studies. Even though many of these studies have enrolled participants from "real-world" community service systems, such as juvenile justice departments, schools, or child welfare, it is unclear if and how they can be made to fit into communities that might be very different from the ones in which they were originally developed. The researchers who have developed these models are typically very concerned about ensuring fidelity of implementation. This is because poor fidelity results in poor outcomes. Studies have shown that if the evidence-based models are changed too much even for good reasons, such as improving the ease with which they fit into practice, they do not work as well (or even at all) in terms of producing positive outcomes.

Community leaders and policymakers considering implementing evidence-based treatments are rightly concerned about being constrained or pushed into methods that might have worked well in the research laboratory but could be irrelevant or even harmful for their particular community. This is especially a problem in places where there is a strong sense of culture and the community members have their own ways of doing things that are rooted in well-established values, traditions, and history. This book is about how a partnership was developed and built between researchers and community members who worked together to create a collaboration that captured the best of both of these worlds (i.e., the strengths of both the science base and the community base).

Since the late 1990s, there has been little doubt that the treatments aimed at improving conduct problems in children and adolescents have progressed rapidly. Strong evidence shows that an increasing number of interventions and prevention programs consistently produce positive outcomes that have long-lasting effects. This progress has prompted decision and policymakers, advocacy groups, funding agencies, and professional organizations to become increasingly interested in the accountability of the services that they endorse. The emerging standard in the United States now requires that the services that communities offer to children and families be grounded in scientific evidence whenever possible. Unfortunately, there are still a number of child and adolescent problems and disorders that are under-researched and for which evidence-based interventions are not yet available. This is not the case, however, for children and adolescents with conduct problems and delinquency. Here, a number of well-researched treatment approaches have shown strong positive enduring effects (although certainly some gaps remain and further improvements in outcomes are needed).

The multisystemic therapy (MST) model has been at the forefront of these effective treatments. Henggeler and his colleagues (Charles Borduin, Sonja Schoenwald, Phillippe Cunningham, Melisa Rowland, Jeff Randall, and Cynthia Swenson) have been instrumental in igniting the evidence-based movement. With their tireless focus on achieving positive outcomes and on using time-limited, cost-efficient methods, they have raised the standard for community-based service delivery. In this book, they take things a step further. Not only do they meet families on their own terms, mapping onto their goals and strengths; they also work together with the existing community forces to energize the entire neighborhood to create a rich array of activities and annual events that fit into the community's unique character, needs, and wants. Underlying all of this are the strong values that the MST team and the community share. Youth can do well if provided with positive opportunities, structure, and guidance. Families are inherently capable, willing, and responsible. People from all walks of life in the community can play a part in creating a vital and supportive neighborhood. What the MST team and the Union Heights community members illustrate here is how widespread, meaningful, and sustainable community-level change can be.

This book tells a story of collaboration and building capacity in the context of partnerships. The partnerships are with community leaders, health professionals, police, and community members from all walks of life. It is a story of the establishment of mutual sensitivities that cross cultural barriers and get down to the business of focusing on improving the daily experiences and opportunities for children, teenagers, families, and elders. It is a story that lays out the broad hope that what happened in Union Heights can be a model that shows researchers and communities a way to coalesce and leverage their resources. This book provides a clear example of how to fulfill the promise that the evidence-based movement makes.

PATRICIA CHAMBERLAIN, PHD
Oregon Social Learning Center

Preface

We are pleased to present this volume to clinicians, academics, policy-makers, community developers, and citizens in any neighborhood concerned about its youth. For mental health professionals, the book is a "how-to" guide for the implementation of multisystemic therapy and other evidence-based practices within a community context. For law enforcement officers, steps are provided for implementing community-policing strategies. For nurses and other health care providers, we outline steps for implementing neighborhood-based health care and outreach. For funders or persons seeking funding, strategies are reviewed for grant writing, fundraising, and creating a nonprofit company to sustain neighborhood gains.

For researchers and program developers, this book is a guide for developing a collaborative process, joining with the people, and planning and implementing programs that meet the goals of a variety of stakeholders. Finally, for citizens who are looking for solutions to violence and crime in their own neighborhoods, we provide many in-depth examples of neighborhood-based violence prevention activities.

The model we describe, "Neighborhood Solutions," goes beyond traditional ideas of behavior change to implement a broad-based model of citizen and professional collaboration to effect neighborhood-wide change. The specific project we use as illustrative material throughout the book developed as a collaboration between professionals and residents of a troubled neighborhood. The residents identified youth criminal activity, substance abuse, and school behavior problems as the most pressing problems affecting families and the quality of life in their neighborhood. In collaboration with the professionals, the neighborhood residents developed and implemented an array of intervention and health-promoting activities that greatly improved the quality of life for children, adolescents, and their families in the neighborhood. Moreover, the collaboration taught the professionals many lessons that we have done our best to convey in this volume.

Acknowledgments

The project on which this book is based began with the vision of Gwen Power, former director of an agency of the State of South Carolina. This vision led us to come together as a group and, through the people of a neighborhood, make a significant, positive change. We thank her for her vision, guidance, and commitment to children growing up in safe neighborhoods with their families. We gratefully acknowledge the work of Debbie Francis, formerly of the same agency, and we applaud and appreciate the commitment of these two women to evidence-based practice in mental health treatment.

As we consider the people involved in this project in one way or another, the list is massive. Many people had a hand in the building, teaching, and learning. We would like to give our most sincere thanks to all of the children, youth, adults, and families in Union Heights, Howard Heights, and Windsor Place who allowed us into your homes and hearts to "school" us. You taught us words we never knew existed, opened our eyes to a culture we were missing, taught us to be humble by example and strong by your grace. You welcomed us in as family, understanding our differences but not allowing them to be a barrier to our work. You rolled up your sleeves, and we had a great time working alongside you, celebrating the successes of the children, raising them as if we were all their parents together—indeed, it does take a village.

The leadership of the Union Heights Community Council at the time of the Project was composed of forward-thinking visionaries who were totally committed to their neighborhood. They were Roscoe Mitchell, Mr. Washington, Rosalee Benekin, Ida Taylor, Isaac President, Oliver Addison, and Elizabeth Addison. We thank them for teaching us, walking the streets with us, keeping us safe, and helping us get past the label of "off-brand people," so that together we could get down to the business of helping children. They truly were equal partners.

Rarely in life does one find drawn together in one place a group of fantastic individuals with a strong commitment to making a difference. In the Neighborhood Solutions Project, we had such an experience. Foremost, we thank Dr. Jeff Randall for his contributions to the project and neighborhood. We appreciate his true MST spirit of doing "whatever it takes." We thank Dr. Sonja Schoenwald for her input in the early days of the project. The community leaders selected the project staff based on their knowledge of the kind of people who would fit in with the community. Although some of the staff were not with us during the entire project, the time they gave us impacted us and left us with a feeling of "family" about them. We express our gratitude to the clinical staff: Coordinator Sarah Edwards; therapists Cynthia Buist, Beth Cunningham, Kristi Macchia, Jay Middleton, and Lee Ann Walters; Activity Director Paul Campbell; Terese Shelton; Family Resource Specialist Stephanie Ramsey; and research staff members Pam Burke, Joe Cunningham, Tony Joyner, Jennifer Kline, and Jennifer Krist.

From the Medical University of South Carolina, we thank President Ray Greenberg, Dr. Carolyn Jenkins, Bernadette Pinckney, and the many nursing students and staff who supported us. We thank the Medical University psychology interns who over the years of the project came through our doors, made a contribution of themselves, and have gone on to be clinical psychologists: Dr. Matt Gray, Dr. Laura Eckhardt Williams, Dr. Kristie Hardie, Dr. Patrick Duffy, Dr. Sonya Batten, and Dr. Ken Ruggerio.

From the City of North Charleston, we greatly appreciate the support of Mayor Keith Summey, Shannon Praete, and James Bell. And from the North Charleston Recreation Department, we are indebted to Director Ed Barfield and supervisor Elizabeth Addison. They supported our activities and provided a community center that was the hub of community activity.

From the courts, we extend a special thanks to Judge F. P. Segars-Andrews and Mr. Julius Scott, who worked closely with our youth through the Charleston County Drug Court. We also greatly appreciate the support of other family court judges, criminal court judges, and magistrates in Charleston and North Charleston. From the Department of Juvenile Justice, we are grateful for the support of director Diana Vaughn (now retired) and all of her staff who worked so closely with us.

From Charleston County School District, we thank superintendents Chip Zullinger and Ron McWhirt and the principals who worked closely with us to keep our children in school: Don Butler, Janis Burchell, Janice Malone, Tommy Mullins. We thank Ruth Harkelroad for coming out to the community to teach, and Officer Terrell Palmer and Coach Tony Eady for always going the extra mile. We thank Daphne Wright for her constant positive attitude, superb teaching of the GED, and sharing her many creative ideas for nontraditional teaching.

From law enforcement, we thank former Police Chief Chad Caldwell, who supported community policing and the many officers who helped us with safety and activities. We are especially indebted to Corporal David Laurie, Detective Donald Ward, and Sergeant Harry Roper, who were there for us no matter the time of day or night, just working to save the children.

We thank Jesse Thrower and Adande Dance Company for teaching all of us a love of African dance and drumming and helping our children find a positive path through the arts. We thank Anthony Bostic for creating the annual Black College Tour that taught our children of the possibilities of college—a concept that at one time felt foreign.

We thank Ellen Blanchard from Clemson University Extension Service and the Johnson and Wales Chef School for their support of teaching our children healthy cooking and eating. We thank Dr. Julie Lipovsky for donating her time to teach soccer and guitar. We thank Sarah Cupit for teaching Spanish and jewelry making. We thank women runners for helping us get our girls on the road: Elizabeth Martin, Kelly Gabriel, Dr. Elizabeth Letourneau, Claudia Hill, Carolyn Murray, Ann Marie Canady, and Dr. Patti Fiero. We thank Mike Aiken and Holley Munnis for their support in kids' running. We thank Burger King, Julian Smith, and Bonita Slau for encouraging and supporting us in the Cooper River Bridge Run. We thank Renee McCuller and the Krewe of Centaur for their support of the Heights Mardi Gras.

A special thanks to people from the neighborhood who went the extra mile—George "Brother Debuff" Jefferson, Rosalyn Rollerson, Coach Roach, Miss Ann Spillers, Eva Grant, Dot Mitchell, Fred Taylor, Ernie D., and Fred Williams—and to Miss Ruby Smith, the Heights' first Mardi Gras Queen, for being a role model for us all.

Regarding media, we thank Mindy Spar and Nadine Parks from the *Post and Courier* newspaper, local news anchor Carolyn Murray, and Sandra Bartlett for airing a piece on the Neighborhood Solutions Project via the Canadian Broadcasting Company.

From the Charleston Eastside neighborhood, we express our gratitude to Shirley Scott of St. Julian Devine Center, Sandy Williams and Arthur Wilson of the Boys and Girls Club, and we recognize the memory of T. C. "Top Cat" Drayton.

We thank Joshua Leblang, Yvonne Johnstone, and Dr. Lisa Saldana for being a resource in the writing phase, and Dawn Cassidy, Ronnie Grubbs, and Amy Mayhew for their help on data entry and management. Regarding sustainability, we thank Toby Smith, Gladys Washington, Jackie Ketchens, and Bonnie Beerman for training us in community development and financial management. We thank Cathy Duffy for, as a volunteer, teaching the neighborhood grant writing and guiding us toward sources for community development. Last, but certainly not least, we would like to recognize the foundations, organizations, and corporations that helped the community develop and sustain its activities via funding: the Junior League of Charleston, the Coastal Community Foundation of South Carolina, the Exchange Club, the Babcock Foundation, Chevron, the Environmental Protection Agency, the Charleston County School District, Weed and Seed, Clemson University Extension Service, Lowcountry Arts Council, and Heery International.

Contents

Neighborhood Solutions for Neighborhood Problems

The Introduction

Dateline 1997: Union Heights neighborhood identified as one of the highest crime areas in the state of South Carolina.

Dateline 2001: community-policing team in Union Heights moved to another area because crime was too low to justify a community policing team.

- How is a neighborhood changed when violence, crime, and substance abuse are taking over?
- How are the odds changed when children are routinely committing school violence, expelled from school, failing to achieve, and dropping out with no apparent job alternatives?
- How is hope given to parents and citizens from a high-crime community when change seems impossible?

Within the covers of this book is one community's answer to these questions.

Flashback to 1997: The Union Heights neighborhood in North Charleston, South Carolina, was identified as one of the highest crime areas in the state. Although near one of the most popular tourist destinations in the nation, drug dealing, crime, and school problems were derailing the youth from success and the neighborhood from unity. The neighborhood had a negative reputation. Throughout the city, this neighborhood was considered "a place you don't go at night and only go with groups of people during the day." The news media were regular visitors for crime reporting.

1

Within the bounds of the neighborhood, the streets were alive by day with children who were put out of school or who chose not to attend because they believed school held nothing for them. Many children saw drug selling as a way to financial security. Bright, talented adults and children lived in the neighborhood, but the conditions and lack of resources did not foster their skills and abilities. Rather, citizens in the neighborhood faced an extremely high rate of school expulsion, drug use, and criminal activity.

Under strong leadership, the neighborhood decided to do something about the situation. Multisystemic therapy (MST) became a part of their efforts. Through neighbors helping neighbors, a strong community-policing program, the creativity of the residents, the schools working in concert with families, the courts and juvenile justice working cooperatively with the therapeutic team, easy access to outreach health care, and much sweat equity, Union Heights changed its children's life trajectories and their ecology.

This book describes a collaborative project that took advantage of the existing social capital (i.e., motivations and talents of residents) in the neighborhood to transform Union Heights into an area of opportunity for children, adolescents, and their families. The neighborhood residents, police, health care providers, schools, and MST team worked together to create a master plan for socially and emotionally revitalizing a troubled neighborhood. This book explains that master plan. As you read it you will find evidence of youth

- Breaking new ground and entering college rather than breaking and entering buildings
- Running in a running club rather than running drugs
- Working a job instead of "working" the system
- Dancing around the city rather than dancing around excuses for not attending school
- Burning designs onto T-shirts rather than burning a joint
- Living their lives with their families rather than living their lives in an institution
- Feeling support from their community rather than support from a deviant peer group
- Recording rap music rather than recording a set of new criminal charges
- Wondering what colleges will be on the college tour this year rather than wondering who will get arrested or shot this week
- Grabbing adults who come into the community center to get help with homework or to read to them rather than grabbing people on the street to take something from them

- Mobbing the streets in a Mardi Gras parade rather than mobbing the streets to watch a drug raid
- Sitting at the community center eating a birthday cake in celebration of their first birthday in 5 years not spent in jail rather than sitting in jail mourning the loss of another year.

As you read this master plan, you will learn of a neighborhood project that was designed by the people of the neighborhood in partnership with professionals. To effect the level of changes that occurred, it took all of us together. A timeline of our efforts follows this introduction. Then the story starts with Chapter 1. Read on.

Neighborhood Solutions Timeline

1993

POLICE   Weed and Seed activities begin in Enterprise communities.

1996

HEALTH   Medical University of South Carolina Nursing Program sets up basic screenings in the Gethsemani Community Center (i.e., blood pressure, cholesterol, blood sugar, health education).

Discussion begins for building a health center in the community.

POLICE   Standard policing procedures in place with some Weed and Seed activities.

1997

HEALTH   A family and the City of North Charleston donate land for site of health center.

Nurses continue weekly health screenings at Gethsemani Community Center.
Nurses increase level of services to include pharmacy.

POLICE   September: PACTeam starts with development of program and 3–4 months of zero-tolerance policing.

MST   December: Dr. Cynthia Swenson makes cold call to Ida Taylor to begin discussions on the Neighborhood Solutions Project.

1998

HEALTH	Nurses continue health services via a weekly clinic at Gethsemani Community Center.
POLICE	PACTeam completes zero tolerance and begins community policing early in the year.
MST	January–February: Meetings with community leaders
	March–May: Individual meetings with ministers, residents, youth, parents, schools, business owners
	June: Begin hiring staff, start-up of prevention activities
	August: Begin MST treatment services with referred youth and their families

1999

HEALTH	Nurses continue health services via a weekly clinic at Gethsemani Community Center.
	Health Center groundbreaking held in spring.
POLICE	PACTeam continues community policing in Union Heights.
MST	Team continues to provide clinical services.
	Team and community continue development and implementation of prevention activities.
	June: nonprofit status attained for Neighborhood Council.
	Team and community leaders begin grant writing and fund raising.

2000

HEALTH	Nurses continue health services via a weekly clinic at Gethsemani Community Center.
	Shell for Health Center building completed.
POLICE	PACTeam continues community policing in Union Heights.
MST	Team continues to provide clinical services.
	Team continues development and implementation of prevention activities.
	December: Neighborhood fully sustaining prevention activities.
	Team and community leaders continue grant writing and fund raising.

2001

HEALTH Leader and neighborhood champion, Roscoe Mitchell, dies on October 6, 2001.

Health Center opens November 5th.

POLICE Calls for service reduced by at least 80%.

April: PACTeam leaves Union Heights.

MST Team continues to provide clinical services.

Team and neighborhood leaders continue implementation of prevention activities.

Neighborhood continues to sustain prevention activities.

July 1: Clinical team ends work in Union Heights.

2002

HEALTH Health center continues to serve neighborhood and area patients.

POLICE Standard policing procedures continue.

RESIDENTS Neighborhood continues to sustain prevention activities.

Neighborhood council continues regular meetings.

2003

HEALTH Health center continues to serve neighborhood and area patients.

Health center enrollment of neighborhood and area families reaches 2,000.

POLICE Standard policing procedures continue.

March: Weed and Seed activities start up in neighborhood.

RESIDENTS Neighborhood continues to sustain prevention activities.

Neighborhood council continues regular meetings.

2004

HEALTH Health center continues to serve neighborhood and area patients.

POLICE Standard policing procedures continue.

RESIDENTS Neighborhood continues to sustain activities.

Neighborhood council continues regular meetings.

PART I

The Empirical and Clinical Background for the Neighborhood Solutions Project

The overriding purpose of Part I is to provide concise overviews of the conceptual and clinical foundations of the Neighborhood Solutions for Neighborhood Problems Project (henceforth the Neighborhood Solutions Project). These include

- Extensive research on the determinants and consequences of community violence and youth criminal activity and substance use (Chapter 1)
- Findings from an extensive body of intervention research addressing youth antisocial behavior (Chapter 2)
- The central clinical aims and emphases of multisystemic therapy (MST; Chapter 3), which are supported by the literatures reviewed in Chapters 1 and 2.

More specifically, Chapter 1 reviews the multiple causes of youth and community violence and shows why comprehensive interventions are required to combat these problems. Topics include how neighborhoods influence the health and well-being of children as well as the prevalence of and costs related to community violence, youth substance abuse, and youth criminal activity. The chapter concludes with a discussion of risk and protective factors that can be used to design interventions.

Chapter 2 summarizes the evidence base for treating criminal behavior and substance abuse in youth. In addition, the types of interventions that exacerbate these problems are considered. Unfortunately, these are among the most widely implemented interventions in the nation. The key features of effective interventions are synthesized.

Chapter 3 provides an in-depth description of MST, the intervention model used in the Neighborhood Solutions Project. This description includes the social–ecological–theoretical foundation of the model, a clinical description of MST, the home-based service delivery model used, and the quality assurance processes implemented to support therapists in obtaining youth outcomes.

CHAPTER 1

The Causes and Consequences of Youth Violence, Substance Abuse, and Community Violence

Safety is a major concern of people throughout the world. Although terrorist attacks represent the most highly publicized safety concern, on a day-to-day basis violence within communities can cause high levels of stress and affect the well-being of children and adults. Many children literally grow up in "domestic war zones." The good news, however, is that violent and troubled neighborhoods can be turned around.

This book describes a collaborative project that helped transform a troubled, disadvantaged neighborhood, in which children and families were at high risk for a variety of serious problems, into a neighborhood that now provides more child and family support per block than many neighborhoods in the affluent suburbs of our city. Before describing the process of the changes that transpired in this neighborhood, it is important to delineate the devastating influences that violence and substance abuse can have on individuals, families, neighbors, and society. Moreover, in order to appreciate the logic and rationale of the interventions discussed in this volume, it is important to examine the known causes of violence and substance abuse. Therefore, this chapter has the following goals:

1. To describe the ways that neighborhoods impact children
2. To provide a background for understanding the prevalence of community violence, youth substance abuse, and youth criminal activity
3. To describe the personal, social, and economic costs of the problems of community and youth violence and substance abuse
4. To discuss known risk and protective factors

9

HOW NEIGHBORHOODS IMPACT CHILDREN

Clearly, the environment in which one lives can have negative and positive influences. Leventhal and Brooks-Gunn (2000) describe three mechanisms through which neighborhoods influence children: institutional resources, relationships, and norms/collective efficacy.

Institutional Resources

Institutional resources refer to the availability, accessibility, affordability, and quality of social, educational, recreational, medical, child care, and employment services in the community. For example, low resources for child care in a neighborhood impacts parents who need it and diminishes their resources for monitoring their children while they go to work. Similarly, the absence of medical services in a neighborhood, in conjunction with poor public transportation, will mean that many acute and chronic medical conditions will go untreated.

Relationships

The mechanism of relationships pertains primarily to parenting skills and characteristics of the indigenous social support available to parents. Living in a dangerous neighborhood is associated with less parental warmth (Furstenburg, 1993), more harsh control and verbal aggression (Earls, McGuire, & Shay, 1994), and restrictive parenting (Jarrett, 1997). While some parents allow their children access to neighborhood influences and attempt to control their children's behavior via harsher discipline, other parents may restrict their children to the home in an effort to limit access to deviant influences.

Norms/Collective Efficacy

Collective efficacy refers to the social cohesion and trust among neighbors (Sampson, Raudenbush, & Earls, 1997). When a neighborhood is close-knit, people take a role in monitoring the behavior of adults and children. For example, neighbors might assure that children skipping school are brought to school, might work together to stop drug selling in the neighborhood, or might combine resources to build a playground for children. Indeed, researchers have found evidence for a relationship between collective efficacy and reduced rates of community violence, violent victimization, and homicide (Sampson et al., 1997). Furthermore, research has shown a negative relationship between collective efficacy and behavioral problems in adolescents (Elliott et al., 1996). Together, these studies indicate the importance of neighbors pulling together to better the lives of children.

Implications for Change

As will be expanded upon throughout this volume, the three mechanisms of influence delineated by Leventhal and Brooks-Gunn (2000) have important implications for focusing efforts to improve the lives and opportunities for children in troubled neighborhoods. These mechanisms suggest that such efforts should

- Empower caregivers and parents, surrounding them with strong indigenous support.
- Bring community stakeholders (i.e., neighbors with shared interests) together in activities of mutual interest.
- Increase the accessibility of formal institutional resources such as medical care.

Contending that intervention efforts should "empower parents" or "bring together neighbors" is easy. The complexity of the implementation, however, is quite another matter. Who, exactly, should come together and how are these individuals accessed? How, exactly, are caregivers empowered, especially caregivers with serious personal problems themselves? Which of the many potential foci of interventions should be targeted for change? A fundamental assumption of this book is that the existing knowledge base on the prevalence and causes of problems as well as research on evidence-based interventions for these problems is the best place to begin answering questions such as these.

COMMUNITY VIOLENCE

Defining Community Violence

Community violence has been defined as "deliberate acts intended to cause physical harm against a person or persons in the community" (Cooley-Quille, Turner, & Beidel, 1995, p. 202). Youth exposure to such violence may be indirect or direct. Indirect exposure includes seeing the violence (e.g., seeing someone beaten) or hearing the violent event (e.g., gunshots, screams) (Buka, Stichick, Birdthistle, & Earls, 2000). Direct exposure includes being a victim of nonlethal violence (i.e., violence committed against a person that does not result in death), or to a greater extreme, being a family member of a homicide victim. Many more children and youth witness violence than experience direct victimization. Scarpa (2001) found that witnessing acts of violence occurred 1.3–4 times more often than being a direct victim.

Prevalence Estimates

Community violence is at epidemic levels in certain neighborhoods in the United States. Particularly in urban areas, rising numbers of children and youth are exposed to life-threatening violence. To understand how often and to what extent children and youth experience community violence, researchers have primarily studied violence in inner-city neighborhoods. The following are results on violence exposure from several of the many important studies in the field.

- Thirty-nine percent of 12- to 21-year-olds interviewed reported involvement in a physical fight during the past year, with 3.3% treated for injuries (National Health Interview Survey; Kolbe, Kann, & Collins, 1993).
- Forty-five percent of 11- to 24-year-old inner-city youth interviewed in Baltimore knew someone who had been victimized by assault with a weapon, robbery, a knifing, or murder, and 67% knew someone who had been shot (Gladstein, Rusonis, & Heald, 1992).
- Sixty-one percent of first and second graders and 72% of fifth and sixth graders surveyed in Washington, DC, reported witnessing violence in their community (Richters & Martinez, 1993).
- One-third of African American school-age children assessed in Chicago reported witnessing a homicide, and two-thirds, a serious assault (Bell & Jenkins, 1993).
- Forty-one percent of young, inner-city adolescents who were assessed reported seeing at least one shooting or stabbing in the past year (Schwab-Stone et al., 1995).
- Ninety percent of sixth graders who were surveyed in a large Southeastern city reported hearing guns being shot and having seen someone being beaten (Farrell & Bruce, 1997).
- Seventy-eight percent of the children in a Washington, DC, Head Start Program reported exposure to at least one incident of community violence (Shahinfar, Fox, & Leavitt, 2000).

As evident from a small sampling of this research, a large percentage of our inner-city youth are witnesses to or victims of community violence. Moreover, boys and minority youth are particularly at risk. The scientific literature is consistent that males tend to experience more exposure to community violence than do females (Cooley-Quille, Boyd, Frantz, & Walsh, 2001; Farrell & Bruce, 1997; Selner-O'Hagan, Kindlon, Buka, Raudenbush, & Earls, 1998), and African American youth experience community violence at disproportionate rates (Attar, Guerra, & Tolan, 1994). Likewise, ethnic minorities are overrepresented in economically disadvantaged urban neighborhoods with high crime rates (Cooley-Quille et al., 1995), and youth living in such neighborhoods report the highest levels of exposure to violence (Selner-O'Hagan et al., 1998).

YOUTH SUBSTANCE ABUSE AND SERIOUS CRIMINALITY

Major federal reports (e.g., McBride, VanderWaal, Terry, & VanBuren, 1999) and academic reviewers (e.g., Bukstein, 2000) have concluded that adolescent criminal activity and substance abuse are highly interrelated. Delinquents are more likely to use drugs, and drug users are more likely to commit criminal offenses. Thus, criminal activity and drug use are both risk factors for and consequences of each other. Indeed, the federal Office of Juvenile Justice and Delinquency Prevention, which is charged with guiding the nation's juvenile justice policy, has labeled substance abuse as "The Nation's Number One Health Problem" (Ericson, 2001).

Defining Substance Abuse and Serious Criminal Behavior

Although substance abuse and criminal activity reflect different aspects of antisocial behavior, the former includes considerably more subjectivity in its assessment.

Substance Abuse

Winters and his colleagues (Winters, Latimer, & Stinchfield, 2001) provide an excellent framework for conceptualizing the continuum from substance use to dependence and for the factors that must be considered in placing a particular youth along this continuum. Drawing from a report by the Center for Substance Abuse Treatment (1999), the 5-point continuum includes the following:

1. Abstinence: no substance use
2. Experimental use: typically minimal use in the context of recreational activities
3. Early abuse: more established use, greater frequency of use, often more than one drug used, negative consequences of use beginning to emerge

4. Abuse: history of frequent use; negative consequences have emerged
5. Dependence: continued regular use in spite of negative consequences, considerable activity devoted to seeking and using drugs

As noted subsequently, the majority of adolescents have used substances; hence, substance use per se is rarely a criterion for intervention. Rather, intensive interventions should be reserved for youth at the abuse and dependence points on the continuum. Importantly, Winters and colleagues (2001) noted that several additional factors should be considered in deciding whether interventions are warranted.

1. Use of some drugs (e.g., heroin) is sufficiently dangerous as to merit intervention even if negative consequences have not emerged.
2. Age should be considered. A 12-year-old experimenting with marijuana may present a very different profile than a 17-year-old.
3. Acute ingestion of large quantities of a substance at any age is sufficiently risky to call for interventions.
4. Use of substances in inappropriate settings (e.g., school, while driving) might justify interventions.

Thus, the general rule for deciding whether interventions for substance use are needed is based on an observed link between substance use and negative life outcomes or high risk for such outcomes.

Serious Criminal Behavior

As discussed by Howell (2003), the Federal Bureau of Investigation's "Uniform Crime Reports" (UCR) serves as a solid basis for defining serious criminal behavior. The UCR includes a Violent Crime Index and a Property Crime Index. Violent crimes include murder and nonnegligent manslaughter, rape, robbery, and assault. Serious property crimes include burglary, larceny-theft, auto theft, and arson. A reasonable definition of a serious juvenile offender, therefore, is a youth who has committed one of the UCR offenses or other serious offenses that are not on the UCR list (e.g., extortion, drug trafficking). A violent juvenile offender is a youth who committed one of the aforementioned violent crimes or a violent offense not on the list (e.g., other felony sex offenses, kidnapping). In general, violent and serious juvenile offenders can present considerable jeopardy to the community and, as such, are often at high risk for out-of-home placement (e.g., incarceration). Such youth, consequently, are prime candidates for intensive community-based interventions to both protect the community and prevent costly (and often iatrogenic) placements.

Prevalence Estimates

Prevalence estimates for substance abuse and criminal activity are based primarily on criminal justice data, large self-report surveys, and crime victim surveys.

Substance Use and Abuse

Although substance use is highly prevalent among adolescents in the general population, especially older youth, substance abuse and dependence are relatively unusual (Weinberg, Rahdert, Colliver, & Glantz, 1998). For example, approximately half of high school seniors report having been drunk at least once during the past 30 days, and about 20% report using marijuana at least once during the same time period. On the other hand, only about 3% of adolescents in the general population have a diagnosable substance abuse or dependence disorder.

Estimates of the prevalence of substance use disorders for youth in the juvenile justice system vary widely. For example, in a large sample of juvenile detainees, Teplin and her colleagues (Teplin, Abram, McClelland, Dulcan, & Mericle, 2002) found that approximately 50% met diagnostic criteria for a substance use disorder. On the other hand, in our work screening large numbers of youth in the juvenile justice system for substance abuse disorders, only 10% have met diagnostic criteria. Regardless of the true prevalence rate, however, by definition, substance-abusing or dependent-adolescents are presenting problems that merit interventions.

Serious Criminal Behavior

Considerable national attention was devoted to the dramatic increase in the UCR Violent Crime Index for adolescents ages 10–17 years in the late 1980s to early 1990s. Juvenile arrest rates for violent crimes almost doubled from 300 arrests per 100,000 juveniles in 1984 to about 550 arrests per 100,000 juveniles in 1994 (Snyder & Sickmund, 1999), leading many to conclude that the nation was experiencing an epidemic in youth violence. Receiving less attention was the fact that juvenile arrest rates on the UCR Property Crime Index remained relatively stable during this time period, and juvenile arrests for violent crimes have decreased substantially in recent years (Howell, 2003). For example, arrest rates for robbery were down more than 50% from 1994 to 1999. Moreover, crime victimization surveys and self-report data do not support the view that adolescents are perpetrating an increasing rate of serious criminal behavior. Thus, while the costs of violent and serious crimes are substantial to victims and society (as discussed subsequently), such offending remains a rare phenomenon (e.g., only 1 in 200 youth was arrested for a violent offense at the peak of the problem in 1994). Nevertheless, the high cost of violence in combination with its low prevalence suggests that identified serious offenders are most likely appropriate for intensive interventions.

Although national statistics indicate that the prevalence of violent crimes is decreasing, several violence-related statistics remain extremely alarming and have great significance for the purposes of this volume. First, homicide is the second leading cause of death among young people in the United States (Centers for Disease Control and Prevention, 1994). Second, lethal violence is especially high among African American adolescent males. The rates of homicide in this group run 10 times higher than for Caucasian counterparts, and homicide is the leading cause of death for African American youth. Third, the rate of homicide among all American males ages 15–24 years is 10 times higher than in Canada, 15 times higher than in Australia, and 28 times higher than in France or Germany. Higher homicide rates are typically only found in war zones (World Health Organization, 1995).

THE IMPACT AND COST OF COMMUNITY VIOLENCE AND YOUTH SUBSTANCE ABUSE AND CRIME

Community Violence

Many studies have shown that children who live in violent and troubled neighborhoods are deeply impacted by the violence they see and experience. Exposure to violence and victimization by violence is linked with several important aspects of functioning.

Externalizing Problems

Children who witness violence are more likely to exhibit aggression and antisocial behavior, regardless of gender (Attar et al., 1994; Bell & Jenkins, 1993; Farrell & Bruce, 1997). Jenkins and Bell (1994), for example, found that girls who witness violence are more likely to use drugs and alcohol, carry guns and knives, and exhibit difficulty in school. Boys who witness violence are more likely to carry a weapon, exhibit problems in school, and engage in fights. Similarly, direct victimization by violence has been related to extreme aggression. Flannery, Singer, and Wester (2001) found that compared to nonviolent high school peers, dangerously violent adolescents (those who have reported shooting or stabbing someone) were more likely to have been a victim of violence.

Internalizing Problems

Exposure to community violence has also been associated with a variety of internalizing symptoms including stress, depression, anxiety, and posttraumatic stress symptoms (Singer, Anglin, Song, & Lunghofer, 1995). For example, high school students exposed to high levels of community violence reported more fears of injury, danger, and the unknown; more trait anxiety and withdrawn behavior; and more somatic complaints than nonexposed counterparts (Cooley-Quille et al., 2001). In part, their fears of danger are real, as children exposed to community violence are also more likely to be rejected and bullied by peers (Schwartz & Proctor, 2000). Moreover, the impact of violence is reaching far beyond adolescence. Infants and toddlers who are exposed to violence show irritability, difficulty with sleep, emotional distress, fear of being alone, and sometimes regression in language and toileting skills (Bell, 1995; Zeanah & Scheeringa, 1996). Exposure to violence need not be direct for children to experience symptoms. Hearing about or witnessing violence has been found to relate to increased stress (Osofsky, Wewers, Hann, & Fick, 1993). Even adolescents exposed to violence in the media are more likely to experience anxiety, isolation, school avoidance, and sleep difficulties (Joshi & Kaschak, 1998).

Physical Health

Preliminary evidence indicates that exposure to community violence has a negative impact on physical health. Neighborhood crime has been related to heart disease in African American adults (James & Kleinbaum, 1976). More recent research found that healthy African American adolescents exposed to community violence had elevated nighttime blood pressure (Wilson et al., 1998).

School Performance

School performance suffers for many children who are exposed to community violence. Especially for children who are experiencing internalizing problems, difficulties with concentration and memory and high levels of fatigue due to lack of sleep can impact motivation and completion of work (Osofsky et al., 1993). In addition to the impact of disturbed sleep, concentration may be reduced by intrusive thoughts of violence observed (Shakoor & Chalmers, 1991). Children, however, need not witness violence nor have it committed against them for school performance to suffer. Poor academic performance has been observed in children who lost a family member to homicide.

Substance Abuse

The relationship between violence in the community and substance abuse is well established (Dawkins, 1997). Witnessing community violence is one of the strongest predictors of substance abuse among adolescents (Kilpatrick et al., 2000). In particular, witnessing severe violence (e.g., murder, explosions) or being sexually assaulted is associated with marijuana and cocaine use (Crimmins, Cleary, Brownstein, Spunt, & Warley, 2000). People who are chronically exposed to violence are thought to self-medicate with substances as a way of coping (Cooley-Quille et al., 1995). Furthermore, people who use drugs are also at risk of being victims of crime (Maher & Curtis, 1995), as they can be easy to victimize when impaired.

Personal and Societal Costs of Youth Substance Abuse and Crime

Adolescent substance abuse and serious criminal activity can have large and enduring personal and societal costs. These costs clearly justify the need to devote resources aimed at altering the life trajectories of youth presenting these problems.

Personal Costs

Youth who persist in their criminal activity through adolescence are at risk of numerous deleterious outcomes as adults (Howell, 2003; Loeber & Farrington, 1998). These include, for example, substance abuse, unemployment and poor job performance, incarceration, unstable relationships, maltreatment of their own children, and psychiatric illness. Importantly, each item in this list also represents an adverse impact on persons in the offender's social network. Thus, personal costs of offending are compounded throughout the offender's life.

Similarly, substance-abusing youth are at high risk for negative outcomes as adults (Newcomb & Bentler, 1988; Office of Technology Assessment, 1991). The role of drugs and alcohol in adolescent suicide, automobile accidents, and drownings is well established. Increased rates of risky sexual behavior, moreover, place substance-abusing youth at risk for contracting HIV. Regarding educational performance, adolescent substance use and hard drug use predict school dropout and decreased later college involvement. Further, adolescent substance use is linked with unemployment and job instability, divorce, increased sexual relationships, and decreased relationship satisfaction in young adults and adults. Together, these findings suggest that substance abuse during adolescence can disrupt developmental tasks and role performance during early adulthood.

Financial Costs

Crime-victim costs, criminal justice system costs (e.g., incarceration costs, costs of an arrest to juvenile justice authorities and juvenile court), and productivity loss (due to incarceration) have been estimated as high as $1.3–1.5 million for an average career criminal (Snyder & Sickmund, 1999). As discussed by Henggeler and Sheidow (2002), monetary costs for the victim and the system-level costs were recently evaluated by researchers at the Washington State Institute for Public Policy (Aos, Phipps, Barnoski, & Lieb, 2001). Victim monetary costs were estimated at over $1 million for a murder, with close to an additional $2 million cost for quality of life. Total costs (i.e., victim costs, victim quality-of-life costs, and system costs) for other crimes were estimated at $180,236 for a single sex offense, $100,966 for a robbery, and $66,273 for an aggravated assault. Similarly, Aos and his colleagues estimated total costs for a 15-year-old offender from offense until age 22 years to be $120,235, based on reoffense rates in Washington of 45.8%, an average number of 2.44 reconvictions during this time frame, and an adjustment for the probability of specific crimes occurring (e.g., murder, 1.3%; rape, 1.3%; aggravated assault, 16.7%).

The deleterious consequences of adolescent alcohol and drug abuse also have significant cost implications. Although the economic costs of substance abuse to society have not been fully delineated for adolescents (Office of Technology Assessment, 1991), available data suggest that such costs are substantial. For example, in 1986 the approximate societal costs for victims of drug-related crime was $5.5 billion, with corresponding law enforcement costs of $12.8 billion (Institute of Medicine, 1990). Moreover, in 1985 the direct costs (i.e., treatment-related expenses) for treating adolescent substance abusers was approximately $2 billion. Although this cost represents only a small fraction of the $50 billion spent on substance abuse treatment across age groups (Rice, Kelman, Miller, & Dunmeyer, 1990), adolescent substance abusers (especially those who are juvenile offenders) probably have a relatively high likelihood of becoming adult substance abusers (Henggeler, Clingempeel, Brondino, & Pickrel, 2002). Effective treatments, therefore, hold the potential of both reducing these serious problems and providing cost savings.

RISK AND PROTECTIVE FACTORS

Risk factors are individual or environmental variables that generally increase the probability of a negative developmental outcome. Protective factors are individual or environmental variables that can help prevent or attenuate the development of negative developmental outcomes.

Decades of excellent correlational and longitudinal research have produced a wealth of knowledge regarding risk and protective factors pertaining to the development and desistance/exacerbation of problems with substance use and criminal behavior in youth. Identified risk and protective factors are very similar for both substance abuse and criminality, and, importantly, have critical implications for the design of effective interventions. The summary of these factors is based on outstanding syntheses of extensive literatures developed by Loeber and Farrington (1998), Howell (2003), and Schinke, Brounstein, and Gardner (2002). Although few in number, studies on witnessing community violence also indicate several factors that increase risk for social and behavioral problems as well as factors that protect children from such problems (Crimmins, Cleary, Brownstein, Spunt, & Warley, 2000; Fitzpatrick & Boldizar, 1993; Freeman, Mokros, & Poznanski, 1993; Pynoos et al., 1987; Song, Singer, & Anglin, 1998; Springer & Padgett, 2000).

Bronfenbrenner's (1979) theory of social ecology provides a useful conceptual framework for organizing the risk and protective factors. This theory posits that youth are embedded in multiple systems (i.e., family, school, peer, community), and that behavior is a function of individuals' reciprocal interactions within and between these systems. That is, each of the systems influences youth behavior, and, in turn, youth behavior influences each of the systems (e.g., youth influence their family and family influences youth). As we consider treatments for community violence, youth violence and substance abuse, a first step is to understand what factors may contribute to or maintain the problem and what factors are preventive.

Community Violence Risk Factors

Risk factors that increase the likelihood that youth who experience community violence will have mental health problems include (1) factors related to the event, (2) family factors, and (3) individual youth factors. Risk and protective factors are summarized in Table 1.1.

Factors Related to the Event or Person Who Experienced the Event

The type, level of exposure, amount of violence experienced, and proximity to the violence can increase the negative mental health impact on a youth. In addition, the closeness of the relationship to the victim can impact a youth. Youth who experience higher levels of violence exposure and witness more severe types of violence show significantly more distress (Shahinfar et al., 2000). Similarly, the closer a youth is to a violent event, the more severe the violence, and the more emotionally connected the youth is to the victim, the more likely he or she will experience emotional

TABLE 1.1. Risk and Protective Factors for Mental Health Problems among Youth Exposed to Community Violence

Risk factors

Event-related
- Higher levels of violence: relates to posttraumatic stress disorder (PTSD) and separation anxiety
- More severe violence
- Closer proximity to violence
- Location of violence: For females, witnessing violence in the community was related to trauma symptoms; for males, witnessing violence at school was related to trauma symptoms.
- Repeated exposure (has an additive effect): New exposures can exacerbate symptoms that have been due to earlier exposures as new events trigger old memories.
- Whether violence is witnessed or experienced: Witnessing mild violence relates to internalizing problems; experiencing mild violence leads to externalizing problems.
- Relationship to victim: The more emotionally connected the youth is to the victim, the more traumatic is the event.

Individual
- The belief that aggression is a positive way to handle peers who provoke
- Low regulation of emotions
- Low perception of neighborhood safety
- Gender: Girls seem to be impacted to a greater degree than boys.
- Age: Younger youth seem to be impacted to a greater degree.

Family
- Not living with mother
- Family violence
- Low support

Protective factors
- Stable, safe family
- Supportive adult
- Safe havens providing a positive climate
- Social support

or behavioral difficulties (Crimmins et al., 2000; Pynoos et al., 1987; Song et al., 1998). The more community violence to which the youth is exposed, the greater the posttraumatic stress disorder (PTSD) symptoms and separation anxiety (Cooley-Quille et al., 2001). When children experience repeated exposure to violence, the effect can be additive. That is, new exposures to violence can exacerbate symptoms that have been due to earlier exposures. This renewal of symptoms may be due to a new event triggering memories of old events (Pynoos & Nader, 1988). Also, one type of violence is compounded by additional types of violence (Horowitz, Weine, & Jekel, 1995). For some children, repeat exposure to violence may have the opposite effect, as they may become desensitized to the violence. That is, when children live with daily, ongoing violence, they get used to it (Fitzpatrick, 1993).

Family Factors

Among children who witnessed violence, those not living with their mother reported higher levels of depression (Springer & Padgett, 2000). In addition, family factors may mediate the relationship between community violence and experiencing PTSD. That is, exposure to community violence has been found to lead to increased family conflict, which led to PTSD (Overstreet & Braun, 2000).

Individual Factors

The individual youth factors that increase risk of mental health difficulties include age, gender, beliefs about aggression, and perception of safety. Younger children and girls exposed to violence seem to be at higher risk for mental health difficulties (Farrell & Bruce, 1997; Springer & Padgett, 2000). Witnessing violence is associated with developing the belief that aggression is a positive way to handle peers who provoke, and, in turn, this belief is associated with increased aggression (Schwartz & Proctor, 2000). When children exposed to community violence experience a decrease in their perception that their neighborhood is safe, this belief of low safety can lead to PTSD (Overstreet & Braun, 2000).

Community Violence Protective Factors

What helps children exposed to community violence to be resilient? Resilience refers to bouncing back or recovering well from difficulty. Howard (1996) presented a triad of protective factors that help make children more resilient in the face of adverse events: (1) personal resource factors (even temper, socially engaging with others, cognitive skills), (2) family factors (warmth, caring, parents who provide guidance and encourage self-esteem), and (3) external support factors (teachers, neighbors, or others who provide support and counsel). The current research literature shows the most support for the latter two factors. A stable and safe family seems to be a child's best defense against the impact of community violence (Richters & Martinez, 1993). But a good relationship with other caring, positive adults can also help buffer the negative effects of violence (Hill, Levermore, Twaite, & Jones, 1996; Osofsky & Thompson, 2000). Furthermore, safe havens within communities, such as churches or community centers, provide a positive climate and mechanism for social support that helps reduce anxiety in children exposed to violence (Garbarino, Dubrow, Kostelny, & Pardo, 1992; Hill et al., 1996).

Youth Antisocial Behavior Risk Factors

The research describing risk factors for youth antisocial behavior links multiple factors, ones similar to conduct disorder (Kazdin, 1987; McMahon & Wells, 1989), delinquency (Elliott, 1994; Thornberry, Huizinga, & Loeber, 1995), and substance abuse (Hawkins, Catalano, & Miller, 1992). These factors have been described through correlational and causal modeling studies (e.g., Elliott, Huizinga, & Ageton, 1985; Henggeler, 1991; Simcha-Fagan & Schwartz, 1986). Risk and protective factors are summarized in Table 1.2.

Individual Factors

Antisocial youth tend to have favorable attitudes toward antisocial behavior and to attribute hostile intentions to others. In addition, antisocial youth show reduced verbal skills and may exhibit psychiatric symptomatology.

Family Factors

Family relations predict youth's antisocial behavior directly or indirectly because they predict association with deviant peers. Families of antisocial youth are characterized by limited monitoring, ineffective discipline, low warmth, and high conflict, and parental problems such as substance abuse, psychiatric disorders, and criminal behavior.

Peer Relations

Association with deviant peers is a strong predictor of youth antisocial behavior. These youth show poor relationship skills and have little opportunity to observe appropriate skills from others due to limited association with prosocial peers.

School

Antisocial youth exhibit low achievement and a lack of commitment to education, and tend to drop out of school. School problems indirectly predict antisocial behavior, in that they predict association with deviant peers.

TABLE 1.2. Risk and Protective Factors Related to Adolescent Antisocial Behavior

Risk factors

Individual
- Early and persistent antisocial behavior
- Favorable attitudes toward antisocial behavior
- Weak verbal skills
- Impulsivity
- Mental health problems

Family
- Caregiver antisocial behavior and mental health problems
- Low monitoring and supervision
- High conflict
- Low cohesion
- Maltreatment
- Weak social support network

Peer
- Association with substance-using or delinquent peers
- Peer support of antisocial behavior

School
- Academic failure
- Low youth commitment to school
- Dropped out
- Disorderly and unsafe schools
- Placement in alternative classrooms

Workplace
- Availability of antisocial coworkers

Community
- Extreme poverty
- Community disorganization
- High rates of transitions (moving)
- Criminal subculture
- Availability of drugs
- Availability of guns

Protective factors
- Higher level of intelligence
- Stable, caring caregivers
- Involvement in positive, prosocial peer activities
- Safe and effective schools

Neighborhood and Community

Antisocial youth tend to receive low support from resources in the community, such as neighbors and church. Their communities are often characterized by high disorganization, high mobility among members, and contain a criminal subculture.

Youth Antisocial Behavior Protective Factors

The research literature on protective factors is much less extensive than that on risk factors. To a large extent, many of the protective factors identified in the literature are the opposite or absence of a corresponding risk factor. For example, intelligent youth living in homes with stable, caring, and competent caregivers, engaging in prosocial peer activities such as sports and community service; and attending safe and effective schools are embedded in numerous protective factors.

CONCLUSION: WHAT DOES ALL THIS MEAN?

This chapter makes several critical points.

1. Neighborhoods influence child outcomes through several interrelated channels—parenting, neighbor-to-neighbor support, and access to formal resources.
2. Children and youth living in troubled neighborhoods witness and experience high levels of community violence, and this violence can have a serious physical and mental health impact on the children.
3. For youth presenting serious antisocial behavior, including crime and substance abuse, these serious problems exact significant tolls for the youth, family, neighborhood, and society.
4. The causes of youth antisocial behavior are related to multiple risk factors within the individual, family, peers, school, and community.
5. Protective factors have been identified that help buffer children and youth from mental health and legal problems, and these factors can be found in multiple systems (i.e., individual, family, neighborhood).

Thus, the overriding conclusion of this chapter is that comprehensive (e.g., parenting, neighbor-to-neighbor support, introduction of formal resources) interventions are needed to address the problems of violence and substance abuse within a troubled community and among its youth. Moreover, these comprehensive interventions should address multiple risk factors and utilize the known protective factors to reduce risk and enhance functioning. That is, we must have the capacity to intervene at the individual youth, family, school, peer, and neighborhood levels.

Next, current evidence-based treatments for youth antisocial behavior and community violence are examined to determine what works and why.

CHAPTER 2

Evidence-Based Treatments
What Works, What Doesn't, and Why

Major advances in the treatment of antisocial behavior in adolescents have been made during the past decade, and these provide consistent findings regarding the nature of effective interventions. In addition, researchers and policymakers are becoming increasingly aware of the limitations of the predominant interventions for youth violence and substance abuse—out-of-home placement and group-based treatment. This chapter has the following goals:

1. To describe what treatments for addressing youth antisocial behavior have an established evidence base
2. To identify what types of interventions can exacerbate the problem of antisocial behavior
3. To discuss the bases of the effectiveness or ineffectiveness of those interventions

EFFECTIVE TREATMENTS FOR YOUTH VIOLENCE

The preeminent reviews of the youth violence treatment literature have been conducted by Elliott and his colleagues in the prestigious "Blueprints" series (Elliott, 1998), sponsored by the Office of Juvenile Justice and Delinquency Prevention and by the U.S. Surgeon General (U.S. Public Health Service, 2001). In the Blueprints series, more than 500 violence prevention and intervention programs were reviewed, and only 3 were found to meet relatively modest scientific criteria of effectiveness in reducing criminal behavior in juvenile offenders: functional family therapy (FFT; Alexander

& Sexton, 2002), multisystemic therapy (MST; Henggeler et al., 1998), and Oregon treatment foster care (OTFC; Chamberlain, 1998). The Surgeon General's report and publications by other leading reviewers (e.g., Kazdin & Weisz, 1998) have identified these same models; Henggeler and Sheidow (2002) provide a review of pertinent outcome studies.

Functional Family Therapy

Developed by Alexander and colleagues in the 1970s (Alexander & Parsons, 1982), FFT has emerged in recent years as one of the most widely disseminated evidence-based treatments, due largely to the efforts of Dr. Sexton. FFT is primarily an outpatient model, with therapists carrying 12–16 active cases with an average treatment duration of 3–4 months. Although all of the evidence-based treatments are family-focused, FFT is most explicitly a family therapy approach. Training in the model emphasizes primarily family systems conceptualizations of behavior, and change strategies concentrate on restructuring family relations in ways that facilitate desired behavior change. Interventions follow a logical sequence of three phases: engagement of family and motivating change, modifying family relations and problem-solving skills to achieve desired goal, and generalization by extending intrafamily change to extrafamilial systems. Importantly, Sexton and Alexander have developed an intensive training and quality-assurance system to support practitioner implementation of the treatment at FFT dissemination sites.

Multisystemic Therapy

MST was developed by Henggeler and his colleagues (Henggeler & Borduin, 1990) in the late 1970s. Currently, MST has been the subject of more than $30,000,000 in research funded by the National Institutes of Health (NIH), and the model has been disseminated to more than 30 states and 8 nations. MST is an intensive home-based treatment, with therapists carrying caseloads of 4–6 families, with treatment lasting an average of about 4 months. MST therefore is used most efficiently as an alternative to out-of-home placement. Although MST is clearly family-focused, the approach is more ecologically oriented than FFT. That is, from the beginning of treatment, considerable attention is devoted to the role of extrafamilial systems (e.g., peers, school, neighborhood, family support network) in determining or maintaining identified problems. MST interventions are generally adapted from existing evidence-based techniques, such as the behavior therapies, cognitive-behavioral therapies, pragmatic family therapy approaches, and even pharmacological treatments (e.g., for attention-deficit/hyperactivity disorder [ADHD]). Similar to FFT, MST has an intensive quality-assurance protocol designed to support therapist fidelity to the model and optimize youth outcomes. The MST approach is discussed more extensively throughout this volume.

Oregon Treatment Foster Care

OTFC was developed in the early 1980s by Patricia Chamberlain and her colleagues (Chamberlain, 1998) at the Oregon Social Learning Center, which is renowned for its research on the development of antisocial behavior in children and adolescents. OTFC provides extremely high-quality foster care placements for youth presenting serious antisocial behavior, and a team of treatment experts (e.g., case manager, family therapist, individual therapist, other resource staff) surrounds each youth. Similar to MST, OTFC provides intensive interventions that focus on the family and key extrafamilial systems. Considerable resources are devoted to assuring close parental monitoring and supervision of youth behavior, appropriate functioning in school, and reduced exposure to antisocial peers. Specific interventions for these aims are primarily behavioral in nature and are based on the aforementioned research at the Oregon Social Learning Center. The OTFC model also includes intensive training and quality-assurance protocols to promote effective implementation at dissemination sites.

Bases of Success across Models

Although these evidence-based treatments were developed independently during the past 20–30 years, they share several key similarities that largely account for their favorable outcomes and dissemination successes (Henggeler & Sheidow, 2002).

   1. *Addressing key risk factors comprehensively and building on known protective factors.* As discussed in Chapter 1, the key determinants of antisocial behavior in adolescents have been well identified through decades of research. Each of the evidence-based treatment models explicitly targets these risk factors. For example, each devotes considerable resources to building effective family relations and reducing youth association with problem peers. Similarly, each model aims to enhance protective factors by, for example, improving family affective relations and youth school or vocational functioning.

   2. *Use of behavioral intervention techniques.* Each model integrates a variety of behavioral intervention techniques (e.g., behavioral parent training, problem-solving training), approaches that have the most support in the broader criminology literature (Gendreau, 1996). Many intervention techniques are at least implicitly proscribed, including, for example, psy-

chodynamic and object relations therapies and confrontative approaches (e.g., positive peer culture).

3. *Commitment to rigorous evaluation.* The developers of each model have sustained ongoing commitments to rigorous evaluations of their respective treatments. Such commitment is critical in determining the limitations of the approaches and in designing and testing model adaptations to overcome such limitations.

4. *Treatment specification.* FFT, MST, and OTFC intervention guidelines have been specified in treatment manuals and clinical volumes. As discussed by Carroll and Nuro (2002), treatment manuals are critical for the implementation and replication of intervention protocols.

5. *Development of quality-assurance protocols.* Intensive quality-assurance protocols have been developed for each model to support the effective implementation of the treatment in community settings. These protocols include several components, such as initial training, booster training, weekly supervision, fidelity monitoring, and outcome monitoring.

6. *Development of organizations dedicated to effective dissemination.* The transport of these treatments to real world practice settings has been accomplished primarily by organizations dedicated to this mission (e.g., MST Services, *www.mstservices.com*). The effective transport of a complex evidence-based practice to field settings requires a different set of skills than those needed to develop and evaluate a treatment approach.

EFFECTIVE TREATMENTS OF ADOLESCENT SUBSTANCE ABUSE

Drawing conclusions about what works is more difficult in the field of adolescent substance abuse treatment than for juvenile offending, for three main reasons. First, relatively few studies have examined treatment effectiveness in the area of adolescent substance abuse. This makes it difficult to discern consistent patterns of outcomes across various treatment approaches. Second, the scientific rigor of much of this treatment research has significant limitations. For example, reductions in drug use of participants in uncontrolled studies (i.e., the treatment has no comparison group) is often given as evidence of the effectiveness of drug treatment, even though many other factors could have accounted for the reductions in drug use (e.g., maturation effects, regression to the mean effects). Similarly, in controlled studies, investigators and reviewers often interpret time effects (i.e., positive change for participants across treatment conditions) as treatment effects (i.e., the change is due to the treatment per se). This conceptual misinterpretation has often led to the unsupported conclusion that "everything works." Third, investigators have tended to overinterpret favorable findings that were observed. For example, favorable outcomes might be obtained for only one of 10 measures, such as self-reported substance use. Yet, this outcome will be highlighted throughout the research report, even though it was not corroborated by the results of the urine drug screen measures on these same participants. With these caveats in mind, several conclusions regarding the nature of effective treatments of adolescent substance abuse are reasonable.

Family-Based Treatments Seem Most Promising

The majority of reviewers have concluded that family-based treatments of adolescent substance abuse have shown the most promise. For example, Williams and Chang (2000) concluded that "outpatient family therapy appears superior to other forms of outpatient treatment" (p. 138); and Waldron (1997) concluded that research findings "provide ample evidence that family therapy is an effective treatment for adolescent substance abusers" (pp. 223–224). The title of Liddle and Dakof's (1995) review, however, best sums up the state of the research: "Efficacy of Family Therapy for Drug Abuse: Promising but Not Definitive."

It must be emphasized, however, that *many* very different family therapy approaches have appeared in the literature, but few have empirical support. The following list of promising approaches is based on summaries and conclusions from the National Institute on Drug Abuse (NIDA, 1999), which is charged by Congress with the mission of developing the research base on the causes and treatments of substance abuse, and the Center for Substance Abuse Prevention (2001; Schinke et al., 2002), which is charged with the mission of disseminating effective intervention programs.

MST

Cited in both reports, MST has had exceptionally high rates of treatment engagement of substance-abusing juvenile offenders (Henggeler, Pickrel, Brondino, & Crouch, 1996), and has produced favorable short-term (Henggeler, Pickrel, & Brondino, 1999) and long-term (Henggeler, Clingempeel, et al., 2002) reductions in drug use. Chapter 6 describes recent adaptations to the MST approach for treating adolescent substance abuse that are further enhancing its effectiveness.

Multidimensional Family Therapy

MDFT (Liddle et al., 2001), cited by NIDA, has been the subject of considerable federally supported research. MDFT devotes substantive resources to building an alliance with each youth (e.g., about 40% of sessions are with adolescent alone), and reestablishing emotional connections between the adolescent and his or her caregivers (Liddle, 1999). In contrast with the treatment models discussed previously (i.e., FFT, MST, OTFC), this approach focuses more on family affective processes and less on behavioral conceptualizations of problems and their solutions. Nevertheless, the roles of extrafamilial systems in maintaining problems are addressed through a case management process.

Brief Strategic Family Therapy

BSFT (Szapocznik & Williams, 2000), cited by CSAP, has also received significant federal research support. BSFT is a structural family therapy approach in which adolescent drug abuse is viewed as the result of several types of maladaptive family interactions (e.g., inappropriate alliances, scapegoating the adolescent). Therapist interventions initially aim at "joining" the family to gain an understanding of the types of repetitive family interactions that are linked with the identified problems. Later, therapists actively restructure family relations with the goal of increasing caregiver authority and facilitating more effective intrafamily communication. Although earlier studies failed to show differential treatment effects for BSFT, a recent report (Santisteban et al., 2003) has demonstrated favorable short-term youth and family outcomes in comparison with group treatment.

Contingency Management (CM)

Cited by NIDA, CM (Donohue & Azrin, 2001) has produced promising results for substance-using adolescents. CM uses behavioral techniques to help youth (1) avoid situations associated with drug use, (2) engage in prosocial activities incompatible with drug use, and (3) change cognitions and feelings associated with drug use. In addition, drug use is tracked through frequent urine drug screens, and caregivers are empowered to reward abstinence and otherwise reinforce desired behavior change. As discussed in Chapter 6, CM has been integrated with MST, and the combination is proving extremely effective at decreasing the drug use of substance abusing delinquents.

FFT

Though cited in neither the NIDA nor the CSAP report, FFT has been adapted by Waldron and her colleagues (Waldron, Slesnick, Brody, Turner, & Peterson, 2001) to treat adolescent substance abuse. The adaptation includes the integration of cognitive-behavioral therapy (CBT) strategies to teach the individual adolescent self-control and drug-refusal skills. CBT

(Carroll, 1998) is a widely used evidence-based treatment for substance-abusing adults. The results of a randomized trial (Waldron et al., 2001) modestly supported the combined effectiveness of FFT/CBT over FFT in the reduction of adolescent drug use. This project is noteworthy, however, because of its integration of evidence-based treatments (i.e., FFT for adolescent criminal behavior; CBT for adult drug use and many other clinical problems) in an attempt to enhance outcomes.

IMPLICATIONS FOR THE DESIGN OF EFFECTIVE INTERVENTIONS

Although the treatment outcome literature does not provide clear guidelines for designing effective services for substance abusing adolescents, the National Institute on Drug Abuse (1999) conducted an extensive review of the treatment outcome research literature in the areas of adolescent and adult substance abuse that is informative. This review identified 13 principles of effective treatment. As noted by Randall and colleagues (Randall, Halliday-Boykins, Cunningham, & Henggeler, 2001), these principles have important implications for conceptualizing the nature of effective services for substance-abusing adolescents.

1. *"No single treatment is appropriate for all individuals."* The choice of evidence-based interventions used for a particular youth and family should be based on the identified risk and protective factors. For example, CBT might be used to address attitudinal barriers to achieving outcomes, whereas CM procedures might be used to track and provide consequences for drug use behavior.

2. *"Treatment needs to be readily available."* Services should have the capacity to address barriers to service access. In a home-based model, therapists provide services in home, school, and other community locations; caseloads are low; therapists are available 24 hours a day, 7 days a week to respond to crises; and appointments are made at times convenient to the family. This approach has enabled MST to have the highest rates of treatment completion achieved in the field (Henggeler et al., 1996).

3. *"Effective treatment attends to the multiple needs of the individual, not just his or her drug use."* Therapists comprehensively address the multiple determinants of the adolescent's problem behaviors across individual, family, peer, school, and neighborhood contexts. Any factor that is a barrier to favorable outcomes should become a target of interventions.

4. *"An individual's treatment and service plan must be assessed continually and modified as necessary to ensure that the plan meets the person's changing needs."* Continuous evaluation of treatment outcomes is a

fundamental feature of evidence-based treatments. Using MST as an example, interventions are developed and implemented collaboratively by the therapist and caregivers based on an understanding of the fit of the identified problems with the adolescent's social network. If interventions are successful, treatment moves on to subsequent goals. If interventions are unsuccessful, the therapist and family reevaluate their understanding of the causes of the youth's behavior. This reevaluation leads to a corresponding modification of the interventions, and the recursive process continues until interventions are effective.

5. *"Remaining in treatment for an adequate period of time is critical for treatment effectiveness."* Each of the promising treatments devotes considerable attention to engagement of family members in treatment, and all provide services for at least 3 months.

6. *"Counseling and other behavioral therapies are critical components of an effective treatment for addiction."* With rare exception, the promising and evidence-based treatments use behavioral change strategies, including techniques based on social learning theory, operant theory, and cognitive-behavioral theory.

7. *"Medications are an important element of treatment for many patients, especially when combined with counseling and other behavioral therapies."* Although most of the evidence-based and promising treatments of antisocial behavior in adolescents do not explicitly incorporate pharmacological treatments (e.g., for ADHD), MST adaptations for youth with serious emotional disturbance (Henggeler, Schoenwald, Rowland, & Cunningham, 2002) have supported the value of such treatments.

8. *"Addicted or drug-abusing individuals with coexisting mental health disorders should have both disorders treated in an integrated way."* Treatment of co-occurring emotional and behavioral problems should be fundamental to the treatment of adolescents presenting serious clinical problems. Some of the evidence-based and promising treatments attend to psychiatric comorbidity, but others do not.

9. *"Medical detoxification is only the first stage of addiction treatment and by itself does little to change the long-term drug use."* A detoxification unit may be used as a safe site for stabilization, but it is not a treatment. The evidence-based and promising treatments are delivered after detoxification is provided, which is a relatively rare occurrence for adolescents.

10. *"Treatment does not need to be voluntary to be effective."* Sanctions or enticements in the family, employment setting, or criminal justice system can increase both treatment entry and retention rates and the success of treatment interventions. Although juvenile court mandates treatment for many adolescent substance abusers, this alone does not lead to engagement or outcomes. Outcomes require developing an active collabo-

ration between the therapist and the family. Regardless of how an adolescent enters treatment, the therapist works to engage the adolescent's family to increase the likelihood that treatment gains will be maintained following treatment.

11. *"Possible drug use during treatment must be monitored continuously."* Through frequent urine drug screens, CM provides continuous monitoring of adolescent drug use. Rewards are provided by the caregivers for clean screens, and negative consequences are given for dirty screens. If the adolescent has a dirty screen, the therapist and caregivers attempt to understand the bases of the "lapse" and design interventions to address them.

12. *"Treatment programs should provide assessment for HIV/AIDS, hepatitis B and C, tuberculosis and other infectious diseases, and counseling to help clients modify or change behaviors that place themselves or others at risk of infection."* To the best of our knowledge, medical evaluations have not been a standard component of any of the evidence-based or promising treatments for adolescents. It seems likely, however, that medical evaluations are provided on an as-needed basis. Nevertheless, in light of the numerous high-risk behaviors presented by substance-abusing adolescents, perhaps the conduct of standard medical exams should be considered.

13. *"Recovery from drug addiction can be a long-term process and frequently requires multiple episodes of treatment."* One of the limitations of the aforementioned treatments (though not from a cost-containment perspective) is that all are time-limited. Many youth and families would benefit from continued access to effective services following treatment completion. Such needs must be addressed in the development of effective community-based programs.

EFFECTIVE TREATMENTS FOR COMMUNITY VIOLENCE

Neighborhood-based services have played an important role in poverty reduction and social reform during the past century (Halpern, 1995), and many comprehensive neighborhood-based programs aimed at reducing community violence are currently being implemented (Garbarino, Kostelny, & Barry, 1998). At this time, however, no well-controlled evaluations of these programs have been published. Nevertheless, findings from research evaluations of individual strategies used in neighborhood-based programs provide valuable information regarding the nature of effective programs. Catalano and colleagues (Catalano, Arthur, Hawkins, Berglund, & Olson, 1998) provide an excellent review of comprehensive community-based interventions aimed toward prevention of antisocial behavior.

Situational Prevention

Situational prevention refers to techniques that physically reduce opportunities for criminal activity and remove inducements for crime. Examples include steering locks, strategic fencing, electronic surveillance, physical barriers for crowd control at events, and immediate cleansing of graffiti. Several studies show reductions in crime that are specific to the strategy used (e.g., less car theft with steering wheel locks). In one study, increased natural surveillance combined with target hardening (implementation of physical barriers) at an apartment complex reduced burglaries by 82% (Meredith & Paquette, 1992).

Mentoring

In mentoring programs, adults or older teens serve as a support and positive role model for a youth. Mentors are generally nonprofessional volunteers who meet with a high-risk youth for several hours about three to four times a month. The research on mentoring shows that when mentors use behavior management techniques, target behaviors such as school attendance improve (Fo & O'Donnell, 1975). Moreover, Howell (2003) has described favorable outcomes associated with other types of mentoring programs (e.g., Big Brothers Big Sisters of America), including decreased substance use and aggressive behavior.

After-School Recreation

After-school recreation programs have been evaluated that target children from low-income neighborhoods. The research, though limited, indicates that well-supervised after-school activities can decrease juvenile criminal behavior in a neighborhood. For example, Jones and Offord (1989) showed that juvenile arrests in a neighborhood providing after-school recreation decreased by 75%, which compared very favorably to the 67% increase observed in a comparison community. These favorable results, however, did not generalize to home or school, indicating that more than an after-school recreation program is required to change antisocial behavior across contexts.

WHAT DOESN'T WORK

The vast majority of existing services and interventions for juvenile offenders and substance-abusing adolescents have either no scientific evidence of effectiveness, or the evidence suggests that these interventions do more harm than good. With rare exception, these are the services that are usually being delivered in practice settings.

Adolescent Criminal Behavior

Howell (2003), in a particularly courageous stance for a former Director of the National Institute of Juvenile Justice and Delinquency Prevention, has, in no uncertain terms, described what does not work in reducing criminal behavior in adolescents. A sampling of ineffective interventions in wide use include the following:

• *Zero-tolerance policies.* These policies call for immediate and severe punishment for rule infractions. School officials can use these policies to justify the expulsion of "problem" students. Such students subsequently have little choice but to stay at home, unsupervised if the caregivers are working, and are at high risk for getting into trouble.

• *Scared straight programs.* Research has shown that these "shock" programs actually increase the criminal behavior of participants.

• *Boot camps.* Though popular among the public for their "get tough" military image, these interventions slightly increase criminal behavior at relatively high cost.

• *Incarceration.* Housing antisocial adolescents together for prolonged periods of time does not increase rates of prosocial behavior, nor is there any logical reason to expect this change. Indeed, incarceration often leads to greater criminal enculturation.

• *Residential treatment and hospitalization.* No scientific evidence supports the effectiveness of these costly interventions that attempt to change youth who have been removed from their natural environment, with virtually no efforts to affect those aspects of the natural environment that were conducive to antisocial behavior.

• *Programs involving groups of antisocial adolescents.* As discussed more extensively later in this chapter, interventions that place antisocial adolescents together in groups, even in the context of a well-conceived treatment, seem to promote antisocial behavior.

• *Specialized sex offender treatment.* No scientific evidence supports the prevailing cognitive-behavioral (e.g., relapse prevention) approaches to adolescent sex offender treatment, and there are good reasons to suggest that these approaches are detrimental.

• *Electronic monitoring.* Although appealing to many juvenile justice professionals, scientific evidence does not support the capacity of electronic monitoring to reduce criminal behavior in adolescents.

• *Wilderness programs.* Again, those programs that remove juvenile offenders from their natural environment, group the offenders together, and do little to change the natural environment have little empirical support for effectiveness.

Why don't these programs work? The answer seems relatively straightforward. These ineffective intervention programs do not address the known risk factors for and determinants of criminal behavior in adolescents. Worse, most of these programs provide interventions that are opposite of those suggested by the known risk factors and implemented by the aforementioned evidence-based approaches. For example, youth spend extended time interacting with other problem adolescents, and no attention is devoted to improving family functioning in ways that provide more effective monitoring, supervision, and discipline for the adolescent.

Adolescent Substance Abuse

As noted earlier, the relative absence of rigorous outcome research in the field of adolescent substance abuse limits conclusions that can be made about the nature of effective and ineffective interventions. Two conclusions about the nature of ineffective services are reasonable, however.

First, *no evidence supports the effectiveness of hospitalization of drug-abusing adolescents*. In the only published randomized trial examining this issue, drug-abusing delinquents treated in the community had at least as favorable outcomes as counterparts treated in inpatient settings (Amini, Zilberg, Burke, & Salasnek, 1982). Liddle is currently evaluating MDFT as a community-based alternative to specialized inpatient treatment of adolescent substance abuse, and we anticipate that the findings will support the relative effectiveness of that family-based model.

Second, three sets of research findings suggest that *group therapy approaches may be harmful with substance-abusing youth*. First, as noted in Chapter 1, association with drug-using peers is a powerful predictor of adolescent substance use. Second, randomized trials with adolescents at high risk for substance abuse have shown that group treatments can increase rates of substance use (Dishion, McCord, & Poulin, 1999; Palinkas, Atkins, Miller, & Ferreira, 1996; Poulin, Dishion, & Burraston, 2001) through deviancy training. That is, antisocial peers react positively to each other's antisocial behavior, and interactions before and after sessions and during breaks negate the possibly positive interactions during sessions (Williams, 2003). Third, as indicated in the previous section on adolescent criminal behavior, extensive research shows the negative effects of grouping antisocial youth together, and there are no compelling reasons for expecting that these findings should vary with the nature of adolescent antisocial behavior (i.e., crime vs. substance abuse).

CONCLUSION

We know what works to reduce adolescent criminal activity and have a reasonable idea of how to reduce adolescent drug use. Services should

- Be family-based
- Remove barriers to service access
- Use behavioral intervention principles
- Include rigorous quality-assurance protocols
- Include well-supervised, structured, neighborhood-based prosocial recreational activities for youth at times of the day when supervision is low (i.e., after school, when the parent is at work).

Unfortunately, the vast majority of interventions provided by the existing service systems and funding structures are not consistent with the knowledge base for effective services. Hence, key stakeholders in several states (e.g., Connecticut, Hawaii, Ohio, South Carolina, Pennsylvania, and Washington) and nations (e.g., Norway) are actively working to change service systems in ways that support the implementation of the evidence-based practices noted in this chapter. In Chapter 3, we present a more in-depth discussion of MST, an evidence-based treatment proven successful in reducing juvenile crime and substance abuse.

CHAPTER 3

Multisystemic Therapy
The Model

This chapter provides an overview of the theoretical and clinical foundations of MST. The goals of the chapter are:

1. To describe the theoretical foundation of MST
2. To provide a clinical description of MST
3. To discuss the service-delivery model
4. To discuss the quality-assurance process
5. To review the role of assessment in MST

THEORETICAL FOUNDATION

The theoretical foundation of MST is rooted in systems theory and social-ecological models of behavior. From these theories, behavior is understood to be multidetermined and driven largely by the relationships that the child or adolescent has with others in his or her natural environment. Based primarily on the work of Bronfenbrenner (1979), Haley (1976), and Minuchin (1974), the MST theoretical framework assumes that (1) children and adolescents are embedded in multiple systems that have direct and indirect influences on their behavior, and (2) these influences are reciprocal and bidirectional.

Children and Adolescents Are Embedded in Multiple Systems

Based on Bronfenbrenner's formulations, Figure 3.1 shows the various systems in which youth are embedded and depicts these systems as a series of concentric circles. The child is in the center, and the family is in the next cir-

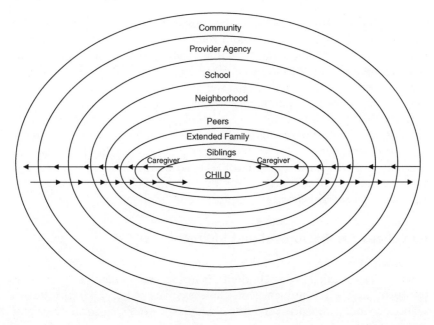

FIGURE 3.1. The ecological environment showing systems in which a youth is embedded.

cle, followed by the extended family, peers, neighborhood, school, provider agency, and greater community. Those systems that are closer to the child are assumed to have more relative power and influence over the child's behavior. For example, the family has influence over the child 24 hours per day, 7 days per week; and family influence extends well into the child's adult life.

Though not as influential as the family, the child also has daily access to peers and other social systems. Peer influence increases as the child ages, and, as noted earlier, association with deviant peers is a powerful predictor of antisocial behavior in adolescents. The school system's influence also can be strong, but school is not in session during the weekend, in the evenings, on holidays, or during summer vacation. Likewise, although neighborhood is an important predictor of the behavior of children, that influence is diffused among the multiple people that live within the neighborhood and by the general characteristics of the neighborhood. Finally, in the outer circle is the greater community with its laws and preferences. Children are certainly influenced by characteristics of the city in which they live and by the region of the country. Nevertheless, the influence of the family and peers remains the greatest.

Very distant from the child is the treatment provider. The relationship between the treatment provider and the child is the least influential relationship when compared with those that occur naturally. Given that service providers have the least influence of all the systems, the MST model assumes that the relationship between the therapist and child is neither necessary nor sufficient to obtain favorable clinical outcomes. This is not to say that the therapist should not have a good working relationship with the child. Rather, the primary relationship for the therapist is with the caregiver(s). The caregivers are (or should be) the managers of the child's ecology. The chief aim of treatment, therefore, is to foster the development of a multifaceted and multilayered context in the natural ecology that supports and reinforces prosocial behavior in children and adolescents.

Influences Are Reciprocal and Bidirectional

As shown by arrows in Figure 3.1, the interactions between each of the systems are reciprocal. That is, children are influenced by each of the systems, but also exert some influence on these systems (e.g., children influence school, school influences children). Similarly, the reciprocal and bidirectional influences extend to the systems. Each of the systems influences the other (e.g., treatment provider influences school, and school influences treatment provider). As discussed later, these theoretical formulations have major implications for the design and foci of interventions within the MST framework.

CLINICAL DESCRIPTION OF MST

Consistent with its theoretical foundation and the nature of the key risk factors for youth antisocial behavior described in Chapter 1, MST is an ecological treatment model that takes into account key systems and their influences in the design of interventions. MST is not a "one size fits all" treatment, applying the same set of interventions to each family. Families are not all alike; they vary greatly in strengths and weaknesses, and virtually no family has the exact same problem manifested in the exact same way. Hence, MST takes a flexible approach wherein interventions are tailored to the specific strengths and needs of each individual family.

In order to facilitate replication studies and the transport of MST programs to community settings, MST implementation procedures have been operationalized and described relatively extensively. These include (1) a set of principles that guide the formulation of clinical interventions, (2) a family-friendly engagement process, (3) a structured analytical process that is used to prioritize interventions, (4) evidence-based treatment techniques that are integrated into the MST conceptual framework, (5) a home-based delivery of services that enables the provision of intensive services, (6) a highly supportive supervision process, and (7) a stringent quality assurance process to promote treatment fidelity.

MST Interventions Follow a Set of Principles

Overall, the clinical practice of MST follows nine principles (see Table 3.1). As discussed later, several studies have shown that youth outcomes are significantly associated with therapist adherence to these nine principles.

  • *Principle 1. The primary purpose of assessment is to understand the fit between the identified problems and their broader systemic context.* Based on this principle, assessment is a process that is ongoing throughout treatment. MST assessment seeks to identify those specific factors within the child's social ecology that are associated with the identified behavior problems. Assessment of the strengths and needs in each of the systems (e.g., youth, family, school, peers, neighborhood) is conducted as one of the first clinical steps, along with the development of hypotheses regarding the key factors that seem to be maintaining the problems.

TABLE 3.1. The Nine Principles of MST

  • *Principle 1:* The primary purpose of assessment is to understand the fit between the identified problems and their broader systemic context.
  • *Principle 2:* Therapeutic contacts emphasize the positive and use systemic strengths as levers for change.
  • *Principle 3:* Interventions are designed to promote responsible behavior and decrease irresponsible behavior among family members.
  • *Principle 4:* Interventions are present-focused and action-oriented, targeting specific and well-defined problems.
  • *Principle 5:* Interventions target sequences of behavior within and between multiple systems that maintain the identified problems.
  • *Principle 6:* Interventions are developmentally appropriate and fit the developmental needs of the youth.
  • *Principle 7:* Interventions are designed to require daily or weekly effort by family members.
  • *Principle 8:* Intervention effectiveness is evaluated continuously from multiple perspectives, with providers assuming accountability for overcoming barriers to successful outcomes.
  • *Principle 9:* Interventions are designed to promote treatment generalization and long-term maintenance of therapeutic change by empowering caregivers to address family members' needs across multiple systemic contexts.

• *Principle 2. Therapeutic contacts emphasize the positive and use systemic strengths as levers for change.* This principle emphasizes the use of a strength focus in treatment by identifying the strengths within each system that can be harnessed to influence behavior change. A strength-focused approach should also extend to all other aspects of program functioning. For example, a negative view of parents will come across in supervision (e.g., comments such as "She's acting so borderline, it's no wonder her kid is acting out") and in behavior toward the family (e.g., canceling appointments, not returning calls in a timely manner). When the therapist has such a negative view of the family, he or she must work with the supervisor to resolve this issue.

• *Principle 3. Interventions are designed to promote responsible behavior and decrease irresponsible behavior among family members.* MST focuses on increasing responsible behavior in the child while also influencing others in the ecology to take active and effective roles in managing the child's behavior and promoting his or her competencies. Increasing responsible behavior in caregivers is often accomplished by altering those behaviors that tend to support and sustain the problem behavior of the child, while increasing behaviors that characterize protective factors. For example, weak parental monitoring and supervision of a child might be changed by interventions that result in decreased parental substance use and increased competency in child management practices.

• *Principle 4. Interventions are present-focused and action-oriented, targeting specific and well-defined problems.* Borrowing from behavior therapy, Principle 4 involves clearly defining the target behavior, determining how to measure the behavior and change in the behavior, and using well-defined interventions that focus on the behavior. The advantage of such specification is that the therapist, family members, and others will know exactly whether the intervention is being implemented and whether it is working. If the intervention is not producing the desired outcomes, the therapist must be able to rapidly determine this and change the course. This principle keeps the key goals and targeted outcomes in the forefront of the case.

• *Principle 5. Interventions target sequences of behavior within and between multiple systems that maintain the identified problems.* Consistent with systems theory, behaviors are viewed as components of sequences of interactions. By defining the sequence of behaviors and making key changes to that sequence, one can change the behavioral outcomes. Importantly, these sequences can pertain to intrafamily transactions (e.g., coercive exchanges) as well as to the family's relations with extrafamilial systems such as the school and family court. In either case, this principle helps the therapist to remember that changes in relations are the keys to changing problem behavior.

• *Principle 6. Interventions are developmentally appropriate and fit the developmental needs of the youth.* The fundamental point of this principle is that interventions should be geared to the developmental needs of the youth. Developmental appropriateness, however, not only refers to what an individual can handle cognitively, but also to where a child or parent is developmentally in the treatment process. For example, the therapist is working with a parent who is having difficulty finding housing and does not have the requisite experience to accomplish this task alone. Here, the therapist determines that the parent is at the early stages in the developmental process of empowerment. Therefore, the therapist works with the parent to demonstrate making phone calls and visiting the housing director. Thus, MST gears interventions to the developmental needs of all in the ecology, including caregivers, by assuring that intervention participants have the requisite knowledge, skills, and support to succeed.

• *Principle 7. Interventions are designed to require daily or weekly effort by family members.* This principle involves engagement of all participants in a series of tasks that produce incremental successes. By accomplishing these tasks on a daily basis, the likelihood is increased that goal-oriented behavior-change tasks will become a part of the family's repertoire. In addition, the assignment of frequent, but clinically pertinent, homework assignments provides valuable information to the therapist regarding family engagement in the treatment process.

• *Principle 8. Intervention effectiveness is evaluated continuously from multiple perspectives, with providers assuming accountability for overcoming barriers to successful outcomes.* Each intervention is designed in a way that allows all participants to monitor progress and success. The therapist collaborates with the participants to design the interventions and teaches them to adapt the interventions based on an ongoing evaluation of effectiveness. The evaluation of the effectiveness comes from the observations and feedback of all the participants involved in the intervention. If the intervention is not producing the desired behavior change, the therapist is responsible for determining the barriers to success and working with the participants to design strategies to overcome those barriers.

• *Principle 9. Interventions are designed to promote treatment generalization and long-term maintenance of therapeutic change by empowering caregivers to address family members' needs across multiple systemic contexts.* The generalization of outcomes means that the caregivers can continue to manage (via interventions) the behavior of the child in the natural ecology when the therapist is no longer present. For therapists to complete treatment and leave families to live their lives, they must give caregivers the tools to solve the child and family's day-to-day difficulties. Thus, families are viewed as the solution to the child's problem. In standard child psychotherapy, the relationship between the therapist and child is paramount. In

MST, the relationship between the parent and child must be more important than that between the therapist and child. Parents are empowered with the knowledge and skills to take care of the clinical needs of their child. They must be empowered to carry out the interventions in the absence of the therapist both during treatment and after treatment is completed.

MST Uses a Family-Friendly Engagement Process

Contrary to standard psychotherapy practice, the MST therapist and clinical team are responsible for family engagement and outcomes (Cunningham & Henggeler, 1999). In the United States, the typical dropout rate is high for a clinic providing outpatient mental health services. In typical outpatient practice, clients who have missed appointments might be contacted by phone or letter, and eventually the case will be closed due to lack of response. Some clinics even implement a "three strikes, you're out" policy. With MST, the therapist must discover how to engage the family and others in the ecology of treatment. In fact, this is the first step in treatment. Until the family is engaged, treatment can neither begin nor progress. At first, families may be hesitant to collaborate with the therapist, as evidenced by behaviors such as not returning phone calls, canceling appointments, and not coming to the door at the time of an appointment. There are, however, many perfectly valid and understandable reasons why a family might not be willing to engage in treatment. For example, family members might not believe that the treatment will help them; they might not trust the system providing the therapy; they might be embarrassed about discussing their problems; or they might have financial or other stressors that are a more important priority. One of the therapist's tasks is to address these reasons to the satisfaction of the family members.

Several aspects of the MST process are designed to promote family engagement in treatment, a crucial step. First, as suggested previously, the strength focus of MST therapists contrasts favorably with the deficit focus that many families have experienced in their interactions with service systems. Second, as noted subsequently, the home-based model of service delivery used in MST helps engagement by overcoming barriers to service delivery. Families are often more comfortable on their own turf than in a clinic setting. Third, treatment is a collaborative process in which families focus on problems that they have identified as important to them. Collaborative relations facilitate engagement. Fourth, therapists never give up on a family or label them as "resistant" or "unmotivated." Rather, the treatment team is charged with the responsibility of assessing and understanding family barriers to engagement. Then new engagement strategies are implemented to overcome these barriers. Fifth, engagement is viewed as an ongoing process rather than a task that is completed and requires no further work. Engagement might be best considered as the ongoing management of a relationship. Thus, therapists are continuously monitoring the family's level of engagement and taking corrective actions when engagement is waning. Engagement is a necessary, but not sufficient, condition for achieving clinical outcomes.

MST Organizes Treatment via a Structured Analytical Process

The MST analytical process depicted in Figure 3.2 is used to operationalize the nine treatment principles. Starting with the identification of referral behaviors from multiple vantage points (i.e., caregivers, youth, teachers, probation officer, other invested parties, and official records), the therapist consolidates the targets for change and measures the current level of these problem behaviors as a baseline. Next, the key individuals in the child's natural ecology are identified and recruited as participants in treatment. Each person is interviewed to gain his or her perspective on the problem, to identify the strengths that he or she brings, and to determine from the person's perspective what changes will be necessary to achieve success. This information is used to develop the overarching goals of treatment in a way that promotes buy-in and participation from all key participants.

The overarching goals define the scope and the end point of MST treatment. When these goals are attained, treatment is complete. Overarching goals must be realistic for the treatment time frame (e.g., eighth-grade child will increase school attendance versus child will graduate from high school). In addition, the goals must be concrete and measurable so that any of the key participants can tell if the goal is met. To remain focused and on task, all subsequent interventions must serve at least one of the overarching goals.

The next step in the analytic process is to prioritize those interactions and relationship changes that are necessary by identifying the "fit" of the problem behaviors within the context of the youth's natural ecology. For example, if the child is having difficulty with anger outbursts at home, the therapist will consider input from each of the systems and use his or her knowledge of the family based on observations to record possible factors that drive the anger outbursts on a "fit circle." The therapist determines the following fit factors: (1) The child has low skills for managing frustration; (2) the parent and child escalate each other in their interactions (i.e., coercive interaction sequences); (3) parental management of the outbursts exacerbates the problem; and (4) the school is frequently leaving messages for the parent concerning the child's difficulties at school, thereby precipitating

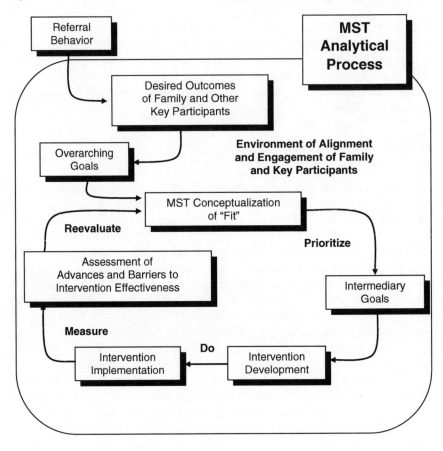

FIGURE 3.2. MST analytical process: The do-loop.

conflict between the parent and child that escalate to outbursts. After the fit factors have been comprehensively identified, the therapist and clinical team determine which of the factors are the primary drivers of the behavior problems. Those factors are targeted initially for change, and those changes are defined as intermediary goals. For example, unintended parental reinforcement of the child's outbursts might be viewed as the primary factor maintaining the problem, and therapeutic attention (i.e., who will do what, when, where, and how) might initially focus on this parent–child interaction. Changes in parental management of the outbursts are viewed as intermediate outcomes—targets that lead to desired changes in the overarching goal. If the anger outbursts are eliminated through more effective parental management of the behavior, it might not be necessary to attend to the other fit factors. Resolving the school difficulties, however, will most likely comprise another of the overarching goals.

The interventions are implemented with all participants monitoring the success and providing feedback to the therapist and caregivers. Throughout the intervention process, the therapist and caregivers compare the intended outcomes with the actual outcomes and measure the successes achieved. If sufficient success has not been obtained, the therapist and treatment participants identify the barriers to achieving the treatment goals. This new information is then compared with or added to the current understanding of how the behaviors "fit" within the natural ecology, and the process is reinitiated each week (i.e., fit—prioritization—interventions—evaluation). The structured analytic process continues until such time as the overarching goals have been completed. At the end of treatment, the therapist and family "true up" the overarching goals. That is, they review each of the goals and the successes in achieving those goals. Throughout treatment, the therapist helps the family to address the problems as independently as possible and to build an indigenous support system that supports the interactional changes that have been achieved.

MST Integrates Evidence-Based Treatment Techniques

A central feature of the MST model is its integration of evidence-based treatment approaches. After the overarching goals are set and the clinical team has an understanding of the "fit" of the factors that relate to or drive the problem, interventions are developed. MST incorporates interventions that have empirical support, such as the cognitive-behavioral therapies, behavior therapies, pragmatic family therapies, and certain pharmacological interventions (e.g., for ADHD). There are several major differences between using these techniques within MST and using them alone, however. First, within MST the ecology is the client rather than the individual child or the family alone. Whereas the aforementioned evidence-based treatments have historically focused on a limited aspect of a youth's social ecology (e.g., individual cognitive-behavioral therapy for anger management), MST integrates those interventions into a broad-based ecological framework that addresses a range of pertinent factors across family, peer, school, and community contexts. Second, because caregivers are viewed as critical to achieving favorable long-term outcomes, interventions are delivered primarily by the caregivers whenever possible. For example, cognitive-behavioral therapy for improving the youth's problem-solving skills might be taught to the father by the therapist, and the father would then teach these skills to his son. Third, as discussed later, and in contrast to how the vast majority of evidence-based interventions are delivered in the field, the interventions are supported by a strong, outcome-oriented quality-assurance system that enhances intervention fidelity and the attainment of desired clinical outcomes.

Although evidence-based techniques are used and high value is placed on treatment fidelity, those techniques must sometimes be adapted to better fit the sociocultural contexts of the families. For example, in cases where skills training is used, the therapist must understand what is feasible for the parent. A parent with intellectual limitations might not be able to implement a complex reinforcement system as part of a substance abuse treatment protocol. Instead, the therapist (with support from the treatment team) might have to adapt the system to its simplest components and provide very concrete cues (e.g., sign on the refrigerator door) and instructions (e.g., pictures versus written information) for implementing the system. Thus, the behavioral techniques might have to be modified to forms that can be implemented by parents of varying strengths and limitations.

MST Provides Intensive Treatment via Home-Based Delivery of Services

MST has been delivered via a home-based model of service delivery in all the MST research studies and across all the MST dissemination sites in the United States and internationally. The home-based model removes barriers to service access and promotes the capacity of interventions to alter the youth's ecology. The key characteristics of MST service delivery include the following:

1. Low caseloads of three to six families per clinician, which allows intensive services to be provided to each family (2-15 hours per week, titrated to need).
2. Therapists work within a team of three to four practitioners, though each clinician has his or her own caseload.
3. Treatment occurs daily to several times a week, with sessions decreasing in frequency as the family progresses.
4. Treatment is time-limited and generally lasts 4–6 months, depending on the seriousness of the problems and success of the interventions.
5. Treatment is delivered in the family's natural environment: in their home, community, or other place convenient to the family.
6. Treatment is delivered at times convenient to the family; thus, therapists work a flexible schedule.
7. Therapists are available to clients 24 hours per day, 7 days per week, generally through an on-call system.

The home-based service delivery system allows the provision of very intensive clinical services that are designed to keep children with their families and prevent out-of-home placements. Although intensive home-based services are more costly than standard, once a week outpatient care, services such as MST are highly cost-effective if targeted to youth at high risk of out-of-home placement (Aos et al., 2001). For example, a therapist who prevents only three $35,000 placements in a year (many residential placements cost much more) pays for his or her salary as well as for all other associated costs (e.g., supervision, office space, travel, phone, fringe benefits). Moreover, implementing an effective community-based treatment (vs. ineffective and costly out-of-home placements) can have many additional benefits for the community (e.g., reduced crime, increased tax support), individual youth (e.g., improved functioning), and family (e.g., reduced stress).

MST Provides a Supportive Supervision Process

The overriding purpose of MST clinical supervision is to help therapists achieve desired clinical outcomes with their families. Within this broader mission, MST clinical supervision explicitly provides therapists with an understanding of the MST model, facilitates adherence to the nine treatment principles, assists in determining ways to engage families and professionals from other systems, assists in learning and implementing evidence-based techniques, and helps identify barriers to the success of interventions. To fulfill these aims, MST provides a high level of weekly supervision (i.e., average 2–4 hours of face-to-face contact with each therapist) along with supervisor availability that matches the therapist schedule—24 hours a day, 7 days a week. When the caseload is comprised of delinquency cases, a 50%-time supervisor is allocated for each MST team (three to four therapists). Thus, the clinical supervisor is available to consult with the therapist when needed and even visit the family with the therapist to address safety concerns or for clinical skill building. Similarly, as specified in the MST supervisory manual (Henggeler & Schoenwald, 1998), the supervisor is responsible for building the therapists' capacity to be effective. This is accomplished by determining the barriers to low adherence, when evident, and developing strategies to overcome those barriers (e.g., additional learning experiences, listening to tapes of sessions, or accompanying the therapist on a family session.)

Weekly supervision sessions are very structured and goal-oriented. Supervision is held in a group format, which assures that each therapist is familiar with every case. Such familiarity is important because the therapists develop an on-call schedule in which they take turns assuming responsibility for crisis response during weekends and vacations. Likewise, therapists have usually met the families in each other's caseloads, which increases the family and therapist's comfort in handling crises at a time that the primary therapist is not available. Prior to supervision, therapists complete a weekly summary sheet (see Figure 3.3) that contains the weekly intermediary goals and notes regarding the family's progress toward achieving each goal as well as any changes in the understanding of fit factors, if pertinent. The supervisor receives a copy of the goal sheet for each family, and these are reviewed before supervision. Supervision generally occurs once a week for about 2 hours. When needed, supervision time is devoted to demonstrating a skill (e.g., marital interventions) or developing solutions to challenging fit factors. Therapists should leave supervision with concrete plans regarding the intervention strategies that will be used to address well-specified intermediary goals for the upcoming week.

MST Uses a Stringent Quality-Assurance Process

Several published studies (Henggeler, Melton, Brondino, Scherer, & Hanley, 1997; Henggeler, Pickrel, & Brondino, 1999; Huey, Henggeler, Brondino, & Pickrel, 2000; Schoenwald, Henggeler, Brondino, & Rowland, 2000; Schoenwald, Sheidow, Letourneau, & Liao, 2003) have demonstrated significant associations between therapist fidelity to MST treatment principles and key outcomes for youth (e.g., avoidance of rearrest or incarceration) and families (e.g., improved functioning). In light of the importance of treatment adherence to MST outcomes, considerable attention is devoted to quality-assurance mechanisms aimed at enhancing treatment fidelity. The quality-assurance system includes (1) an orientation training week, (2) quarterly booster training, (3) weekly on-site MST supervision, (4) weekly consultation from an MST expert, (5) feedback on adherence ratings from parents and therapists, and, in MST clinical trials, (6) feedback via expert ratings of audiotaped therapy sessions. With the exception of MST treatment that is provided within the context of research programs in clinical trials, all components of the quality-assurance system are provided by MST Services (*mstservices.com*), which has the exclusive license for the transport of MST technology and intellectual property through the Medical University of South Carolina.

• *Orientation training week.* Prior to beginning an MST program, therapists, supervisors, and administrators participate in an initial 5-day orientation. This training provides an overview of the MST treatment model and carefully reviews the treatment manual (Henggeler, Schoenwald, Borduin, Rowland, & Cunningham, 1998). The week includes some didactic instruction along with role play of techniques and group exercises to provide practice.

• *Booster training.* Clinical teams participate in booster trainings on a

Family: _____ Therapist: _____ Date: _____

Weekly Review

Overarching/Primary MST Goals

Previous Intermediary Goals   Met   Partially   Not

Barriers to Intermediary Goals

Note: These should correspond to intermediary goals

Advances in Treatment

Note: These should correspond to intermediary goals

How has your assessment of the fit changed with new information/ interventions?

New Intermediary Goals for Next Week

FIGURE 3.3. Case summary for MST supervision and consultation.

quarterly basis, with the content of the training specific to the needs of the team. Examples of the types of booster training that occur include specific techniques for working with maltreated children and their families, treatment for serious mental illness in caregivers, school-based interventions, and engagement strategies.

• *Weekly on-site supervision.* As noted earlier, weekly supervision is intensive and geared toward helping therapists achieve the overarching goals for each family.

• *Weekly consultation from an MST expert.* Following the MST consultation protocol (Schoenwald, 1998), an MST consultant who is distal to the program site provides weekly consultation to the team with the aim of promoting positive client outcomes through adherence to the MST treatment model. This is a phone consultation that generally requires 1 hour per week. As in the supervisory process, the consultant receives faxed copies of the status of each case (i.e., goals, progress, barriers) prior to the conference call for review. Feedback is received through adherence ratings from parents and therapists. Standardized ratings measuring adherence to the nine principles are completed by the caregivers on a regular basis. The Therapist Adherence Measure (TAM; Henggeler & Borduin, 1992) is completed by the parent during the second week of MST and once every 4 weeks thereafter. Feedback is given to the therapist regarding how closely the model is being followed, and corrective strategies are developed when treatment adherence is low. Likewise, the Supervisor Adherence Measure (SAM; Schoenwald, Henggeler, & Edwards, 1998) is completed by the therapists 1 month after the MST program begins and every 2 months thereafter. The SAM evaluates the supervisor's adherence to the MST model of supervision. The TAM and SAM and their scoring are available on the MST Institute website (*www.mstinstitute.org*).

• *Feedback via expert ratings of audiotaped sessions.* In MST clinical trials, where treatment fidelity is absolutely critical for the validity of the research, therapists audiotape every treatment session. On a weekly basis, a session tape is randomly selected and rated by an expert to measure adherence to the nine principles. Therapists are given feedback on the adherence ratings, and comments are provided on adherence to each principle.

THE ROLE OF ASSESSMENT IN MST

Assessment conducted within the MST framework differs from that conducted in typical psychotherapy practice. The main functions of MST assessment are to determine (1) the problem areas requiring intervention and strengths that can support the interventions, (2) the factors that seem to be driving or maintaining the problem areas, (3) whether the interventions are working on a daily to weekly basis, and (4) the change in key variables over time in the youth, family, and ecology. Thus, while valid assessment is critical to the design and implementation of interventions within MST, assessment is tailored to the individual youth and his or her ecology rather than being the product of a compilation of measurement instruments.

Assessment of a Family's Strengths and Needs

The function of the therapist's initial contact with the family is to begin the engagement process and gather information about the concerns of the youth, parents, and others in their ecology. A standard intake assessment obtains detailed information on the presenting problem, a history of prior services (inpatient and outpatient), the child's developmental history (language, social development, motor skills), a medical history (accidents, injuries, allergies, health problems), a school history (grade, special services, expulsions/suspensions, behavioral problems), and a trauma history (abuse or neglect, accidents, community or family violence). Furthermore, a mental status examination is conducted with the child to gain an understanding of possible psychiatric symptoms, and a genogram (e.g., Figure 3.4) of the family is developed to gain an understanding of who is in the family as well as the makeup of social supports, including extended family, close friends, and neighbors.

Strengths and needs are assessed regarding each of the systems in the life of the child. To do so may require an interview with grandparents, teachers, and other community resources. Figure 3.5 shows a completed strengths and needs summary. As treatment begins, the factors on the needs

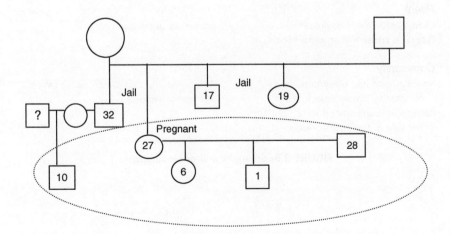

FIGURE 3.4. Family genogram.

Family: _Arbutus_____   Therapist: _Rumsay_____   Date: _9/17/03___

Systemic Strengths

Individual

Desire to attend school

Industrious and independent

Friendly and mannerly

Bright

Enjoys football

Helps care for siblings

Family

Caregiver had him since infancy

Male caregiver has a job

Family has transportation

Caregivers affectionate to child

Involved grandmother

Involved extended family

School

School has good relationship with
  caregiver

Child completes homework

Performs at grade level

Respectful toward teachers

Peers

Liked by children in neighborhood

Prosocial cousins in neighborhood

Community

Neighborhood has playground and
  community center near home

Parents in neighborhood watch out for
  the kids in the neighborhood

Systemic Weaknesses/Needs

Limited prosocial activities

Doesn't communicate needs

Runs away

Steals

ADHD—behavior problems:
  inattention/impulsivity

Sets inappropriate limits for
  developmental level

Economic difficulties

Marital communication problems

Female caregiver depressed

No rules/consequences

Female caregiver overwhelmed by child
  care tasks and overuses child as
  babysitter

Child has math and behavior problems:
  poor attention, tapping, talking out

Access to antisocial peers

High crime and substance abuse rates

Community violence

FIGURE 3.5. Strengths and needs summary.

side are targeted for intervention, and the factors on the strengths side are used to help with change. For example, a strong after-school program (community strength) might be used to partially compensate for low parental monitoring (a parental need). The therapist would work with the parent to make use of this strength *and* meet the need by helping the parent enroll the child at the after-school program. As treatment progresses, the strengths side of the list should grow and the needs side should diminish.

Assessment of the Fit of the Problem

Assessment of the factors driving the key problems is completed after those problems are identified. Figure 3.6 shows an example of a "fit circle," which organizes the fit assessment. The problem behavior (e.g., school truancy, low monitoring, conflict between parent and child) goes in the circle—this is the identified problem. To assess fit factors of the behavior in the circle, the therapist, based on information obtained from multiple sources, hypothesizes factors that contribute to the target behavior. These factors can come from any of the systems surrounding the youth (e.g., parents, siblings, school, peer, neighborhood) or from characteristics of the youth (e.g., depressive symptoms). Next, the therapist describes the evidence supporting the role of each fit factor in the identified problem, based on direct observation and information from key individuals in the child's social ecology.

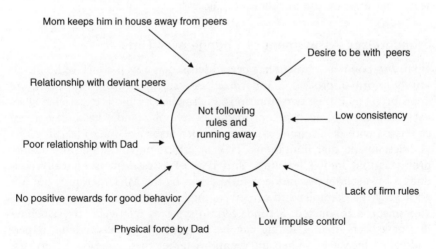

FIGURE 3.6. Fit circle.

The fit factors are very important in MST because they become the proximal target of interventions aimed at ultimately ameliorating the identified problems. Furthermore, as treatment progresses and the therapist gains a more complete understanding of the family and its ecology, the delineation of pertinent fit factors will change. Therefore, therapists keep a weekly record of changes in understanding the factors driving the identified problems. Finally, circumstances can change during the course of treatment that have implications for the delineation of fit factors (e.g., grandparent becomes critically ill, and working parents no longer have help in monitoring their teenager's after-school time). In such cases, the therapist considers the relative influence of the new fit factor and prioritizes that factor for intervention.

Ongoing Assessment of Intervention Success

The assessment of clinical progress is ongoing throughout treatment. Using standard behavioral strategies, a baseline measure is taken of the target behavior. For example, if truancy is the target behavior, school records would be obtained to determine days the youth attended school and days absent. Attendance would be measured each week to see if the intervention is working. A second example is a target behavior of parental cocaine use. Urine drug screens are taken on a weekly basis to determine whether the parent is successfully avoiding drug use. When behaviors are not improving, continuous assessment gives the therapist a timely opportunity to determine the barriers to the lack of progress and to alter interventions in ways that increase the likelihood of success.

Standardized Assessment of Change over Time

Up to this point, assessment has been discussed as a well-conceived, but relatively informal, process. Standardized assessment measures, however, are appropriate in at least two situations. First, when a child is experiencing severe behavioral or academic problems in school, standardized assessment can assist with determining whether the problems are due to learning disabilities, intellectual limitations, lack of effort, or emotional and family problems that inhibit learning. This type of assessment is typically conducted by a school psychologist rather than by the MST therapist, but advocacy by the therapist and caregivers might be needed to assure that the assessment is conducted. Second, certain types of relatively covert behaviors or aspects of functioning can be assessed with well-validated paper-and-pencil measures. When interventions target these types of behaviors, corresponding assessment instruments can be used to monitor progress. For example, when cognitive-behavioral therapy or medication is being used to reduce childhood depression, the Children's Depression Inventory (Kovaks, 1981) can be used to track outcomes. Similarly, the Brief Symptom Inventory (Derogatis, 1993) can be used to monitor success in treating caregiver emotional distress.

CONCLUSION

MST is based primarily on a social-ecological model of behavior that considers the reciprocal effects of all of the systems pertinent to the life of a child. These systems are considered in the assessment of the strengths and needs of the family, in the assessment of the fit factors that contribute to the identified problems, and in the interventions based on these analyses. Intervention techniques are selected from the array of interventions that have at least some evidence base, and can be applied to problems identified in each system (i.e., school, family, individual child). These interventions are tailored to the specific characteristics, strengths, and target problems of a particular family in the context of the strengths and limitations of their social ecology. The application of interventions is conducted in a very structured, organized, and intensive way by highly trained and supported therapists who follow a stringent quality-assurance process.

The application of MST has typically been with individual families in varying neighborhoods. This book represents the first project in which MST was implemented neighborhoodwide. Before describing how MST principles were implemented in an entire neighborhood to address violence and drug abuse, it is first helpful to discuss how the neighborhood was engaged in this collaborative process.

PART II

Implementing Prevention and Intervention Programs in Collaboration with Neighborhood Residents

The overarching purpose of Part II is to provide a comprehensive description of the wealth of interventions provided within the Neighborhood Solutions Project and how these interventions combined to be mutually supportive.

This section includes

- Guidelines for engaging neighborhood residents and partnering with key stakeholders (Chapter 4)
- MST treatment protocols that were used to address youth criminal behavior, substance abuse, and school expulsions (Chapters 5–7)
- Overviews of supportive initiatives provided in collaboration with other community stakeholders, including health and wellness activities, health care, and community policing (Chapters 8–10)

More specifically, Chapter 4, written primarily by the neighborhood leaders with input from the day-to-day experiences of the project director, describes the development of the Neighborhood Solutions Project. A step-by-step guide is provided for engaging a neighborhood and partnering with key stakeholders. Common issues that must be addressed by outsiders are reviewed, including issues of trust, safety, race, culture, and conducting research in a black community.

Chapters 5–7 describe the MST approach to managing three types of clinical problems with youth: antisocial behavior, substance abuse, and problem behavior in school. Each chapter starts with a brief review of the scientific literature illustrating the success of MST for the corresponding problem domain. Then a description is given of applying MST for each of the problems within the context of the Neighborhood Solutions Project. The MST process for treating each type of problem is illustrated through case examples.

Chapters 8–10 describe services other than MST that were included in the Neighborhood Solutions Project. Chapter 8 discusses health and wellness activities that were designed by the neighborhood leaders and residents (some of whom were youth) and implemented as violence and substance abuse prevention activities. Chapter 9 presents steps for implementing and methods for financing neighborhood-based primary care health services. Finally, Chapter 10 reviews community policing and describes a corresponding program that was a part of the Neighborhood Solutions Project.

CHAPTER 4

Implementing a Neighborhood-Based Project

When researchers or program developers wish to join with a neighborhood to implement a neighborhood-based program, knowing how to engage the neighborhood and secure support for the project is essential. Several common elements are critical to the start-up of any neighborhood-based program, yet each neighborhood is unique and the culture of individual neighborhoods will guide the tailoring of project development. In this chapter the reader is guided through steps to engaging a neighborhood and developing partnerships with key stakeholders. The chapter goals are

1. To describe the background of the "Neighborhood Solutions Project" as an example of a neighborhood-based project addressing youth crime, substance abuse, and community violence
2. To present steps for engaging a neighborhood and securing support from its leaders
3. To discuss common issues related to outsiders coming in to a neighborhood and strategies for overcoming barriers these issues present

BACKGROUND OF THE NEIGHBORHOOD SOLUTIONS PROJECT

The Neighborhood Solutions Project was developed and implemented in North Charleston, South Carolina, as part of a Healthy South Carolina initiative funded through the state. The major purpose for this project, from the perspective of the funders, was to reduce costly out-of-home placements (i.e., incarceration, residential care, long-term hospitalization) among youth who were high risk for such placements and to approach this goal by working with key persons in the youth's natural ecology. Researchers responsible for this project (Scott W. Henggeler, Principal Investigator; Cynthia Cupit Swenson, Project Director) were tasked with (1) identifying neighborhoods in South Carolina with very high rates of crime, juvenile arrests rates, maltreatment reports, and poverty, and (2) designing a study to evaluate the effects of developing and implementing a collaborative project using evidence-based interventions to address these neighborhood problems.

Dr. Sonja Schoenwald, Associate Director of the Family Services Research Center, took the lead in identifying neighborhoods across the state that had these negative social indicators. She used census data, Department of Juvenile Justice records, child protection data, and crime statistics to develop a list of the most challenging neighborhoods. The Project team drove through several of these neighborhoods, noting visible resources and size of the neighborhood. Union Heights was randomly selected from the list of high-crime neighborhoods as the first neighborhood to approach for participation in the project. If they were not interested, a second neighborhood would be randomly selected. They were interested.

The Staff

Project staff included the project director, two master's-level therapists, a bachelor's-level family resource specialist, and an activity director. The family resource specialist grew up in the neighborhood and knew many of the leaders and families in the neighborhood. The project director had a PhD and licensure in clinical and school psychology and served as the MST clinical supervisor.

The Funding

The funding included approximately $600,000 spread across 3 years. This amount covered all of the clinical positions, pagers, cell phones, supplies, and laboratories for regular urine drug screens, and equipment and materials to carry out the prevention activities.

The Evaluation

Four groups of participants contributed to the research evaluation of the Neighborhood Solutions Project. The first group, labeled the Neighborhood Solutions clinical sample (NS–clinical) consisted of youth ages 10–16 years who were referred by community leaders for their criminal activity and substance abuse. To assess the progress of these youth, weekly urine drug screens were taken, and an assessment battery was administered pre and post treatment and every 3 months until aftercare was complete. This battery measured ultimate outcomes (i.e., arrests) as well as youth functioning, community violence experiences, parent functioning, and family functioning.

The second group of youth, labeled the Comparison clinical sample (Comparison-clinical), served as a control group for the NS–clinical youth. This second group of youth was referred by leaders from a nearby neighborhood with similar crime problems. The age range and referral criteria were similar as for the NS–clinical sample, and the research staff gave families information for treatment referrals. These youth and their caregivers completed the same assessment battery as the NS–clinical youth, but urine drug screens were not collected. Work was conducted to engage the comparison community. Although extensive efforts were made to recruit a group of high-risk youth in the comparison neighborhood, subsequent analyses showed that these youth had significantly lower rates of criminal activity and behavioral problems than did their NS–clinical counterparts. These preexisting differences greatly attenuated the value of the Comparison-clinical youth as a control condition.

The third group of participants consisted of youth referred to the Neighborhood Solutions Project due to imminent risk of suspension or expulsion from school (NS–school). The school personnel made referrals initially, and later parents self-referred. A pre– and post treatment assessment battery was administered that contained the same measures as those used with the NS–clinical sample.

The fourth group of participants was a well-adjusted sample of youth living in the neighborhood (NS-healthy). Leaders in the target community developed a list of children and youth who were "doing well." These youth were assessed once per year over the course of the project for a total of three assessments. The assessment batter contained the same measures as those used with the other groups of participants.

The Neighborhood

The Union Heights Community is comprised of roughly 2,500 individuals living in the Union Heights, Howard Heights, and Windsor neighborhoods of North Charleston, South Carolina. Ninety-nine percent of residents are African American. The majority of residents have low incomes (median household income = $13,583). A single parent heads 56% of families in the neighborhood. According to state demographic data, 75% of residents did not complete high school. School district records show that only 30% of elementary and middle school students meet minimum standards for reading. Many of the neighborhood youth are involved with the Department of Juvenile Justice (DJJ). The 17 DJJ-involved youth referred for clinical treatment by the community leaders had a total of 67 (M = 3.9) arrests in their history, representing 154 (M = 9) legal charges. Community-policing records indicate that over 200 calls for service in a month were common. Finally, the children in the community face a future of health concerns because the families suffer from high rates of diabetes (13% of adults in the neighborhood) and hypertension (40% of adults in the neighborhood).

The Outcomes

NS–Clinical Participants

Pre–post treatment outcomes are reported on arrest data and self-reported criminal activity. Because youth from the comparison community had significantly fewer arrests, and thus were not an adequate comparison group, between-groups comparisons were not conducted. As shown in Chapter 5, only 29% of youth in the NS–clinical group (N = 17) were rearrested during the intensive MST treatment phase, and none of these arrests were drug related. In addition to arrest data, self-reported youth criminal activity decreased significantly from pre to post treatment for the NS–clinical youth. As shown in Chapter 6, youth who were having problems with cocaine and marijuana use (N = 13) showed marked reductions in use of these drugs. Also, youth showed significant reductions in self-report of drug use and association with peers involved with drugs.

In addition to reductions in criminal activity and drug use, youth in the NS–clinical group endorsed marked pre–post treatment reductions in experiencing and witnessing violence over the past 6 months. These changes pertained to

- Seeing people selling drugs: 88% to 38%
- Being asked to sell drugs: 38% to 13%
- Being slapped, punched, or hit: 69% to 13%
- Being beaten or mugged: 19% to 0%
- Seeing someone else be beaten or mugged: 69% to 19%
- Being shot: 13% to 0%
- Seeing someone being shot: 50% to 6%
- Seeing someone being killed: 25% to 0%

NS–School Participants

Among youth referred for being at imminent risk of expulsion (N = 16), only 1 student was expelled. This student was quickly enrolled in an alternative school program and was able to continue academic progress. Further, youth in the NS–school group reported substantive reductions in perpetrating crimes against persons and school delinquency.

NS–Healthy Participants

This normative group consisted of 31 youth. Fifteen of these youth moved out of the neighborhood during the course of the project, and data were collected only so long as they lived there. Youth who lived in the neighborhood during the entire project increased the number of leisure and recreational activities in which they were involved from Year 1 to Year 2 and showed even further increases from Year 2 to Year 3. Regarding experiences with community violence, although the percentage of youth initially reporting that they witnessed or experienced violence was lower than those in the clinical group, a large portion of youth still endorsed these experiences. The number of youth exposed to these experiences of violence decreased at Year 2, and the decrease was maintained at Year 3 for most "witnessing violence" experiences. Seeing someone else being beaten or mugged increased slightly in Year 3 but did not reach Year 1 levels. Significantly, none of the muggings reported at Year 3 took place in the community. They took place at either school or places outside the neighborhood (e.g., mall, another town). Following is a summary of violence experiences at Year 1, Year 2, and Year 3:

- Seeing people selling drugs: 63% to 56% to 50%
- Being slapped, punched, or hit: 47% to 24% to 25%
- Seeing someone else being slapped, punched, or hit: 41% to 12% to 13%
- Being beaten or mugged: 24% to 0 to 6% (1 youth)
- Seeing someone else being beaten or mugged: 53% to 24% to 31%
- Seeing someone being attacked with a knife: 12% to 0 to 0
- Seeing someone get shot: 18% to 0 to 0
- Seeing someone being killed: 6% to 0 to 0

It is interesting that the NS–clinical participants who received MST showed greater decreases in physical assault experiences than did the normative group.

DOING THE GROUNDWORK

Several early steps were critical in identifying and engaging neighborhood stakeholders.

Identifying Neighborhood Leaders

The first step in engaging the neighborhood was to identify the leaders and stakeholders. Our initial contact was with the mayor's office to request information regarding neighborhood associations, identified formal leaders, and the city government's knowledge of informal leaders—the "movers and shakers" of the community. In the Union Heights neighborhood, the Gethsemani Community Center, directed by Ida Taylor, was identified by the mayor's office as the hub of activity. In addition, Roscoe Mitchell was identified as the president of the Neighborhood Council. The mayor's office provided necessary contact numbers and addresses.

Contacting Key Neighborhood Leaders

The second step toward getting into the neighborhood was to contact a key leader. The mayor's office suggested that we contact Ida Taylor. A cold call was made to Mrs. Taylor, and she agreed to meet with the project director. In preparation for this meeting, a list of questions was developed to learn as much as possible about the community and to begin to formulate the next steps toward determining whether the community might want to engage in a project. During the first meeting, the project director noted how the community leader introduced her and how she referred to the other leaders. Doing this allowed a show of respect for the formality or informality of the initial relationships. For example, Mrs. Taylor referred to her neighbors using the title of Mr. or Mrs. and their last name. These titles were used until leaders in the community expressed a desire that our communication be on a first-name basis. In African American neighborhoods nicknames are fairly commonplace. Over time the relationship between project staff and the community developed to the point that some staff members were assigned nicknames (e.g., Dr. Swenson = Doc). In addition, nicknames of neighborhood leaders became known (e.g., Ida Taylor = Shorty Rock) and could be used by project staff. Some neighborhood members were introduced by their nicknames, and staff never knew their actual names. Using those nicknames is a sign of affection and is part of being an integral part of the family of a neighborhood.

Meeting with Neighborhood Leaders as a Group

The initial group meeting, and third step, was between project staff and approximately 10 leaders from the community. The meeting was conducted at the community center. The primary purpose of the meeting was for the potential collaborators to get to know each other and to discuss the opportunities presented by the project. During such meetings, the "outsiders" must come "one down" with a willingness to learn about the neighborhood and the leaders' concerns as well as an eye for highlighting the strengths of the participants. The community leaders of Union Heights emphasized that all neighborhoods are different and that outsiders should not approach a neighborhood with the attitude of "I can fix your community." People in troubled neighborhoods do not view themselves or their neighborhood as "broken." Nevertheless, neighborhood stakeholders are keenly aware of difficulties and generally welcome help in resolving problems if they can trust the outsiders bringing the help.

Communities that experience economic disadvantage, however, must have proof that outsiders are not coming in to take from the community and give little in return. That is, researchers cannot expect to be welcome to conduct research for research's sake. There must be a substantial benefit for the community, and that benefit must meet the goals and desires of the people. Leaders must feel comfortable that the research collaborators are committed to helping meet the goals specified by neighborhood residents and that the researchers are not planning to "hoodwink" the neighborhood.

Discussing Change Priorities

During the initial and subsequent group meetings, project staff emphasized that we wanted to join in implementing a project to address what the leaders viewed as the foremost needs of their youth and families. The leaders later reported that the most important behavior of the project staff in facilitating engagement was to allow the leaders to express their concerns about their community and their youth, to list out those concerns, and to prioritize. The leaders noted that researchers commonly come into African American communities with "canned" projects and impose them on the community, regardless of whether these programs fit the community's goals. Similarly, researchers will place the name of a neighborhood on their grant application, use the "disadvantaged" statistics of the community to obtain funding, and never provide any substantive services. In fact, the leaders showed us a brochure on which their community was listed and said they had never even met the director of the project described on the brochure.

After considerable discussion, the neighborhood leaders reached consensus that the most pressing problems facing youth and families in the neighborhood were youth substance abuse, youth crime, and youth suspension/expulsion from school. These were the priorities that the neighborhood leaders wanted to address, and, significantly, these priorities were consistent with the aims of the state-funding source. The project staff was clear that they would set the project up any way that the community wanted, but that project staff specialized in interventions for antisocial behavior using a treatment approach called MST. Thus, it was likely that

MST principles would play an important role in the design of any interventions programs.

Subsequently, a valuable contribution to engagement was the ability of project leadership to show evidence that the proposed treatment model had a strong track record for reducing youth crime and drug use. This allowed the neighborhood leaders to feel confident that they were not guinea pigs trying out a new treatment, but that proven interventions would be used. Thus, community leaders were given copies of the publications from MST clinical trials. The results of the past research were explained. Researchers or anyone implementing a project should never underestimate the capacity of people who are not researchers to understand study outcomes and the logic of study design, and to demand high-quality services. In fact, the public deserves no less. In addition, researchers must realize that community leaders know the most about their own neighbors, and a neighborhood-based project cannot get off the ground or survive without this knowledge. The balance of knowledge that each side brings to the table is what creates a working team.

Communitywide Meeting

After neighborhood leaders had an understanding of what the project staff would bring to the table, and the project staff had an understanding of the goals and desires of the leaders, the next step was to meet with the community as a whole. The primary aims of this meeting were to introduce the idea of a project, listen, answer questions, and ask questions regarding what the residents want and their priorities. In addition, this meeting began a broader relationship with the neighborhood residents. Thus, project staff did what was necessary to make participants feel comfortable and welcome. For example, the neighborhood leaders identified the optimal day, time, and place for the meeting.

The project staff was told not to become alarmed if residents were not on time. Leaders informed us that people would likely be late because part of their culture included a concept known as "CPT" or "Colored People Time." They explained that people of color, at least in their community, do not always operate on a standard time for meetings, but generally come after the stated starting time. So, we should relax and not be anxious with the empty room at the time a meeting is scheduled to start. Refreshments should be provided, and these should include food that is common to the culture of the people. The project staff should introduce themselves and tell about their personal backgrounds. We came to understand that when people are considering welcoming you into their neighborhood, this is a relationship that takes on a very personal, intimate quality. They must feel comfortable about you as a person and, consequently, they want to know personal things about you such as where you grew up, a little about your family, where you went to school, and how much experience you have. In effect, the researchers have to sell themselves to the community as human beings (i.e., as mothers, husbands) and as researchers. Moreover, in answering questions from the neighborhood residents, the leaders should be summoned to help. This shows the neighborhood residents that the proposed project is a collaborative venture, and not just a bone being tossed out by a university without the blessing of the leaders. When trust is developed and people in the community see that the project staff are "here for a good reason," they will be more likely to work with the project.

In the initial neighborhoodwide meeting of the Neighborhood Solutions Project, we were directed by the residents to meet further with their leaders and others to discuss project specifics and to come back to the community and draw the project for them on a poster-size piece of paper. Toward the goal of determining what the project should look like, one of the leaders, Oliver Addison, agreed to serve as a "cultural guide." Through him we came to understand the common issues concerning outsiders coming in to a neighborhood, strategies for overcoming barriers these issues present, how to determine the specifics of the project, and how to secure support.

Laying the Foundation: Many Individual Meetings with Many Stakeholders

The single most important strategy for determining the specifics of a project and securing support is to take the time and devote the energy needed to gain the trust of collaborators. Researchers should not rush into a project, even though funding structures include clear time parameters. Spending the time talking and developing relationships up front can prevent the failure of a project down the line.

In the Neighborhood Solutions Project our cultural guide directed us to meet one-to-one with many different individuals including (1) all ministers within the bounds of the community (there were 17 churches), (2) school personnel including principals, teachers, cafeteria line staff, cleaning staff, school board members, and the county school superintendent, (3) the mayor and other city officials, (4) family court judges, (5) other judges in the county, (6) business leaders, (7) the recreation department director, (8) department of juvenile justice staff, (9) the sheriff, (10) the police chief, (11) local police officers, (12) local residents, (13) elders of the community, (14) parents, and (15) drug dealers working in the community. The cultural guide set up and accompanied us to each of these meetings, which was an essential show of support for our credibility. Roughly 6 weeks of daily meetings, sun up to sun down, were required to meet all of the people noted here, find out what they felt the project should look like, and answer their questions. Most of these individual meetings took place in church sanctuaries, offices, schools, cafeterias, the jail, and courtrooms. For the elders, meetings occurred on porches, piazzas, and in lawn chairs. For drug dealers, the meetings were usually spontaneous and transpired on street corners or in private places out of public view. In keeping with the MST model, we met with people at times and in places that were convenient for them. In addition to one-to-one meetings with ministers, we attended church services with community leaders at several different churches. Doing so allowed us to describe the project for the church members and to secure their support. Finally, following the individual meetings, school personnel, judges, and others from outside the neighborhood were invited to the community center to visit the neighborhood, meet residents, and secure their support.

The Second Neighborhoodwide Meeting

Upon completion of the groundwork, a second neighborhoodwide meeting was held, and the specifics of the project were shown in a drawing (see Figure 4.1) and detailed aloud by the project director and community leaders. The community was asked to vote on implementing this project. The decision to proceed was passed with a unanimous vote. In addition, throughout this process we had been clear that there was a research component to evaluate our work. The project director laid out the research plan and the community voted on the research plan, which was approved unanimously.

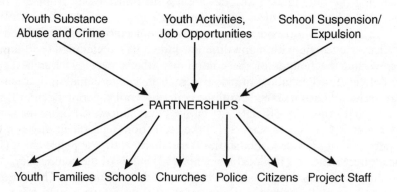

FIGURE 4.1. Targeted problem areas and systems involved in the solutions.

During the groundwork process and once the project was approved, our cultural guide began to help us with common issues related to outsiders coming into a neighborhood and strategies for overcoming barriers these issues present. These issues include trust, safety, cultural understanding, and conducting research with minorities.

DEVELOPING TRUST

The issues of trust in implementing a neighborhood-based project, especially in an economically disadvantaged neighborhood comprised primarily of people from a minority background, relate to race, police, the schools, and the nature of counseling.

Early in the project, Ida Taylor gave us the following rules for gaining the trust of the neighborhood residents:

1. Listen.
2. Never promise something you cannot deliver.
3. Don't do too much too soon.
4. Don't throw money at us, instead empower us and give us your time.

These rules became the guiding principles of our relationship with the community and underlie the trust developing strategies discussed here.

Race

For black Americans, issues regarding trust for white Americans come from a long history of inequality and exploitation. Aside from a history of blacks being owned by whites in the time of slavery and the mistrust that comes from ownership of a human being, in recent years other events have contributed to lack of trust. The community leaders of the Neighborhood Solutions Project told of the days when white insurance agents would come to the homes of black people to sell life insurance policies. The agents would come by on a regular basis and collect money on the policies. When a loved one died, however, the family would not receive benefits and had no recourse for correcting the situation. The insurance sales occurred at a time when it was common for outsiders to come into neighborhoods selling anything from food to furniture to floor linoleum at Christmas time, and everything was put on a "payment plan." People bought the items because they did not have the financial means for going out to a store, and it helped to be able to pay for the purchase over time. Similar to the insurance scams, neighborhood residents would buy furniture on a long-term payment plan at exorbitant interest rates and receive cheap products that did not outlast the payments. Blacks felt duped by whites and learned to be wary of dealing with any whites. Likewise, many neighborhood residents believed that whites initially introduced drugs into their community, as few black people had the financial means to finance the drug trade. Today, it is not uncommon for white people to bring drugs into a black community or to come into that community to buy drugs. Many blacks have been left with the feeling that although whites originally brought drugs into the black community, it is the neighborhood that has primarily suffered and now has the bad reputation.

As a result of many of the events that have occurred and prejudices in our world, in some black communities white people are not safe. In the site of the Neighborhood Solutions Project, the leaders related that white people might not be safe to walk the streets because residents did not know them or know their business. People felt suspicious of why whites were there, and there was a risk that they might be robbed, especially at night. The neighborhood had a reputation as "a place you don't want to be at night" and a place where white people were not welcome. This reputation was not entirely correct, but was indeed the reputation of the neighborhood. In this context, a project staff that included several "outsider" white university employees intended to go into homes to work with families, take urine drug screens from residents with drug use problems, be available for crises at night, and help with evening and weekend activities in the neighborhood. Developing trust, therefore, was essential to achieving our goals.

Our plan to gain trust started with "walkabouts." That is, the cultural guide and other leaders would take us on walks around the community. We would stop and talk with residents, drink iced tea or Kool-Aid, and sit and chat on porches or the street corner. Initially, we gained trust by getting to know people. For example, the drug dealers advised us to have a block party with hamburgers, hot dogs, sodas, chips, and music. They told us to set up on a certain street so we would not be viewed as being partial to one part of the community over the other. The community leaders who were with us agreed, and we held a block party. Some of the drug dealers showed up to help flip burgers. Their girlfriends helped pass out buns and chips. Having this party allowed us to begin relations with the drug dealer network that would have future benefits for the project.

A second strategy for gaining trust was to provide a consistent show of respect and not expect acceptance too soon. Respect was demonstrated by always speaking with people when we saw them, spending time playing with the children in the park and recreation center, listening, and always keeping ourselves in the role of student, regardless of our education levels and publication records.

As a third strategy, the clinical staff (described subsequently) moved into the community center very early in the project. Doing so gave us a constant presence in the neighborhood, easy contact with the children and adults of the community, and helped us to become part of the community rather than professionals coming out from the university. The easy access to the staff also meant that neighborhood residents did not have to navigate the bus system, traffic, the huge maze of buildings of the university and, mostly, did not have to see us "in an office" to work with us.

These strategies, along with consistent support from the community leaders, helped families trust project staff enough to participate in the relatively intensive treatment procedures described in subsequent chapters. Throughout the entire project, only one person declined treatment for one of her children, but she accepted treatment for her other child.

As the project continued, trust was earned by the actions of staff. When a child was recommended for expulsion from school, three carloads of neighborhood stakeholders were driven to the expulsion hearing to support the family. We had to prove that urine drug screens were being used to help adolescents get off drugs, not to have them arrested. Court hearings were attended to advocate for youth and support their parents, and project staff attended every school meeting with parents regarding child behavior problems. Medical appointments were attended with some of the adults to explain what the doctor said or to help them ask appropriate questions. For example, a family member who was an intravenous drug user believed that she had AIDS and was dying. She had taken an AIDS test a year earlier, and no one ever got back to her with the results. She assumed that that meant she had AIDS. A project staff member, along with Dr. Carolyn Jenkins, the director of a nursing program in the community, attended a medical appointment with the young lady and supported her in asking the medical resident to read through the chart for the past year. In doing so, she learned that she did not have AIDS. This information, understandably, reduced the stress on the family tremendously.

Over time, the children in the neighborhood stopped seeing the project staff as different. Our white staff was referred to as "light skinned." Our differences became less obvious than our similarities and common goals.

Police

In a neighborhood-based project aimed at crime reduction, working with the police is essential to successful outcomes for youth. However, in the black community the police are often not trusted because of a belief that they come into the neighborhood to arrest, not to help. Some officers have been overly aggressive toward youth and adults, and, consequently, the police are often viewed as vehicles of harm. In addition, many police officers are white, and this gives them a double whammy of distrust. In fact, at the current site of the Neighborhood Solutions Project, the police department had previously built a substation that was burned down the night that it opened. In sum, the neighborhood residents do not generally know the police as people, which is not conducive to trust.

Our task was to figure out how to work with the police in a way that project staff would not be viewed as police surrogates, but that helped the police develop relationships with the community to support neighborhood goals of reducing crime and drug use. Project staff could not be so involved with the police that staff looked like informants or were perceived to be "5-0" (i.e., undercover officers) by residents. On the other hand, we needed to develop a working relationship with the police that the community could see was beneficial to their own goals. We began by meeting away from the neighborhood with the police who worked in the neighborhood. The officers told us that every interaction we had with them would be watched. If project staff should pass officers on the street, staff should say hello, but not stop and talk with the officers. If we stopped to hold conversations, we would be viewed as informants. The police officers also told us that if staff were meeting with a family or were anywhere in the neighborhood when there was a drug bust, staff should immediately get on the floor, allow the officers to handcuff and arrest them, and the situation would be worked out later. If staff did not get arrested, they would be viewed as informants. The police also indicated that under no circumstances should project staff go into their pockets or purses to produce identification because this might lead to a shooting.

Following this advice, our peripheral interactions with the police helped families to understand that we were not reporting them or their children to law enforcement authorities. In addition, as we worked in the Neighborhood Solutions Project, the police department stationed a community-policing group in the neighborhood (see Chapter 10 for an extensive discussion of community policing) that had a very favorable impact on their relations with neighborhood residents. These officers took time to talk to the children and get to know the residents. In addition, they would call project staff if one of our clients was where he or she should not be, and we would call the parents to go get their son or daughter to prevent a possible problem. Occasionally, when needed, officers would even participate in family sessions. For example, when one of our parents was arrested on an old, outstanding warrant, an officer met with us to reassure the children and to help problem-solve how we could assist the parent and the family. When families learned that the police were working to help the community achieve its goals, they began to trust the police to a greater degree.

In addition to peripheral interactions on the street and intense interactions to work clinically with the police on specific cases, the community began to involve the police in recreational activities. For example, the police served food at a father–son breakfast. Father was defined as any male in the life of a child, regardless of whether the relationship was biological. Another example of trust developing and nontraditional police involvement in the neighborhood was "Beatdown in H-Town," a basketball game between neighborhood teenage youth and officers from the local police station. Such activities sparked a spirit of fun and camaraderie between the police and residents.

The Schools

Community leaders reported that neighborhood residents had a very low level of trust in the schools their children attended, and that a primary driver of this mistrust was a history of negative interactions between school personnel and neighborhood families. Specifically, families thought that teachers and principals believed the negative stereotypes of the children's neighborhood and families, did not welcome or value relatively uneducated parents as collaborators in their children's education, were intimidating, and wanted to put their children on medication as a quick fix rather than to work out problems with the families. Similarly, many neighborhood parents believed that their children would benefit if instruction was more "out of the box" and delivered in a more nontraditional approach. When children did not perform well with traditional instruction and did not "fit in the box," the parents thought that teachers viewed the child as "the problem." Further compounding the school–neighborhood cultural gap was the fact that most of the middle-class teachers had been raised differently than are children from high-crime inner-city neighborhoods, and the teachers rarely sought a cultural understanding of their students' home environments.

Principal tasks of the Neighborhood Solutions Project, therefore, were to establish trust with the schools, help parents improve their relationships with the schools, and better connect the schools with the community. To establish trust with the schools, project staff met with key school personnel and gave them a voice in the design of interventions to decrease school-related problems for the neighborhood youth. These interventions are described extensively in Chapter 7, but as an example, a direct referral process was arranged so that Project staff was available to school personnel by pager 24 hours a day. When teachers called asking for help, project staff provided immediate access to resources (e.g., immediately traveled to the school to provide support). The teachers and administrators expressed that they had never had any other professionals this accessible to help manage acute child behavior problems, and that this service was the difference between seeking intervention and having the child arrested.

To develop more collaborative relationships between parents and teachers, when project staff were called by the school to intervene, the child's caregivers were contacted immediately and arrangements were made to join forces with the parents to help work out the problem. If the parent was working and could not leave work, we arranged a meeting between the teacher and parent or principal and parent at a later time. Concurrently, project staff worked with school personnel to change negative beliefs about families from the neighborhood. In cases where parents were put down by school personnel or called names, we advocated for the parent and worked with the school to treat parents differently. In cases where the parent put down the school or called names, we worked with the parent to manage his or her relationship with the school more productively. When children were in need of medication (e.g., for ADHD) to help them focus attention more effectively in school, project staff talked with parents about the research and the benefit of medication for certain well-specified medical disorders. On special teacher recognition days, community stakeholders were notified and some of the members would make cakes or take food to the teacher's lounge with a note saying from which community the food came. Finally, teachers, principals, and other school staff were invited to the community for special events.

After the first year of the project, a school official confided to the project director that the school had been watching the staff closely to see "what we are made of" and "when we are going to give up." Similar to the process that transpired with neighborhood residents, project staff had to prove that they were tough and competent enough to handle the problems, were not going to give up even in the face of direct attacks on parents or us by school personnel, and could outlast problems without becoming unconstructive. Project staff had to demonstrate a continuous focus on "doing the right thing" for the children.

Counseling

According to community leaders in the Neighborhood Solutions Project, lack of trust in mental health and substance abuse counselors was due to several different concerns. First was the question of whether "this person in authority has my best interest at heart, will help me help myself, or will take information I give and do something to hurt me." Second, people in the black community may hold the belief that if problems arise, God will fix them, and not relying on God is a sign of lack of faith in or respect for God. The third concern is a fear of stigmatization. Individuals who receive mental health counseling fear their family members and friends might view them as crazy.

To show that we had the best interests of clients at heart, project staff practiced visibility, accessibility, persistence, and flexibility, and always took the time to listen. In response, community residents indicated that they appreciated the fact that we "were not all about technical terms and the mandate, but were about the client." Project staff was told that their persistence showed that the work was serious, and "standing our ground" showed that we were tough enough to handle the problem or any situation. Parents did not have to take off time from their jobs to participate in treatment, and this erased many barriers to participating (e.g., transportation, child care). Neighborhood residents also indicated that we proved that their best interest was at heart by including in treatment everyone who was in the child's life, such as extended family, ministers, and teachers.

As project staff worked closely with families in the neighborhood, they were very careful to respect the role of God in the families' lives and in the solution to their children's problems. After project staff attended several churches of differing denominations in the community early in the project, we were told that doing this had shown respect for the role of God in the community and lives of the people. During church services and when ministers were involved in treatment, they expressed to families that "God brings people in your life to help you as God's way of taking care of you." In a powerful endorsement, ministers were very clear that they felt God had put our team in this neighborhood. Similarly, community leaders indicated that the project had helped change the perception that residents had about accepting help to that of "we have to help ourselves and God gives us others to do so."

Providing the neighborhood leaders with a solid understanding of the MST treatment model also fostered trust. For example, prior to project implementation, one of the community leaders completed the 1-week orientation training that is provided to all new MST therapists. After this week of training, he was highly knowledgeable in representing the treatment model to his neighbors. Moreover, having this leader go through the initial MST training showed that we were confidant that the intervention model was family- and neighborhood-friendly, and that residents would view MST favorably.

A strategy that seemed effective in combating the stigmatization of mental illness was to hold sessions in nontraditional ways. Treatment sessions were rarely held in an office or even called treatment sessions. Assessments and intervention planning were usually conducted in cars, on the street, at the church, in the mall, at the community center, at the parent's job (e.g., helping the parent fold clothes while we talked), at Grand-mother's, and in the family's home. Families clearly understood that our work focused on keeping their children out of hospitals, residential pro-grams, and jails; and keeping them in their neighborhood with their fami-lies. As residents got to know and trust project staff and understand the pragmatic focus of our work, the word got out. Families told other families how we worked, and the endorsement from neighbors went a long way to-ward gaining trust for participating in counseling.

Two initially contentious treatment issues, however, were that MST uses urine drug screens in cases of substance abuse and that sessions are audiotaped for treatment adherence ratings (as part of quality assurance). Being taped and checked for drugs was difficult for families to deal with at the start of the project, and we had to extend considerable effort to earn trust. To help, when possible, staff were hired who had grown up in the neighborhood and surrounding area. For example, one staff member, hired as a family resource specialist, had been raised in the neighborhood, knew many of the current residents, and had gone to high school with some of the parents. Families felt that they could trust this person since she had truly walked in their shoes. This staff member led the way in helping other project staff gain trust around the treatment requirements. With her help and with the families seeing that a dirty urine screen did not lead to an ar-rest, trust increased enough for families to self-refer. In addition, at least one of the neighborhood leaders was involved in all job interviews for new staff. Job applicants had to pass neighborhood leadership review to be of-fered a position.

PROJECT STAFF SAFETY

In a neighborhood where crime is high and drug selling and use are com-mon, safety is an issue to keep in the forefront. Safety risk is highest for persons who are not known in the community and whose business is sus-pect (i.e., buying drugs, informant). Although the dangerousness of certain inner-city neighborhoods is often exaggerated by media hype, it was impor-tant for project staff to take regular precautions and use good common sense.

Community leaders used several strategies to keep project staff safe. As noted previously, the first strategy was for staff to walk the streets with community leaders. They introduced project staff to residents and ex-plained our business in the community. At the start of the project these walks were taken on a weekly basis and at various times during the day. The goal was to get our face and business known to community members so that people did not think we were there to buy drugs or harm anyone.

As a second strategy, the neighborhood leaders identified safe houses for project staff. These were houses at various places in the community that staff members could go to and be taken care of if they felt unsafe. For the first month of the project, staff did not go into the community without a guide from the community. As new staff was hired, even in latter stages of the project, a known person always accompanied them in the neighborhood until they were known. As we became part of the community, existing staff were able to serve as guides for the new staff.

A third strategy to promote safety was to have peace with the drug dealers. We met with some of the dealers, talked with them about why we were in the community, asked their opinions on what the project should look like, and listened to their advice. What we learned immediately was that drug dealers in this community were not small-time crime lords, but instead were people trying to find solutions to their lack of education and lack of power in their lives. The drug dealers had excellent insight on what might have turned them away from drug selling when they were younger, and most did not want their family members to take the route they had taken. Some even wanted to start a different way of life, and project staff pledged to support that decision if it were made. Seeking out the drug dealers, not identifying them as drug dealers but as people who knew the community and could give us advice, and listening to them led to referrals of their family members and, in some cases, problem-solving relationships that led some of them away from drugs. But mainly this approach contributed greatly to the safety of our staff. Because many of the drug dealers truly cared about the children in the neighborhood, they kept an eye out for our staff and would flag us down if we were going the wrong way on a one-way street or had a headlight out, to get us on a correct path. At a time when the community could not secure sports equipment for a football program, the drug dealers donated the equipment. To maintain a positive relationship with the drug dealers and with most people in the community, however, project staff had to exercise extreme caution in their interactions with law enforcement. As the drug dealers began to trust us, some of them allowed project staff to help them enroll in GED programs. This had to be done in secret, as they could not allow their peers to know they were seeking a GED until the test was passed. Otherwise, the peer pressure not to pursue education would be too great for the individuals to continue.

PROJECT STAFF–NEIGHBORHOOD CULTURAL DIFFERENCES

Often, professionals who provide treatment come from different cultural backgrounds than their clients. Cultural differences are apparent in food, language, and music as well as in child rearing, management of life problems, and ways of viewing the world. As the Neighborhood Solutions Project started, it was apparent that the majority of the project staff had a limited understanding of the culture of the neighborhood. Although most of the staff members were also African American, their backgrounds were quite different than those of the neighborhood residents. For example, project staff did not understand much of the language, as many of the neighborhood residents spoke Gullah/Geechee, nor did staff understand many of the slang words used by the children. Gullah is a language brought to the area by African slaves; it is still spoken on the South Carolina Sea Islands and has influenced the language of people living in many coastal communities in the state. Gaining an understanding of the language was imperative, as misunderstanding the meaning of words can lead to negative outcomes for children. For example, early on we learned that "stick you" means to hit you. Luckily we had this understanding when attending a school meeting where a teacher was trying to have a child arrested for threatening to stab another student. The child had stated, "If you don't give me my bookbag back, I'm gonna stick you." The teacher thought he meant stab, and this conjured up images of murder. Project staff was able to correct this misunderstanding, along with teaching the child that threats to hit a classmate were not the best way to handle frustration. A second common example of the importance of understanding language is use of the word "beat"—"I beat my child." In the culture of the neighborhood, the word "beat" means "give a spanking to." However, the word connotes a much harsher action in many other neighborhoods. Understanding the language in this case might prevent an unnecessary report to Child Protective Services.

To learn more about the language and music, project staff talked with people about what certain words meant and received regular language lessons from residents. Neighborhood youth even put together a list of important words and made this list into a T-shirt for neighborhood residents to wear. The youth sold these T-shirts to earn money for the Black College Tour.

An important lesson when beginning to learn about a different culture is never to pretend you know what someone is talking about if you do not, and always to ask questions. People are generally happy and proud to teach about their lives and their culture. Project staff also spent time listening to music at the community center with the children and even took CDs home or listened to them in their cars. Gaining such cultural familiarity helped staff learn more of the language and what the children valued. One of the community leaders said, "You have to go in and come down to the level of the people you are going to serve. If you stay up high and mighty, people will not feel they can talk to you."

In addition to differences in language, cultural differences are apparent in foods of a specific neighborhood. Food is a central part of activities in many neighborhoods. Eating with people is considered "fellowship" and is very important to developing trust and becoming a part of the family of the neighborhood. People will generally understand if your tastes are different and perhaps eating pigs' feet is not possible for some professionals, but trying the food is important, especially when it is homemade for you by someone in the community. Sharing a meal is a sign of acceptance on both sides of a relationship. In the Neighborhood Solutions Project, food was used to welcome people at the early meetings. Had the staff brought in food that was not familiar to people in the neighborhood, the welcome would not have been as strong and doing this would have been a sign that "we don't understand you." As we progressed through the project, many meals were consumed, and we learned about "Lowcountry" cuisine typically prepared in the neighborhood and nicknames for dishes. Sharing these meals was a truly enjoyable part of engaging with the community.

Another cultural difference that needed to be addressed was the sense of priorities. For example, one of our staff was highly alarmed over broken glass on the basketball court. While no one in the community wanted the children to play around broken glass, it was not a critical issue for the neighborhood residents, which exasperated the staff member. Similarly, people in the neighborhood may have had a different concept of supervision, monitoring, and parenting than do project staff. For example, parents commonly viewed the neighborhood as a whole as a monitor for their children. Thus, when a 4-year-old boy came to the park unsupervised, some of the staff was upset. The community leaders, knowing the family, the neighborhood, and the child, helped us understand that this behavior was the norm and that the child was indeed safe. On a clinical level, however, as we worked with individual families to increase their monitoring and supervision of problem adolescents, we had to help them understand that their problem teen needed more monitoring than a child usually would need in the neighborhood.

Project staff also came to understand that many negative events (e.g., school expulsion) might seem less serious to people in the neighborhood than they do to the staff. The staff, therefore, must not misinterpret the family's feelings about the importance of an event. For example, when a large drug bust occurred on the streets during a girls' running group Saturday run, the children and parents did not seem overly concerned, but the staff was a bit shaken. A second example is the day that a therapist was conducting a therapy meeting in a family's home and a drug dealer from the street ran into the house to hide, with the police in hot pursuit. The young man was thrown to the floor, handcuffed, and hauled away. The family was not fazed by this event, but the therapist was clearly rattled.

Project staff also learned about neighborhood culture by understanding the "informal mainstays" of the community and getting to know those individuals. For example, Darrie, an adult in the community, was unable to speak or hear, but was very friendly and accepted by all in the neighborhood. Although not a formal leader, he was a mainstay in the community. Being accepted by him helped us gain acceptance in the community. To be accepted, the director of the project learned how to communicate with him on the street. The communication started with him writing messages on a piece of paper, if one was handy. This changed to writing with his finger on the director's wrist. He gave important information about the community and about the children in the community that helped with treatment planning and the development of trust.

Overall, when implementing a neighborhood-based project, the culture of the neighborhood must be embraced and evident in all the work that occurs. According to the community leaders in the Neighborhood Solutions Project, a defining moment was when we learned the values of the community, the language of the community, and dealt with residents on their level. We had to focus on the client, the entire family, and the extended family. We had to figure out how each person in the family and even extended family viewed life, parenting, monitoring, and family. Trust gave the community an avenue for teaching us their culture. They could not teach us until they felt we were ready to receive the lessons.

CONDUCTING RESEARCH IN A BLACK COMMUNITY

For black Americans, the word research connotes exploitation and possible harm. Historically, research with black Americans did create harm. A prime example is the Tuskegee Syphilis Study that ran from 1932 to 1972 (Rothman, 1982). Three hundred and ninety-nine disadvantaged, rural black men were deliberately infected with syphilis, and then monitored over time to examine the course of the disease. They were not informed as to what disease they were suffering, but were told they were being treated for "bad blood." Even after effective treatment was developed, these research participants were left untreated and were even prevented from receiving appropriate treatment. This study set a negative precedent for trust in research with black Americans. Today, 30 years after Tuskegee, blacks living in inner-city communities often view research as a vehicle for professionals to come into a community, gather information for grants that shows the community desperately needs certain resources, obtain grant dollars, and never provide any substantive benefit to the community with those dollars.

To battle the past harm and mistrust created by research, the Neighborhood Solutions Project team was very clear at the outset of the program that research would be conducted. Community members were informed that the research was not about taking information and not giving services, but instead was an evaluation of the services we were implementing. Nothing was hidden with regard to what the research would involve. Copies of research instruments were provided for review, and we explained that data would be collected on crime and drug use—the primary aims of the project. Essential to gaining community collaboration, the investigators spoke plain English (i.e., did not use psychobabble), solicited questions and concerns, asked for input, and allowed the community to vote on the research plan. In addition, with the utmost respect for the intellect of people in the community, proof of the worth of the interventions (i.e., empirical evidence) was provided, and plans for the evaluation methods of the project were described. Also, investigators explained the lengths to which we would go to protect the confidentiality of the research data. In contrast with almost all of our other research projects over the past 25 years, participants were not paid to complete research interviews. Gaining the trust and support of the whole community was essential to cooperation and participation.

BARRIERS, CHALLENGES, AND PITFALLS
TO IMPLEMENTING A NEIGHBORHOOD-BASED PROJECT

Several issues experienced in implementing the Neighborhood Solutions Project were discussed previously. This section summarizes those challenges and presents additional challenges or pitfalls. Although the development and implementation of the Neighborhood Solutions Project went fairly smoothly, the process was not easy. Tremendous effort was required on the part of the clinical team, nurses, police, and especially, the neighborhood leaders. These leaders and their neighbors led the way in negotiating solutions to potential pitfalls. Although the outsiders provided some resources and certain types of expertise, their initial decisions were often doomed to failure. Rather, we outsiders came to appreciate that the neighborhood leaders and residents understood the best ways of leveraging the resources that we brought.

The first major challenge in developing the project was getting all groups of stakeholders on board. For example, all of the ministers were invited to a meeting at a place (i.e., the community center) and time (i.e., the evening) we thought were convenient. None attended. We learned afterward from neighborhood residents and several ministers that we should have first arranged individual meetings at times and places of each minister's choosing. Hence, we subsequently arranged approximately a minimum of 17 meetings with ministers at their churches and various other places. This strategy helped bring all members of this important stakeholder group on board.

A second major challenge was earning the trust of people in the community. This trust was needed to enable the clinical staff to work in the neighborhood and engage families in treatment. The strategies for earning trust involved following the advice of the leaders, showing respect in every interaction with the youngest to the oldest resident, listening, following through on what the staff said they would do, standing up for youth and families who were in crisis with other systems (e.g., court), locating staff at the community center, being available at convenient times, and respecting cultural differences. Outsiders and residents spending the time getting to know each other best facilitated the development of mutual trust. Trust was maintained by delivering high-quality services that helped families.

A third challenge involved the likelihood of staff being viewed as police informants because we were new to the community. This problem was managed by following the directions of the leaders, youth, and police, as discussed previously. The staff needed to act with care and caution consistently when interacting with the police.

A fourth challenge was getting people involved in activities early in the project. The main strategy was to schedule the activities at convenient times and places and to conduct outreach in signing youth up for events. Being persistent and never giving up even when events were not well attended overcame this challenge.

Although, fortunately, it was not a substantive challenge in the Neighborhood Solutions Project, another set of concerns could pertain to the nature of the neighborhood leadership. For example, a particularly difficult challenge to implementing a neighborhood program would come into play if the leaders did not get along, had divergent goals, or had power and control issues. In such cases, a respected person from outside the neighborhood might need to be brought in to resolve conflict and negotiate a plan for moving forward. Similarly, implementing a neighborhood project would be challenging if neighborhood leaders were apathetic or afraid that their influence was going to be diminished. Apathy is often related to low empowerment or not believing that resources that make a difference can come to the community. Apathy or low empowerment must be met with persistence in attempting to bring needed resources to the community. Although leaders might be fearful of losing power or working "outside the box," project staff must continually respect the roles of these individuals. Their support should be slowly cultivated, and the leaders should be credited for any emerging success. At times, having an outside consultant teach different ways of working (e.g., grant writing, fund raising) can help leaders feel comfortable with new approaches.

CONCLUSION

Implementing a neighborhood-based project requires completion of several successive and time-intensive steps to join with the residents of that neighborhood as well as to overcome barriers that may be in place due to past experiences of the community. Through lessons learned from the Neighborhood Solutions Project and direct teachings from the neighborhood leaders and residents, strategies were presented for getting into a neighborhood and engaging the neighborhood leadership and residents in a collaborative process. The key lesson in the engagement process is to take the time to complete the groundwork needed to earn the trust of the neighborhood stakeholders. Project staff and neighborhood residents have different roles in such a project, and each side brings much to the table. The support of the entire neighborhood is needed to make the project successful, and this support will only come if residents trust the project staff and believe that they have the community's best interest at heart.

After the community gives its blessing for the project, the clinical work to address the problems of interest to the neighborhood can begin. The next six chapters of this book discuss interventions for the clinical problems addressed in the Neighborhood Solutions Project. Before leaving Chapter 4, however, we must note that the thesis of this chapter is so important that it bears repeating: The clinical work cannot be successful if it comes before joining with the neighborhood and establishing a collaborative relationship with the residents.

CHAPTER 5

The MST Approach for Reducing Youth Antisocial Behavior

Historically, antisocial behavior has been a very difficult problem to treat. In fact, at the time that MST was developed in the late 1970s, the prevailing assumption in the fields of criminology and mental health was that "nothing works" in the treatment of juvenile offenders. As research on the causes and correlates of adolescent antisocial behavior emerged, however, reasons for the failure of the predominant treatment at that time—individual therapy—started to become evident. As described in Chapter 1, investigators were consistently finding that adolescent criminal behavior is multi-determined. The causes were found not only in characteristics of the youth, but also in family, school, peer, and neighborhood factors. Understanding the multiple determinants of antisocial behavior made it clear that treatment that focused on the individual or only one of the systems would yield little gain on the average. Rather, to be successful, treatment needed the capacity to address pertinent factors across the multiple systems in which youth are embedded. Recognition of the need for treatment to address multiple systems led to the development (and naming) of multisystemic therapy (MST).

This chapter addresses the application of MST to the problem of youth antisocial behavior. The chapter goals are

1. To present evidence that MST works for reducing antisocial behavior in adolescents
2. To describe what the Neighborhood Solutions Project added to traditional MST
3. To demonstrate the application of MST in the Neighborhood Solutions Project through a case example

THE EVIDENCE THAT MST WORKS
FOR REDUCING ANTISOCIAL BEHAVIOR

As noted in Chapter 2, MST has been cited as an effective treatment of adolescent antisocial behavior by the Surgeon General (U.S. Public Health Service, 1999, 2001), Elliott's prestigious Blueprints series (1998), and leading reviewers (e.g., Farrington & Welsh, 1999; Kazdin & Weisz, 1998). These distinctions are based on the outcomes of several well-controlled and scientifically rigorous studies that examined the capacity of MST to reduce symptoms of conduct disorder and rearrest in juvenile offenders. The first MST outcome study was published by Henggeler et al. (1986), and showed that MST was more effective than juvenile diversion services in decreasing the behavior problems of juvenile offenders as well as improving their family relations and decreasing association with deviant peers. As noted in Chapter 1, family relations and association with deviant peers are important determinants of adolescent antisocial behavior. Hence, these early results foretold the potential of MST to impact adolescent criminal activity.

Indeed, shortly after this initial publication, Borduin and his colleagues (Borduin, Henggeler, Blaske, & Stein, 1990) published a small (i.e., 16 youth and their families participated) randomized trial of MST with juvenile sexual offenders. This study showed dramatic decreases in sexual and other criminal rearrests for youth in the MST condition at a 3-year follow-up, in comparison with youth who received individual therapy. Though not yet published, these findings for sexual offenders have been replicated in a randomized trial conducted by Borduin and colleagues with a larger sample. Moreover, Henggeler, Borduin, Letourneau, and Schewe are currently collaborating with the state attorney's office and others in Chicago to conduct a major randomized trial of MST with juvenile sexual offenders.

More pertinent to the present discussion, the strongest evidence supporting MST in the treatment of adolescent antisocial behavior is provided by three randomized trials of MST with violent and chronic juvenile offenders conducted in the 1990s. In the Simpsonville, South Carolina, Project, Henggeler, Melton, and Smith (1992) studied 84 juvenile offenders who were at imminent risk for out-of-home placement because of serious criminal activity. Youth and their families were randomly assigned to receive either MST or the usual services provided by the Department of Juvenile Justice (DJJ). At posttreatment, youth who participated in MST reported less criminal activity than did their counterparts in the usual services group, and at a 59-week follow-up, MST had reduced rearrests by 43%. In addition, usual services youth had an average of almost three times more weeks incarcerated (average = 16.2 weeks) than MST youth (average = 5.8 weeks). Moreover, treatment gains were maintained at long-term follow-up (Henggeler, Melton, Smith, Schoenwald, & Hanley, 1993). At 2.4 years postreferral, twice as many MST youth had not been rearrested (39%) as usual services youth (20%). This study is one of the first in the field to demonstrate long-term reductions in criminal activity among serious juvenile offenders.

In the second of the three trials, the Columbia, Missouri Project (Borduin et al., 1995), participants were 200 chronic juvenile offenders and their families who were referred by the local DJJ. Families were randomly assigned to receive either MST or individual therapy (IT). Four-year follow-up arrest data showed that youth who received MST were arrested less often and for less serious crimes than counterparts who received IT. Moreover, while youth who completed a full course of MST had the lowest rearrest rate (22.1%), those who received MST but prematurely dropped out of treatment had lower rates of rearrest (46.6%) than IT completers (71.4%), IT dropouts (71.4%) or treatment refusers (87.5%). In addition, Borduin currently has a manuscript under review describing the favorable MST outcomes from a 10-year follow-up of this sample.

In the third trial, the Multisite South Carolina Study, Henggeler et al. (1997) examined the role of treatment fidelity in the successful transport of MST to community mental health clinics. In contrast with previous clinical trials in which the developers of MST provided ongoing clinical supervision and consultation (i.e., quality assurance was high), MST experts were not significantly involved in treatment implementation, and quality assurance was low. Participants were 155 chronic or violent juvenile offenders who were at risk of out-of-home placement because of serious criminal involvement, and their families. Youth and their families were randomly assigned to receive MST or the usual services offered by DJJ. Not surprisingly, MST treatment effect sizes were smaller than in previous studies that had greater quality assurance. Over a 1.7-year follow-up, MST reduced rearrests by 25%, which was lower than the 43% and 70% reductions in rearrest in the previous MST studies with serious juvenile offenders. Days incarcerated, however, were reduced by 47%. It is important to note that high therapist adherence to the MST treatment protocols, as assessed by caregiver reports on a standardized measure, predicted fewer rearrests and incarcerations. Thus, the relatively modest treatment effects for rearrest in this study might be attributed to considerable variance in therapists' adherence to MST principles.

The capacity of MST to reduce adolescent antisocial behavior has been replicated in other recent studies as well. In a randomized trial with substance-abusing juvenile offenders discussed more extensively in the next chapter, MST reduced recidivism by 26% at a 1-year follow-up, which was not statistically significant (Henggeler, Pickrel, & Brondino, 1999). MST reductions in violent crime, however, were significant at a 4-year follow-up for this sample (Henggeler et al., 2002). Similarly, in a randomized trial of

MST as an alternative to the psychiatric hospitalization of youth presenting mental health emergencies (i.e., suicidal, homicidal, psychotic), MST was more effective than emergency psychiatric hospitalization at decreasing the externalizing symptoms of youth in the short term (Henggeler, Rowland, et al., 1999). Finally, in a multisite randomized trial in Norway, MST has been more effective than usual services at reducing youth conduct problems (Ogden & Halliday-Boykins, 2004), and Ogden is currently preparing a manuscript describing favorable MST outcomes at a 2-year follow-up.

In summary, across the three trials with violent and chronic juvenile offenders, MST produced 25–70% decreases in long-term rates of rearrest, and 47–64% decreases in long-term rates of days in out-of-home placements. These outcomes have resulted in considerable cost savings. The Washington State Institute on Public Policy (Aos et al., 2001) concluded that MST produced $31,661 in reduced placement and juvenile justice costs per participant. Further savings from costs to victims increased this figure to $131,918 per participant. Moreover, the capacity of MST to reduce adolescent conduct problems has been demonstrated in several other populations of youth presenting serious clinical problems.

PROVIDING MST IN THE CONTEXT OF THE NEIGHBORHOOD SOLUTIONS PROJECT

The most important concern of neighborhood leaders was criminal activity among youth. Specifically, neighborhood youth were selling drugs, stealing, and committing violence. Hence, one of the primary aims of the Neighborhood Solutions Project was to provide MST services to chronic juvenile offenders and their families in the neighborhood. Providing these services in a single neighborhood, however, required modifications in the usual MST referral, engagement, and intervention processes.

The Referral Process

Traditionally, juvenile offenders are referred to MST programs through community agencies or the courts. The referral process for antisocial youth in the Neighborhood Solutions Project, however, was at the neighborhood level. First, neighborhood leaders identified the youth that were struggling and involved with the juvenile justice system. Next, the leaders visited the family without the MST team to enlist the caregivers' support. Then, the leaders asked the MST team to contact the family to discuss treatment options. During the early phases of the project, when many of the families did not know about the Neighborhood Solutions Project, prior contact by the neighborhood leaders was essential to endorsing the services and supporting families' efforts to work with the treatment team. As time passed, care-givers and youth self-referred through the community center director or through notes sent directly to the project director or treatment team.

Engagement

Rather than focusing solely on a single family, per traditional MST, engagement was also extended to the broader neighborhood. On one hand, the MST team used the usual family engagement strategies, such as going by the house multiple times until a connection was made, getting to know everyone in the ecology, treating the family with the utmost respect, and addressing the family's primary clinical concerns (Cunningham & Henggeler, 1999). In addition, however, the therapists maintained a presence in the neighborhood to further support engagement. This presence included attending community events; helping prepare food for community dinners; helping clean up after events; patronizing neighborhood businesses; playing with the children at the center; walking the streets with a neighborhood leader; attending weddings, wakes, and funerals; periodically attending the ministers' monthly meeting; and attending church services. Moreover, the team was located at the community center and available during off-hours to formal clients and others in need of advice or consultation.

Intervention Support

The clinical team was fortunate to have the support of the whole neighborhood. Although confidentiality of clients was maintained, the support of neighbors and other community stakeholders was enlisted when caregivers gave permission to the team. Having access to "inside" information often helped in the design and implementation of effective interventions. For example, neighbors were in a position to make round-the-clock observations of a youth and family. When a youth went out the window at night or did not attend school, unbeknownst to the working parent, the stay-at-home neighbor knew about this behavior. Including neighbors in the treatment provided a forum for them to tell of their observations of the youth, thus promoting interventions related to the misbehavior, which otherwise might go unchecked.

Provision of Aftercare

Traditionally, MST programs provide intensive services for 4–6 months. After this intensive phase, youth who need continued treatment are usually referred to local mental health centers or other clinics. In the Neighborhood Solutions Project, however, referring the youth outside the neighborhood was not viewed as optimal. Thus, the team began providing less-intensive home- and-community-based MST for youth who needed longer-term clinical involvement. Such youth included those who were involved with drug court, were taking medication, or whose terms of probation included continued treatment. In addition, some of the youth had serious emotional difficulties that required longer-term services to sustain gains.

Outcomes for Referred Youth

Through the Neighborhood Solutions Project, 17 youth with involvement in the juvenile justice system were referred to the MST team. These youth averaged 3.9 arrests: 10 (59%) had been arrested on drug charges; 12 (71%) on violence charges; 5 (29%) for theft; 6 (35%) for destruction of property; 8 (47%) for school-related charges; and 6 (35%) for a variety of other charges. Of these youth, only 29% were rearrested during the intensive MST treatment phase, and none of these arrests were for drugs. In addition to arrest data, youth criminal activity, according to self-report, decreased significantly. Finally, youth reports of witnessing violence (e.g., seeing someone killed or shot) and experiencing it (being slapped, hit, punched, mugged, or shot) decreased dramatically during treatment.

CASE APPLICATION OF MST

The following example represents a fictionalized composite of the Neighborhood Solutions Project cases. Because this book is based on clinical work within a single neighborhood, individuals familiar with that neighborhood might be able to identify a case example. Thus, case circumstances have been changed to protect confidentiality.

In presenting this case, the MST analytical process seen in the do-loop in Figure 3.2 (Chapter 3, p. 48) is followed, and the weekly paperwork used in MST supervision and consultation is shown.

Step 1. Referral Behavior

The reasons for referral are recorded on the Initial Contact Information form (see Figure 5.1). The neighborhood leaders referred Nosmo King Henderson, a 15-year-old male, to the clinical team. He had a history of five arrests (three for assault), multiple stays in juvenile detention, 6 months in a state training school, and was under probation with the DJJ. Nosmo King was referred because the community was concerned that he was getting involved, yet again, with selling drugs. He also had been engaging in physical fights with peers in the community and was verbally aggres-

Family: Henderson   **Therapist:** Beech   **Date:** 9/20/03

Genogram

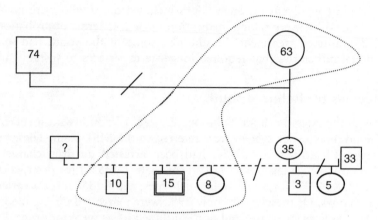

Reasons for Referral

1. Physical aggression in the community—assault of a peer
2. Verbal aggression in school—cursing teachers, suspended multiple times across the school year
3. Selling drugs in the community—arrested for possession, denies drug use

Initial Goals/Desired Outcome

Participant	Goal
Nosmo King	Stay out of jail, finish my education
Grandmother	Stop beating up kids in the neighborhood, stop cursing the teacher, do what I tell him to do, stay away from those boys on the corner
Neighbor	Stay off the corner, stop fighting other kids, stay out of jail
Teacher	Stop verbal threats and cursing, do his work
Probation Officer	Stop physical and verbal aggression, no more arrests for drug possession
MST Therapist	Stop verbal and physical aggression, Stay away from drug-selling peers

FIGURE 5.1. Initial contact information.

sive toward teachers at school. This latter problem had resulted in multiple school suspensions and very high risk for permanent expulsion.

Step 2. Desired Outcomes of Key Participants

The desired outcomes are gathered by interviewing each key participant. First, the therapist meets with the parents or legal guardians to identify key individuals in the child and family's social network. Releases of information will be obtained from the caregiver to allow these individuals to communicate with the therapist about Nosmo King.

Genogram

A genogram (McGoldrick & Gerson, 1985) is developed to document the family context and provide an overview of the extended family. As shown in the genogram in Figure 5.1, Nosmo King lives with his grandmother, 10-year-old brother, and 8-year-old sister. His mother is separated from her husband (Nosmo King's stepfather), who is the custodial parent for their two younger children. The mother's whereabouts are unknown, and Nosmo King does not know his biological father. Nosmo King's grandmother is separated from his grandfather, but the grandfather is interested in having a meaningful relationship with his grandchildren. The family is very close to Miss Ruth, who lives next door. Hence, the participants in treatment are Nosmo King, his grandmother, his grandfather, Miss Ruth, the probation officer, and a teacher.

Intake

The initial interview and assessment of the caregiver and child are generally conducted individually. During these interviews, the child's developmental, health, behavioral, trauma, criminal, and treatment histories are taken. The presenting problems are discussed and defined, and the therapist determines how often and for how long the target problems have been occurring. A mental status examination is conducted to determine if the child is experiencing suicidal or homicidal ideation, if there is any indication of psychosis, or if there are red flags regarding cognitive functioning (e.g., memory, general fund of information). Finally, the therapist obtains information regarding the caregiver's parenting style and techniques.

During this first visit, time permitting and as appropriate, the therapist might ask the caregiver and child to complete standardized measures to obtain a baseline of functioning. For example, the parent might complete a behavioral rating scale and the child might complete a depression checklist.

If problems are occurring at school, the teacher will also be interviewed to obtain specifics such as the behavior of concern, when and how often it happens, and interventions the school has implemented. The teacher might also complete a formal measure assessing behavioral symptomatology.

Strengths and Needs

A crucial step in the assessment process is to identify the strengths and needs of each system. Figure 5.2 shows the strengths and needs in each of the individual, family, peer, school, and community systems related to Nosmo King. At the start of treatment, the weaknesses side of this list is usually longer than the strengths side. At the end of treatment, if successful, the strengths side should be longer than the weaknesses side.

The strengths and needs assessment for Nosmo King and his family revealed several significant strengths that can be used to facilitate treatment goals. Although this young man is a 15-year-old in the eighth grade, he has not given up on school. His strength and interest in math may be helping him maintain interest in school. He is liked in the community and shows some responsibility at home, helping to care for his siblings. Nosmo King's interest in basketball might help him become more involved in school and other constructive activities. In addition, he has several adults in his life who can support his efforts. The principal can help with school behavior; the grandmother is highly committed; and the grandfather wants a relationship with him. Likewise, prosocial activities are available in the community and school. His two prosocial peers can help Nosmo King stay away from criminal activity, and Miss Ruth, the neighbor, can support the family's efforts to increase their monitoring of Nosmo King.

On the weaknesses side, information from multiple participants indicates that physical aggression, verbal aggression, and drug activity are key areas of concern that must be addressed. Moreover, further assessment should be directed at clarifying the detrimental effects of possible reading problems, the grandmother's conflictual relationship with the school, and Nosmo King's inability to control his anger. Finally, the grandmother's lax monitoring and discipline in the home, the grandfather's lack of involvement, and Nosmo King's association with several antisocial peers might exacerbate these difficulties.

Initial Goals

As each participant is interviewed, he or she is asked to identify desired changes in the youth's behavior and interpersonal relations. The desired goals are recorded on the Initial Contact Information form (see Figure 5.1) and are synthesized to formulate the overarching goals.

Family: Henderson   **Therapist:** Beech   **Date:** 9/20/03

Systemic Strengths	Systemic Weaknesses/Needs
Individual	
A desire to improve in school	Weak skills in reading
Well liked in the community	Poor management of anger
Helps care for siblings	Poor problem-solving skills
Strong math skills	Verbally aggressive
Interest in basketball	Involved with selling drugs
	Physically aggressive
Family	
Grandmother cares for children	Low monitoring of Nosmo King
Affective bond between grandmother and Nosmo King	Negative interactions with grandmother
Interested grandfather	Mom's whereabouts unknown
	Limited contact with grandfather
	Lax discipline at home
School	
Sports available	Teacher and grandmother do not get along
Interested principal	No reading assistance given
	No behavioral plan
Peers	
Two prosocial peers in community	Antisocial peers plentiful
Community	
Strong community center with a lot of activities	High crime rates
Desire of the people to rid the neighborhood of drugs	Economic disadvantage
Interested neighborhood	Drug selling regular on the streets

FIGURE 5.2. Strengths and needs summary.

Step 3. Overarching Goals

The overarching goals set the direction for treatment, and achieving them signifies the end of treatment. Thus, the goals must be objective and defined in such a way that all stakeholders understand them in the same way. In Nosmo King's case, the overarching goals pertained to physical and verbal aggression and drug selling activity (see Figure 5.3). The key index of physi-

Family: Henderson   **Therapist:** Beech   **Date:** 9/20/03

Weekly Review

Overarching/Primary MST Goals

1. Nosmo King will stop physical aggression in the community as evidenced by no further charges for assault and by parent report.
2. Nosmo King will stop verbal aggression at school as evidenced by teacher report.
3. Nosmo King will eliminate drug activity as evidenced by no further arrests for drug possession and by parent report.

Previous Intermediary Goals	Met	Partially	Not
1. Grandmother to identify rules and expectations for home behavior	x		
2. Nos and grandmother will meet with coach and center director to sign up for activities	x		
3. All teachers will collect baseline data on verbal threats	x		
4. Grandmother to meet with teacher to set initial intervention for aggression	x		
5. Grandparents and Nos will check out jobs	x		

Barriers to Intermediary Goals
None Identified

Advances in Treatment*

1. Grandmother identified and wrote down rules and expectations.
2. Nos signed up for basketball and tutoring.
3. Baseline verbal threats were low frequency and toward the teacher and peers, and work avoidance was a fit.
4. Meeting successful—Grandmother and teacher have agreement on contingency.
5. Nos hired at the car wash.

How has your assessment of the fit changed with new information/interventions?
Grandmother unfamiliar with parenting strategies—low skills.
Work avoidance is a fit factor for school verbal aggression.

New Intermediary Goals for Next Week

1. Grandmother and Nos to meet to settle discipline plan
2. Grandmother and Nos will follow up on basketball and tutoring
3. Grandmother, Grandfather, Miss Ruth to meet to discuss transportation and monitoring plan
4. Nos and grandmother to meet with teacher to set intervention
5. Grandparents to work out transportation for Saturday job

FIGURE 5.3. Weekly review for MST supervision and consultation. *Numbers correspond to those of previous intermediary goals above.

cal aggression was reports from various respondents (e.g., neighbors, teachers, other children) regarding Nosmo King's physical confrontations and possible assaults and rearrest. The measure of verbal aggression was based primarily on teacher reports, because school was the main context for this problem. The measure of drug selling was based on the observations of the family and neighbors, any evidence that Nosmo King had acquired resources that could not be accounted for legitimately, and rearrest. When the overarching goals are set, they should be reviewed with the family to make sure that they are consistent with the family's desires. Therapists should also note that additional overarching goals may be set during the course of treatment if desired. Overarching goals are reviewed throughout the course of treatment, and progress toward achieving these goals is evaluated consistently. In the closing treatment session, the therapist and family will "true up" the goals. That is, the success of each goal is discussed.

Step 4. MST Conceptualization of Fit

After overarching goals are established, fit factors are developed for the targeted problems. The fit factors are those variables within or across systems that contribute to the targeted behavior. In Nosmo King's case, the key problems were physical aggression, verbal aggression, and drug-selling activity (see Figure 5.4). To begin the assessment of fit, the therapist brainstormed potential factors based on the intake and on the strengths and needs assessment that were conducted. Drafts of fit circles were drawn and brought to supervision for the team to review. During supervision, the therapist reported on which of the fit factors were backed by evidence (her observation or that of another participant) and which were more speculative and required additional assessment.

Physical Aggression

Regarding the determinants of physical aggression, an identified fit factor was negative peer association. The physical aggression occurred when Nosmo King had been visiting with peers on the street corner and they would fight amongst themselves or would prey on children walking around the neighborhood. When he associated with the two prosocial peers, this aggression did not occur. Family factors included a lax discipline system, negative interactions with the family, and low monitoring. Nosmo King's grandmother worked into the early evening and at times on weekends. She had no structure set up for the children in terms of a schedule, curfew, rules, or consequences for appropriate or inappropriate behavior. At times she expected Nosmo King to stay home and at other times she allowed him to make his own decisions about his whereabouts and curfew. When he did

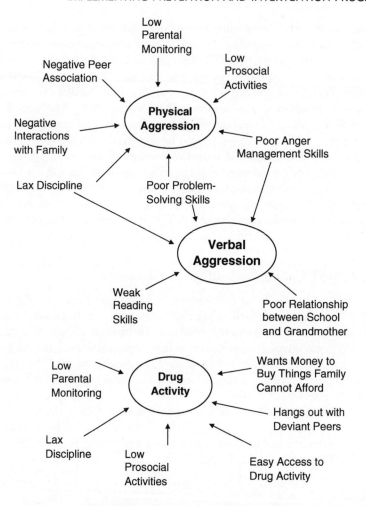

FIGURE 5.4. Fit circles for Nosmo King.

not meet his grandmother's expectations, she would yell at him, he would verbally escalate, and she would tell him to get out, resulting in him leaving the house to hang out with peers on the street corner. The lax discipline system did not support association with prosocial peers. Individual factors included little involvement in prosocial activities, poor anger management skills, and poor problem solving. Although Nosmo King was interested in basketball, he was not involved in sports. Instead, his social activities involved hanging out with deviant peers on the street corner. He was unable to give alternatives to aggression when angry and showed limited skills in thinking through a problem and coming up with potential solutions.

Verbal Aggression

Verbal aggression seemed to be driven by some overlapping fit factors. Family factors included a lax discipline system. The evidence gathered by the therapist indicated that Nosmo King, having limited rules at home, expected not to have to follow rules at school. As with his grandmother, when the teacher placed demands on him, to get his way Nosmo King verbally escalated to quiet others. Individual factors included poor problem-solving skills, poor anger management, and weak reading skills. When angry at school or home, Nosmo King was unable to develop alternatives for managing the problem. At times, he was verbally aggressive to mask a serious reading problem and save himself the embarrassment of peers finding out about this skill deficit. School factors included conflictual relations between the school and his grandmother. Her contention was that the school called her "every day" about problems. Because her grandson was not pleasant at school, she believed that the school did not like him or her. She related that she never knew when he was doing something positive at school, as they did not call her about positive behavior.

Drug Activity

Overlap with the fit factors was also seen for drug activity. First, family factors included ineffective monitoring and discipline. Since Nosmo King was allowed to make his own rules and curfew, he hung out in high-risk situations. Individual factors included a desire for money to buy things the family could not afford and low availability of prosocial activities. Since Nosmo King did not earn his own spending money and received no allowance, he reported that selling drugs was a viable means for buying clothes and jewelry. He had bought several gold chains and removable gold tooth covers. He had plenty of free time to participate in drug sales, as he was not involved in community activities. Peer factors included association with other drug-using and drug-selling peers. On a daily basis, deviant peers stood on the street corner near his home and welcomed him in their association. He enjoyed interacting with these young men. Community factors included easy access to drug activity, which was going on at multiple sites in the neighborhood.

After determining the fit factors, the next step is to prioritize them for intervention. Priority goes to factors that (1) are the most proximal or immediate cause of the problem; (2) are the most powerful or consistently connected; (3) occur in the present; (4) are important to the participants; (5) need to be addressed to be able to address other factors; (6) have support as risk factors in research; and (7) have practical solutions. In light of the fact that parenting practices (i.e., lax monitoring and discipline) contributed significantly to each of the identified problems and could be used to help address other proximal determinants (i.e., negative peer association, access to drug activity), the team prioritized the development of more effective parenting practices.

Step 5. Intermediary Goals

The intermediary goals should link directly to the overarching goals. Figure 5.3 shows an example of the weekly review sheet. This sheet is completed weekly by the therapist and presented at clinical supervision.

Overarching Goal 1

Nosmo King will stop physical aggression in the community as evidenced by no further charges for assault and by parent report.

Intermediary Goal 1

The strongest fit factors related to physical aggression were identified as lax discipline and association with deviant peers. An initial intermediary goal was set to address these fit factors and included his grandmother identifying rules and expectations for the children regarding home behavior, curfew, where they may go when she is not home, and consequences for following rules and for breaking them. As shown under the advances in treatment, his grandmother successfully identified the rules and expectations. Setting up consequences was difficult, and through this session a new fit factor became apparent. Low parenting skills were a fit factor for the lax discipline. Grandmother had never set up a discipline plan with her own children or her grandchildren. However, she was open to doing so. The next goal would involve Nosmo King and his grandmother coming to an agreement on the discipline plan.

Intermediary Goal 2

Deviant peer association and low prosocial activities go hand in hand in this case. To address the deviant peer problem, his grandmother reported that Nosmo King will need to start with alternative activities, especially during after-school hours. To find an alternative of interest, he and his grandmother will talk with the director of the community center and the coach at school and sign up for desirable activities. As shown under the "Advances in Treatment" heading, Nosmo King and his grandmother signed him up for basketball at the city recreation department. This activity would take him off the streets two afternoons per week. However, since his grandmother was working, transportation needed to be addressed. Back to the strengths assessment—his grandfather had an interest in getting involved, and the neighbor, Miss Ruth, was available to help. A new intermediary goal would be set to involve Grandfather and Miss Ruth in the transportation and basketball program. Regarding further alternate activities, Nosmo King's school grades were not high enough for him to engage in basketball; this was a barrier to participation in school sports. Grandmother learned from the community center that he could participate in tutoring three afternoons per week. Doing so might help increase his grades and would also provide further monitoring. The next goal set was to begin tutoring.

Overarching Goal 2

Nosmo King will stop verbal aggression at school as evidenced by teacher report.

Intermediary Goal 3

The initial intermediary goal involved gathering baseline data on the verbal aggression at school to determine how often this was occurring and to try to develop a further understanding of fit factors. As shown under "Advances in Treatment," the teacher kept a baseline that showed that verbal aggression was a low frequency behavior, but when it occurred it was aimed toward the teacher and peers. The therapist met with the teachers to define verbal aggression. Agreement among the teachers indicated that verbal aggression meant saying in a loud voice, "You can't tell me what to do, I do what I want to do" or calling the teacher a name such as "baldhead" or "crackhead." The data kept by teachers indicated that the verbal aggression was specific to reading and social studies classes. The classroom observation revealed that the aggressive comments generally occurred at times that Nosmo King was attempting to avoid his work. During the 1-hour reading class, Nosmo King made two verbally aggressive statements directed toward the teacher. During social studies, he made two verbally aggressive statements directed toward other students. Work avoidance was identified as a fit factor.

Intermediary Goal 4

The poor relationship between Grandmother and the school was a strong fit factor, yet they would need to work together to change the problems Nosmo King was experiencing. An intermediary goal was set for Grandmother and the teacher to meet face to face to discuss the verbal aggression and set an initial intervention. The therapist, of course, would be present to help make interactions positive and the meeting productive. The "Advances" section shows that the meeting took place and, although interactions were initially negative, the teacher and Grandmother came to an agreement that Nosmo King would only be able to attend the school dances if he showed no verbal aggression the week prior to the dance. The next goal was set for the teacher and Grandmother to meet with Nosmo King to formalize this intervention.

Overarching Goal 3

Nosmo King will eliminate drug activity as evidenced by no further arrests for drug possession and by parent report.

Intermediary Goal 5

The fit factors of low parental monitoring, lax discipline, association with deviant peers/low prosocial activities are already being addressed. One additional fit factor that is very reinforcing for Nosmo King is obtaining money to buy things he wants. Nosmo King related that he would like to get a job because it was important for him to have his own money. Grandmother agreed that he could work on Saturday but not during the school week. A goal was set for Grandmother, Grandfather, and Nosmo King to check into Saturday jobs at the local grocery store and car wash. Under Advances, the review notes that Nosmo King was hired at the car wash. The family needed to problem-solve around transportation, and the goal was set to meet with Grandfather to determine a solution.

Step 6. Intervention Development

Interventions are applied to the fit factors that have been identified as contributing to the target behavior. Most interventions conducted within the context of MST are practical and problem-focused. For example, low caregiver monitorng (Grandmother was not available until 6:00 P.M.) was a key fit factor in Nosmo King's after-school drug-selling activities. To increase monitoring, practical solutions were crafted that capitalized on the identified strengths of the systems. Thus:

1. Prosocial after-school activities of high interest to Nosmo King were identified to occupy his time.
2. Grandfather, who was interested in becoming more involved with Nosmo King, was recruited to provide transportation to the activities.
3. Grandfather and the neighbor, Miss Ruth, agreed to provide direct supervision on days when activities were not available.

4. The community center had both supervised after-school activities and academic support available almost every day.
5. Nosmo King thanked his grandfather and neighbor for their support by helping with yard chores.

Thus, creative and practical solutions can be crafted with participants working together to provide monitoring during a high-risk time of day. Although such interventions are not manualized in the traditional sense, the process of their conceptualization and operationalization is consistent with that used by most evidence-based treatments, especially the behavior and cognitive-behavioral therapies. That is,

1. Target behaviors are well defined and specified.
2. Primary drivers of the targets are identified.
3. Interventions aim to change the drivers.
4. Outcomes are examined to evaluate effects.
5. Interventions are modified to improve outcomes, and so forth.

The difference in using this process within MST, however, is that MST makes considerable use of resources in the social networks surrounding the youth. That is, MST takes a comprehensive view of both determinants of problems that might be targeted for change and the resources available to support such change. In addition, as discussed in Chapter 3, MST surrounds these interventions with a strong quality-assurance system to promote outcomes, an organizational commitment to overcome barriers to family engagement and service access, and the philosophy that caregivers are the most important and sustainable change agents in children's lives.

Step 7. Intervention Implementation

As noted in Chapter 2, the process of developing and implementing MST interventions has much in common with evidence-based behavioral approaches. Indeed, in the case of Nosmo King and his family, the therapist provided empirically supported treatments to address several problems that have been the focus of evidence-based treatment techniques: ineffective parenting, negative interactions within the family, and poor anger control.

Developing More Effective Parenting Strategies

When working with caregivers to set up a discipline system, the therapist should determine why such a system is not already in place. Is the absence of effective discipline due to a lack of knowledge or to some other barrier (e.g., caregiver knows how to set up a system but is too depressed to do so)? If the reason is low knowledge, the therapist can take the parent through some basic steps. Several excellent manuals are available to help therapists set up behavior management systems with caregivers (Clark, 1985; Munger, 1993; Patterson, 1976). The central thrusts and key components of these systems are described extensively in the MST treatment manual of antisocial behavior (Henggeler et al., 1998). On the other hand, as suggested previously, ineffective discipline might be driven primarily by caregiver problems such as drug abuse and psychiatric problems. In such cases, more intensive interventions for caregivers are needed, and these are described in the MST treatment manual for serious emotional disturbance (Henggeler, Schoenwald, et al., 2002).

The primary barrier to developing effective parenting in the Neighborhood Solutions Project, however, was that many of the caregivers were overwhelmed with daily life tasks. Before one more "burden" could be added, the caregivers had to believe that the effective parenting strategies were practical, doable, and sustainable. Such characteristics are also necessary to assure that the new parenting practices are maintained over time. Thus, therapists had to strive for simplicity. Several steps can be taken for increasing the effectiveness of parenting (structure, monitoring, and discipline) in families referred to the MST team.

1. Set a daily schedule. A daily schedule can be drawn up so that each family member knows what is expected to occur at what time. This schedule will include time for waking, leaving for school, meals, and going to bed. Adherence to the schedule need not be rigid, but the schedule helps the family member to get better organized.

2. Set rules, especially for the problem behaviors that prompted the referrals. Caregivers and children can set these rules together, and some of the rules might be negotiated with teens. For example, Nosmo King's grandmother expected him to complete his homework daily, but never made this rule explicit. Her rules, then, would include complete his homework and have his grandmother check it daily. Other rules might pertain to household chores and curfew times, and these can be added to the family schedule as well.

3. Set consequences for following rules and for breaking rules. Oftentimes families will focus solely on the punishment side of consequences, as applied to breaking rules. However, the importance of providing positive consequences for following the rules cannot be overestimated. Positive consequences can be as simple as praise, smiles, or a hug; or as complicated as an increase in privileges. Potential rewards and sanctions should be decided during the family meeting, but the parent has the final approval. The rewards and sanctions should be written down, with clear links to corresponding behaviors.

4. Teach the use of contingencies. Most parents understand Grandma's rule—you must finish your dinner before you get dessert. Although parents can learn to apply this basic rule, support is sometimes needed to assure that the rewards for good behavior are provided *after* the desired behavior. Many parents provide many rewards and privileges for their children, irrespective of the children's actual behavior. That is, many children presenting antisocial behavior still receive ample rewards from their caregivers. Hence, the therapist must work with the caregivers to clearly identify rewards and privileges and to link these explicitly with desired youth behavior. In other cases, deciding on the best negative contingency can be difficult. For example, when a youth on probation is ordered to attend school and that youth refuses, the parent might want juvenile justice authorities to provide the punishment for that behavior. However, to become stronger in the eyes of the youth and set the stage for more effective long-term discipline strategies, the parent might set a "What Mama says goes" rule. That is, if the youth does the right thing and goes to school with no trouble, Mama will be happy and things will be good. However, if there is a problem and the probation terms are not being followed, Mama will not be happy and will intervene in unpleasant ways. These interventions might include riding the bus to school with the youth, accompanying the youth to class, or having Grandmother sit in class with the youth. The message is that Mama can be just as, if not more, powerful than the probation officer.

5. Set the stage for regular family meetings. The therapist can demonstrate for the family how to have one. During family meetings someone can present a particular problem or a positive event. For problems, the family conducts basic problem-solving steps to resolve the issue at hand. These steps include defining the problem, determining a desired outcome, examining potential solutions, selecting a viable solution, and implementing that solution. Each member of the family has an opportunity to express how he or she feels about issues in the family. This meeting can also be a time to follow up on the rules and consequences that have been developed. After the family has learned the structure of the family meeting, a family member can lead and the family can continue without the therapist.

Family Communication and Problem Solving

Verbal conflict can turn physical when negative interactions in the family escalate. In such cases, parents and their children need to learn how to communicate in ways that solve problems rather than create more of them. Robin, Bedway, and Gilroy (1994) developed an excellent procedure for teaching family problem solving and communication skills. For example, the family is led through several problem-solving steps as applied to their own situation. The steps include (1) defining the problem, (2) generating alternative solutions, (3) evaluating and deciding on the best solution, and (4) implementing that solution and evaluating its effectiveness. To enhance communication skills, the family starts by identifying negative communication habits (e.g., yelling, name calling) and evaluating how these impact family members. They are then taught more constructive and positive communication skills (e.g., turn taking, requesting nicely), and these are practiced during treatment sessions. Finally, the family learns how to challenge unreasonable thinking. First they learn the connection between extreme thoughts, angry affect, and arguments (i.e., extreme thoughts lead to extreme feelings that lead to fights). For example, when parents attribute a child's behavior to malicious intent (e.g., he turned his stereo up loud to get back at me), the resulting anger contributes to an argument. Next, families learn to identify unreasonable beliefs they may have (e.g., my parents are always unfair to me) and to challenge their validity. This is done through a series of questions such as "Is there evidence supporting my belief?" or "Am I making a mountain out of molehill?"

Youth Self-Control Training

In general, cognitive-behavioral therapy (CBT; Feindler, Ecton, Kingsley, & Dubey, 1986; Lochman, Burch, Curry, & Lampron, 1984) has some empirical support for improving self-control in children. Common techniques in CBT self-control training include (1) assessing typical management of anger by assessing the sequence of events that led up to aggression, (2) determining inside and outside anger cues that indicate escalation of negative thoughts and feelings, and (3) teaching physical and cognitive skills that decrease escalation of negative thoughts and feelings. Although CBT is usually provided in individual treatment sessions, when used with MST the caregivers should be involved in learning the skills and supporting their child's efforts to use new strategies for coping with anger.

To assess how a youth typically manages anger, recent examples of when his or her anger escalated and the youth lost control should be examined. During this exercise, the therapist notes how the youth reported handling anger and whether a pattern of behavior emerges across incidents. Functional analyses are conducted to understand the sequence of events that surrounded recent "loss of control" incidents. In these functional analyses, the therapist learns the ABCs of the situation: that is, the *antecedents* (what happened before the anger began to escalate), including what the youth was thinking and feeling; the *behavior* (how the youth handled the situation), and the *consequences* (positive or negative outcomes of the loss of control). In addition, corresponding feedback should be obtained from the caregivers or other family members. These individuals will often have less biased views of the incidents.

To clearly delineate triggers for escalating anger, the therapist also engages the youth and caregivers in a discussion of situations, people, or things others say that make the youth "hookable" (i.e., things that provoke anger) (Swenson & Brown, 2000). Knowing the triggers of escalation helps the youth watch for situations in which he or she needs to leave or begin to manage the escalation. In addition to identifying triggers, the youth and caregivers should determine inside (physiological and cognitive) and outside (what others see in the youth) cues that signal an escalation in anger. Here, the youth lists the ways his or her body feels when anger is starting to escalate, and the caregivers note how the youth looks when he or she starts to get angry. The physiological cues are written down and reviewed each week in case additional cues are discovered. If the youth is unable to report physiological cues, examples (e.g., heart beating fast, eyes watering, feeling tension in the arms or neck) can be given to facilitate such identification. If nothing still comes to mind, watching for physiological cues can be a homework assignment. Generally, cognitive cues to escalating anger are easier to identify—the youth expresses what he or she is thinking as anger grows. For example, the thought "this burns me up" might precede the thought "I'm gonna hurt him," which, in turn, precedes physical aggression. Once the physiological and cognitive cues are determined, they are rank-ordered. Doing this helps the therapist understand the feeling or thought that starts the escalation process and, thus, when in the process intervention needs to occur.

To directly manage anger, physiological and cognitive deescalation skills are taught. Physiological deescalation procedures involve teaching the youth relaxation skills. Several protocols are available for youth relaxation training (e.g., Kolko & Swenson, 2002; Ollendick & Cerny, 1981). Careful planning and practice should be conducted to determine which techniques can be used in public without seeming too obvious. Cognitive deescalation skills involve the substitution of coping statements for the cognitions that escalate anger. For example, "It's not worth it" replaces "He better shut up or I'll stick him." The coping statement should come from the youth, not the caregiver or therapist, as it must be meaningful to be used. A second cognitive deescalation strategy is to think ahead to the negative consequences of escalated anger (e.g., school expulsion, upsetting parents, arrest, jail). The youth is taught to recognize triggers early in the escalation sequence and to immediately think ahead to the negative consequences of escalation. The thought that is maladaptive (e.g., "This burns me up") is quickly substituted with thinking ahead (e.g., "If I do this I will get arrested").

Finally, self-control training should include extensive role play and even videotaped practice if possible. The new behaviors will not be automatically taken into the youth's "anger management repertoire." Practice will help the youth develop a level of comfort with using the techniques in real situations. Further, to assess progress, the youth and parent should chart the number of anger incidents, triggers for escalation, and how the youth managed the incident. This information should be reviewed regularly with the therapist.

Step 8. Assessment of Advances and Barriers to Intervention Effectiveness and New Fit Factors

The therapist reports advances on each intermediary treatment goal to the supervisor and consultant on the weekly summary sheet (Figure 5.3). The therapist also describes the fit of the advance, that is, what caused the advance. If the intervention is not working, the therapist attempts to identify barriers to progress or to carrying out the intervention. The team might hypothesize additional barriers, and interventions are altered to overcome these barriers. With the identification of new information regarding systemic strengths and challenges, the fit circles (Figure 5.4) are revised during supervision. For example, during a family session, low parenting skills became an apparent new fit factor for the lax parenting. Therefore, the therapist will need to work closely with the grandmother to implement parenting strategies that are unfamiliar to her.

The MST assessment–intervention–evaluation recursive process continues around the steps of the do-loop until the overarching goals are met, if possible. By then families have developed the skills and indigenous resources to manage their own difficulties, and treatment is complete. In other cases, however, youth and their families need long-term treatment or case management. For example, children taking psychiatric medication will need ongoing monitoring. In those cases, the MST therapist assists the family in finding follow-up care or case management programs that are as theoretically and clinically compatible with MST and other evidence-based practices as possible. The MST therapist stays with the family through the transfer of the case to facilitate a positive transition.

Treatment Strategies for the Case of Nosmo King Henderson

The preceding description provides several snapshots of the case of Nosmo King. These snapshots, however, do not adequately represent the continuous and evolving analytical and treatment processes that underlie MST. In this case, as well as in the vast majority of MST cases, a broad and integrated range of interventions are implemented to address the identified problems. These interventions are sometimes delivered sequentially and other times delivered concurrently. Sometimes the interventions are successful, sometimes they are not. When unsuccessful, new interventions are developed and implemented based on observed barriers to success.

The following interventions were provided to Nosmo King and his family.

For Physical Aggression

- Behavioral intervention to increase the effectiveness of the parental discipline system
- Strategies with the grandmother to break his link with deviant peers
- Strategies to increase his involvement in basketball and other prosocial activities
- Family communication and problem-solving training
- CBT for helping Nosmo King control his temper

For Verbal Aggression

- A caregiver-imposed and teacher-coordinated discipline system to reward alternatives to verbal aggression at school
- Additional strategies to improve the relationship between his grandmother and the school
- CBT for helping Nosmo King control his temper
- Tutoring in reading at the community center and other academic assistance at school

For Drug-Selling Activity

- Ongoing strategies to break the link with deviant peers
- Strategies to increase monitoring by his grandmother and others in the ecology
- Behavioral intervention to increase the effectiveness of the parental discipline system
- Strategies to help Nosmo King find activities for which he might earn legitimate money (e.g., job)
- Participation in Men of Distinction (see Chapter 8) and strategies to increase involvement in other prosocial activities

CONCLUSION

This chapter aimed to provide an overview of the use of MST to treat adolescent antisocial behavior in the Neighborhood Solutions Project. In particular, the case of Nosmo King was used to exemplify the pragmatic, multifaceted, and theory-driven nature of the interventions provided in many MST cases. As indicated by the preceding list of interventions, several evidence-based clinical interventions were delivered to Nosmo King and his family, though, as noted previously, these were adapted for the MST conceptual framework. On the other hand, several pragmatic services were also provided (e.g., helping him find employment, connecting with neighbors, attaining tutoring), and these are often beyond the purview of usual clinical practice. Finally, in the larger picture, the therapist attempted to help Nosmo King and his grandmother change their social networks in strategic ways that would promote long-term success. Positive peer activities were substituted for negative peer activities. Improved academics and employment opportunities were emphasized. Extended family, neighbors, and teachers were united to achieve mutually agreed goals. Finally, Nosmo King was taught different strategies for controlling his aggressive impulses. Together, these broad multisystemic changes are intended to be mutually reinforcing and supportive.

CHAPTER 6

The MST Approach for Treating Adolescent Substance Abuse and Dependence

As described in Chapter 1, substance abuse has been labeled as the "The Nation's Number One Health Problem" (Ericson, 2001). Substance-abusing youth present many serious social problems, including high rates of psychiatric symptomatology, poor school performance, and relationship disturbances, and these often lead to unfortunate long-term developmental trajectories. Moreover, the problems presented by substance-abusing youth are extremely costly to many segments of our society, including the justice system, schools, mental health system, and child welfare system. Hence, the implementation of effective strategies to treat substance abuse is a public health priority.

The goals of this chapter are:

1. To present evidence that MST reduces substance use in substance-abusing and -dependent adolescents
2. To describe the implementation of MST within the context of the Neighborhood Solutions Project
3. To demonstrate the application of MST for adolescent substance abuse via a case example

THE EVIDENCE THAT MST WORKS FOR REDUCING YOUTH SUBSTANCE ABUSE

Reviewers have noted the promise of MST in treating substance-abusing youth (e.g., McBride, VanderWaal, Terry, & VanBuren, 1999; Stanton &

113

Shadish, 1997). The National Institute on Drug Abuse (1999) and the Center for Substance Abuse Prevention (2001) have noted that MST is one of the few treatments of adolescent substance abuse with empirical support.

FINDINGS FROM CLINICAL TRIALS

Engagement and Retention in Treatment

Although treatment retention rates have traditionally been quite low in the area of substance abuse treatment (Stark, 1992), MST retention in a study (Henggeler, Pickrel, & Brondino, 1999) with juvenile offenders who met formal diagnostic criteria for substance abuse (56%) or dependence (44%) was excellent. Fully 100% (58 of 58) of families in the MST condition were retained for at least 2 months of services, and 98% (57 of 58) were retained until treatment termination at approximately 4 months postreferral, averaging 40 hours of direct clinical contact with an MST therapist (Henggeler, Pickrel, Brondino, & Crouch, 1996). The effective MST family engagement strategies are described by Cunningham and Henggeler (1999).

Drug- and Alcohol-Related Outcomes

Several clinical trials of MST have evaluated drug- and alcohol-related outcomes.

Outcomes with Serious Juvenile Offenders

Substance-related outcomes were examined in two randomized trials of MST with violent and chronic juvenile offenders (Borduin et al., 1995; Henggeler, Melton, & Smith, 1992), and these findings were published in a single report (Henggeler et al., 1991). Findings in the first study (Henggeler et al., 1992) showed that MST significantly reduced adolescent reports of alcohol and marijuana use at posttreatment. In the second study (Borduin et al., 1995), substance-related arrests at a 4-year follow-up were 4% in the MST condition versus 16% in the comparison condition. In a meta-analysis of family-based treatments of drug abuse (Stanton & Shadish, 1997), the MST effect sizes were among the highest of those reviewed.

Outcomes with Diagnosed Substance-Abusing or Substance-Dependent Juvenile Offenders

The effectiveness of MST was examined in a study with 118 juvenile offenders meeting Diagnostic and Statistical Manual of Mental Disorders,

3rd edition, revised (DSM-III-R; American Psychiatric Association, 1987) criteria for substance abuse or dependence and their families (Henggeler, Pickrel, & Brondino, 1999). Participants were randomly assigned to receive MST versus usual community services. MST reduced self-reported marijuana and alcohol use at posttreatment, incarceration by 46% at 6-month follow-up, and total days in out-of-home placement by 50% at follow-up. Reductions in criminal activity, however, were not as large as have been obtained previously for MST. Examination of treatment adherence measures suggested that the modest results of MST were due, at least in part, to low treatment adherence—a problem addressed successfully in a subsequent study of MST and juvenile drug court. Nevertheless, this earlier study provided the first demonstration of long-term treatment effects from a randomized clinical trial with substance-abusing adolescents. At a 4-year follow-up (Henggeler, Clingempeel, Brondino, & Pickrel, 2002), results from urine screens repeated twice during 12 months showed significantly higher rates of marijuana abstinence for MST participants: 55% versus 28% of young adults.

Juvenile Drug Court Study

Although a comprehensive description of this project is beyond the scope of this section, an important aim of the drug court study is to determine whether integrating an evidence-based practice (i.e., MST) into juvenile drug court enhances the outcomes of drug court (Randall, Henggeler, Cunningham, Rowland, & Swenson, 2001). More than 150 substance-abusing juvenile offenders and their families have been recruited for participation, and, thus far, the findings at 1-year postrecruitment are among the strongest achieved in MST clinical trials to date. Significant treatment effects favoring the MST conditions have been observed for each of the self-report and biological measures of substance use. For example, MST youth have tested positive for drugs on only 13% of their drug court appearances, whereas counterparts receiving community services have tested positive on 39% of such appearances. Likewise, on a measure that has important economic implications, youth in the community services conditions were incarcerated for an average of approximately 8 weeks during the year, in comparison with less than 2 weeks, on average, for MST counterparts. Based on caregiver reports, MST youth have also shown greater decreases on externalizing symptoms than have youth receiving community services. Finally, even on those measures that have not shown significant treatment effects, the direction of change favors MST (e.g., self-reported delinquency), and treatment effects might emerge from more sophisticated analyses when the study is complete.

Cost Savings

Within the context of the randomized trial with substance-abusing or -dependent juvenile offenders (Henggeler, Pickrel, & Brondino, 1999), the incremental costs of MST were examined, and these costs were related to observed reductions in days of incarceration, hospitalization, and residential treatment at approximately 1 year postreferral (Schoenwald, Ward, Henggeler, Pickrel, & Patel, 1996). Results showed that the incremental costs of MST were nearly offset by the savings incurred as a result of reductions in days of out-of-home placement during the year.

WHAT THE NEIGHBORHOOD PROJECT ADDED TO THE STANDARD MST

Referral Process

The referral process was similar to that described for adolescent criminal activity with one exception: Several cases were referred directly by the presiding judge at the Charleston Juvenile Drug Court. She was the primary judge supporting the aforementioned MST juvenile drug court study, and welcomed the opportunity to refer cases residing in Union Heights to the MST program in that neighborhood. Some unusual referral methods were used as well. For example, one young man who was in detention for a weekend due to a drug court sanction met up with another youth from the neighborhood who had been arrested on drug possession charges. The weekend detainee called a family member collect and patched through to the project director's cell phone. The purpose of the call was to refer the other young man to treatment, as he did not have a counselor or anyone to advocate for him. Although the MST team was supporting the parents and drug court in administering consequences (i.e., weekend detention) to the first youth, he still recommended the program for his neighbor.

Engagement

Engaging families in treatment for substance abuse is a challenging task, and treatment completion rates in the field of substance abuse are very low (Stark, 1992). Moreover, engagement can be especially difficult in neighborhoods where trust of counseling or "the system" is low. In the Neighborhood Solutions Project, for example, families were initially hesitant to give urine drug screens for fear of what project staff might do with those results. In keeping with standard MST protocols, however, families were fully informed of the consequences of dirty screens. Indeed, even for youth in drug court, the team did everything possible to have negative consequences come from the caregivers rather than from the court. Moreover, individuals in the neighborhood helped the team engage challenging families by speaking on the team's behalf, even when not requested to do so. Interestingly, becoming a topic of neighborhood gossip also worked to the team's advantage. Newly referred parents often knew about existing MST cases from the neighborhood grapevine, and asked veteran MST parents about the team and what was being done with the urine screens. Trust from one family transferred to another family, which helped with engagement. Of the families who participated in the Neighborhood Solutions Project due to their child's substance abuse problem, all 13 completed at least 4 months of treatment, with 12 of 13 fully completing treatment. Only one youth left treatment before goals were completed.

Intervention Support

Having the eyes and ears of the neighborhood on the targeted youth helped the team and family meet treatment goals. For example, people in the neighborhood would call the center director when they were concerned about a particular youth, and that information was relayed to the team. One day an anonymous phone call came to the team from a neighborhood resident indicating that a youth in treatment was in a high-risk deviant-peer situation. The therapist called the parent and together they picked up the youth, preventing a potential arrest. Finally, the community policing team became a source of support for MST interventions. The policing team had a strong commitment to turning the youth in the neighborhood around and would work with the MST program to prevent rearrest (versus taking a zero-tolerance approach).

Partnering with Drug Court

Of the 13 substance-abusing youth referred for MST, 8 were enrolled in the Charleston County Juvenile Drug Court, under the direction of The Honorable F. P. Segars-Andrews. The key features of drug court are (1) weekly appearances by caregivers and youth before the judge to review therapeutic progress, (2) weekly drug testing, (3) engagement in community-based "drug abuse" treatment, and (4) positive or negative consequences provided by the judge based on drug-testing results and counselor reports of compliance with drug abuse treatment. Youth who meet their goals and produce a clean screen receive an acknowledgement in the form of verbal praise or other rewards (e.g., movie tickets) from the judge. If this success continues, the youth advances up a levels system to graduation. If, on the other hand, the youth produces a dirty screen or is not meeting behavioral goals at home or school, he or she receives a sanction from the judge. This consequence might be mild, such as writing an essay on substance abuse or, if dirty screens and treatment noncompliance continue, more intensive, such as community service or spending a weekend in the detention center. Failure to stop drug use or change problem behavior over time can result in even stricter consequences, such as juvenile justice placement.

Unfortunately, as suggested in Chapter 2, few community drug treatment programs are evidence-based, and many provide services that research has shown to increase substance use (e.g., services that combine substance-abusing teens into groups). In the present case, however, the evidence-based nature of MST interventions could be integrated with the significant strengths of drug court (i.e., frequent monitoring of substance use, judicial support for community treatment) to provide a particularly potent intervention. The court backed the clinical aims of the MST team and caregivers, which provided caregivers with additional leverage to influence their adolescents. Likewise, the MST team and caregivers supported the aims of the court. Drug court and MST together, as demonstrated by the preliminary outcomes of the drug court study noted previously, can be a particularly effective combination of services in the treatment of adolescent substance abuse.

Outcomes for Referred Youth

Thirteen youth were referred to the project by neighborhood leaders or juvenile drug court due to an extensive history of marijuana and cocaine use. Eight of those youth were enrolled in drug court. All 13 youth completed an intensive phase of MST ranging from 3 to 9 months. As youth successfully completed treatment, they were phased out of urine drug screen collection. For some youth the intensive phase ran longer because they were in drug court, which has a usual duration of 12 months. For other youth, the intensive phase was lengthened by difficulty sustaining reductions in marijuana use. This latter problem led to the development of a less-intensive phase of MST—one that followed the intensive phase and aimed to sustain adolescent abstinence with greater efficiency and less cost by reducing the frequency of client contacts.

Results of weekly urine drug screens evidenced reductions in cocaine and marijuana use, especially the former. By Week 7, all youth were abstinent for cocaine, and the majority of youth were abstinent for marijuana (85%). These outcomes were generally maintained across 22 weeks of treatment. Furthermore, from pre to post treatment, youth showed significant reductions on self-reported personal involvement with chemicals, social and recreational drug use, preoccupation with drugs, and having a peer group that is involved with drugs (i.e., Personal Experience Inventory; Winters & Henly, 1989).

CASE APPLICATION OF MST

A fictionalized case of a substance-abusing adolescent enrolled in juvenile drug court and referred to MST is provided. The format of the presentation follows that used in the preceding chapter, including the sequence of the MST analytic process depicted on the Do Loop (see Figure 3.2, Chapter 3, p. 48).

Step 1. Referral Behavior

Tywan Echo, a 16-year old male, was referred to the clinical team by the neighborhood leaders. As indicated on the Initial Contact Information form (see Figure 6.1), Tywan was referred for drug possession and use, school failure, and noncompliance at home. He had a history of four arrests for possession of controlled substances and was on the cusp of going into the adult system. The school principal viewed Tywan as a "street thug" and was highly concerned that he would bring a gun to school. At the time of referral by neighborhood leaders, he had just been arrested for possession of marijuana and cocaine, and had been referred to drug court by juvenile justice authorities.

Step 2. Desired Outcomes of Key Participants

The desired outcomes are gathered by interviewing each key participant in the youth's and the family's social network. The consent to treat and appropriate releases of information are signed at the initial meeting, where caregivers also identify the key participants. Gathering information on the desired outcomes usually occurs across several meetings, as all the key players are rarely present at the first meeting.

Genogram

The genogram (McGoldrick & Gerson, 1985) is drawn to document the family context and to give an overview of the extended family. As shown in the genogram in Figure 6.1, Tywan lives with his 36-year-old mother, twin 10-year-old brothers, and an 8-year-old brother. His parents are divorced, and his father is in prison in New York, having been convicted for drug

Family: Echo   Therapist: Forest   Date: 4/16/03

Genogram

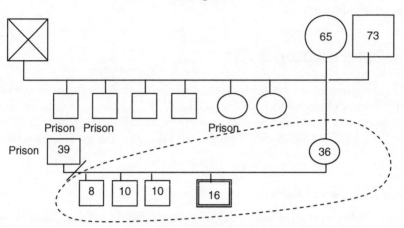

Reasons for Referral

1. Arrested for possession of drugs. Uses cocaine and marijuana
2. Failing in school—sleeps in class
3. Does not do what he is told to do at home

Initial Goals/Desired Outcome

Participant	Goal
Tywan	Stop getting arrested, get my mama off me, pass in school
Mother	Tywan to stop using drugs, mind me, get along better with the family, and do better in his schoolwork
Grandmother	Tywan to get off drugs, stay home at night, and do better in school
Teacher	Tywan to stay awake in school and do his work
Probation Officer	No more arrests for drug possession, attend school, improve his grades, follow rules at home, stop drug use
MST Therapist	No further arrests, improve school performance, improve relationship with family and follow the rules at home, stop drug use

FIGURE 6.1. Initial contact information.

possession, manufacturing controlled substances, and intent to distribute controlled substances. The maternal grandmother is involved in Tywan's life. She remarried to Rocky 4 years after her husband's death. Tywan has two uncles and one aunt in prison for drug trafficking.

Strengths and Needs

As described in the previous chapter, initial interviews and assessments identify important aspects of the youth's history, presenting problems, and psychosocial functioning. A crucial step in this process is for each participant to report on the strengths and needs of each system. Figure 6.2 shows the strengths and needs identified in each of the systems related to Tywan. On the strengths side, Tywan truly seemed to want to stop his drug-involved lifestyle, despite his family's significant drug-related history. Tywan's mother was employed, and she had a good relationship with his grandmother. Further suggesting family competency, the siblings were well behaved and not involved in drugs. Tywan rarely missed school, cared about school, and wanted to pass. Moreover, Tywan had won the heart of a school counselor, who wanted to help despite his lack of progress. Regarding prosocial activities, Tywan was interested in running, and track teams were available at his school and in the neighborhood. Finally, a prosocial cousin lived in the neighborhood.

On the weaknesses side, Tywan had been using drugs since 9 years of age and engaged in regular marijuana and cocaine use. He often stayed out all night and had never followed a curfew, even when on probation. His lack of sleep spilled over into school, where he slept most of the time. Although he attended regularly, Tywan felt disconnected at school, as he believed the majority of people there did not like him and wanted to put him out. His mother rarely responded to requests for help from the school. Several significant weaknesses were also evident in the family. The mother was rarely home, even when not working, and the children basically took care of themselves. The mother was often irritable and engaged in screaming and yelling, which made it difficult to talk with her children in a positive tone. Home life was minimally structured and family cohesion was low. The mother continued to feel extensive grief over her father's death 5 years earlier, and Tywan and his siblings had no contact with their father. With regard to peers, Tywan tended to associate primarily with friends who sold and used drugs. They were his lifelong peer group.

Initial Goals

As each participant is interviewed, he or she is asked to give desired goals. These are the changes that the participants in the youth's ecology would

Family: Echo   Therapist: Forest   Date: 4/16/03

Systemic Strengths	Systemic Weaknesses/Needs
Individual	
A desire to pass in school	Drug use
Wants to stay out of trouble	Failing in school
Bright and has capacity to pass in school	Doesn't follow parent's rules
Would like to participate in running	Not following curfew and sleeping little at night
Regular school attendance	
Family	
Concerned grandmother	Low family cohesion
Mom and grandmother get along	No discipline plan
Siblings are well behaved	Low monitoring
Mom is employed	Negative interactions
	No contact with Dad
	Mom's extended grief
School	
Sports available	Poor relations between Mom and school
School counselor wants to help	Low connection between school and Tywan
Peers	
Prosocial cousin in neighborhood	Hangs out with drug-using peers
Community	
Strong community center with a lot of activities and running	High crime rates
Desire of the people to rid the neighborhood of drugs	Economic disadvantage
	Drug selling regular on the streets

FIGURE 6.2. Strengths and needs summary.

like to see happen through their participation in MST. The desired goals are recorded on the Initial Contact Information form (see Figure 6.1). The desired outcomes of each participant are integrated to denote the overarching goals.

Step 3. Overarching Goals

The overarching goals set the direction for treatment, and achieving these goals would signify the end of treatment. In Tywan's case, the overarching goals pertained to his drug use, school performance, and noncompliant behavior at home (see Figure 6.3). Moreover, the goals must be objective and defined in such a way that participants have a shared understanding. In Tywan's case, the goals were defined as follows:

- Drug use was measured by random urine screens.
- School performance was indexed by grades.
- Compliance with family rules was based on reports from his mother and a grandparent.

After the overarching goals are delineated, the therapist reviews them with the family to make sure that they are consistent with family desires. As noted previously, additional overarching goals can be set during the course of treatment. For example, the therapist later learned that the mother was abusing substances, so maternal drug abstinence was added as an overarching goal. Finally, in the closing treatment session, the therapist and family will "true up" the goals. That is, the success of each goal is evaluated.

Step 4. MST Conceptualization of FIT

Once the overarching goals are established, fit factors are developed for the overarching goals (see Figure 6.4).

Drug Use

Association with drug-using peers was the major peer factor, and evidence indicated that this was a strong factor. The family had lived in the neighborhood all of Tywan's life, and his negative peers were his lifelong peers. Hanging out with them and using drugs was a regular way of life. Family factors included lax discipline, low parental monitoring, and low family cohesion. Mom was rarely at home to monitor the children and they lived by their own rules, cooked their own meals, and decided their own curfew. Mom reported Tywan did not follow rules, but she was unsure really what the rules were. Since Tywan's father was in prison for life under the Kingpin

Family: Echo _____ Therapist: Forest _____ Date: 4/16/03 _____

Weekly Review

Overarching/Primary MST Goals
1. Tywan will stop drug use, as evidenced by 12 weeks of clean urine drug screens.
2. Tywan will follow rules at home, as evidenced by parent and grandparent report.
3. Tywan will increase school performance, as evidenced by raising all grades to passing.
4. Ms. Echo will stop drug use, as evidenced by 12 weeks of clean urine drug screens (UDS).

Previous Intermediary Goals

	Met	Partially	Not
1. Tywan will complete a baseline UDS	x		
2. Mom/Grandma/Tywan will meet to set up a Community Reinforcement Approach (CRA) contract	x		
3. Tywan will attend drug court	x		
4. Tywan will identify activities of interest	x		
5. Mom will set rules and consequences			x

Barriers to Intermediary Goals
Mom reports low energy and feeling overwhelmed.
Mom acknowledged cocaine use.

Advances in Treatment*
1. Tywan readily gave a UDS.
2. Family set up CRA contract with rewards to earn for clean screens.
3. Tywan attended drug court and reported on UDS and progress.
4. Tywan identified running and karate.

How has your assessment of the fit changed with new information/interventions?
Mom revealed drug use.

New Intermediary Goals for Next Week
1. Mom and Grandma to meet to set up CRA for Mom.
2. Mom will give a baseline UDS.
3. Tywan will give a UDS.
4. Tywan will enroll in karate and running at the community center.
5. Mom and grandma will meet to assess the children's monitoring needs and establish a plan for monitoring.
6. Tywan and Grandmother will attend drug court.

FIGURE 6.3. Weekly review for MST supervision and consultation. *Numbers correspond to those of previous intermediary goals above.

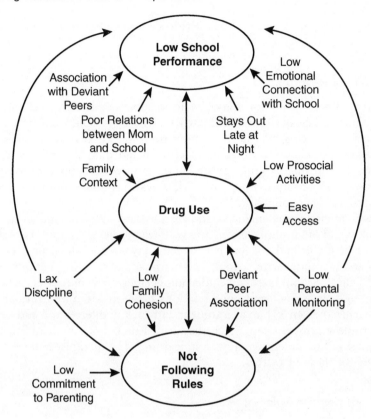

FIGURE 6.4. Fit circles for Tywan.

act, Tywan had taken on the role of father and the women in the family did not try to give him rules. Grandmother had stepped in with the younger children and they spent time at her house. She had not imposed discipline on Tywan. Mom's low parental monitoring contributed directly to the deviant peer association. The peer group had in effect replaced the family. Since the children had little time with Mom, they did not feel close to her. Another important family factor was that the context of this particular family was one of high drug use and drug selling. The past could not be changed, but the family was accustomed to drug use and not nearly as alarmed as the therapist. Individual factors for drug use were low prosocial activities and low school performance. Tywan just spent his time with his drug-using peers, so he was hesitant to engage in any structured activities away from them. He was not doing well in school, though he wanted to do well. His frustration with failure was generally handled by drug use. Community factors included easy access to drugs. Evidence was gathered for all of the fit factors.

Low School Performance

A potential peer factor for school performance was negative peer association. None of Tywan's friends did particularly well in school and when one of them was successful, the remaining peers teased the student. Tywan wanted to continue to fit in. Family factors included lax discipline and low parental monitoring. No rules existed in the family that supported completing homework or improving grades. Mom was not home enough to monitor any level of schoolwork.

Individual factors included staying out late at night and drug use. Tywan would often smoke marijuana with friends before school. He stayed out late at night, and cocaine helped him stay awake. He slept very few hours and was fatigued at school. The marijuana reportedly kept him from being "edgy." School factors included a low emotional connection between Tywan and the school and poor relations between Mom and the school. The teachers perceived him as a student with lack of interest and had begun to just allow him to sleep. Since they had little contact with Mom, they were unsure how to engage Tywan in learning. The therapist had evidence for each of these fit factors.

Not Following the Rules at Home

Again, the peer factor of deviant peer association seemed to be a strong predictor in that Tywan was hanging out on the corner with peers late at night. Family factors included low parental monitoring, lax discipline, low commitment to parenting, and low family cohesion. Given that little monitoring was going on and no rules were enforced, Tywan did not know what rules to follow. Instead, he lived life as an adult. Clearly there was little cohesion in the family, and the therapist hypothesized that since Mom had little involvement with her children, the commitment to parenting them may be low. An individual factor driving Tywan's not following rules was the drug use. When using substances, Tywan was not in the mood to hear about rules. The therapist gathered evidence for each of the hypothesized fit factors except low commitment to parenting.

Fit factors were prioritized based on proximity to the overarching goal, strength, and other criteria noted in Chapter 5. The three most important fit factors in the identified problems seemed to be low parental monitoring, deviant peer association, and lack of structure at home. Low parental monitoring left Tywan on his own, where deviant peers were readily available to fill his time. Since Tywan rarely received consequences for staying out late, drug use, or other misbehavior, he had little motivation to behave more responsibly. Likewise, because he rarely received positive consequences for responsible behavior, he had little incentive to behave maturely. In essence, Tywan was embedded in a social context that was highly conducive to antisocial behavior.

Step 5. Intermediary Goals

The intermediary goals link directly to the overarching goals. The intermediary goals may apply to more than one overarching goal. Figure 6.3 shows an example of the weekly review sheet that is completed by the therapist and presented at clinical supervision. The intermediary goals for this week focused on the fit factors of low parental monitoring, deviant peer association, and lack of structure at home, as these were viewed as the most important determinants of the overarching problems.

Overarching Goal 1

Tywan will stop drug use, as evidenced by 12 weeks of clean urine drug screens.

Intermediary Goal 1

A drug use monitoring system needed to be established to allow the treatment team to track Tywan's drug use accurately. Based on the strengths and needs assessment, his grandmother was recruited to help with collection of urine specimens, as she had favorable relations with both her grandson and daughter. This system began with a baseline urine drug screen conducted in the home by the grandmother. Tywan was compliant with the collection process and proceeded to provide urine samples weekly.

Intermediary Goal 2

To further address Tywan's drug use and the monitoring of that use, the second goal involved Tywan and his mother and grandmother. They met with the therapist to begin substance abuse interventions for Tywan. A contingency management program (described later in this chapter) was implemented. This intervention begins with completion of a contract that details how substance use will be monitored. Under the "Advances in Treatment" heading in Figure 6.3, it can be seen that the family met and the contract was established.

Intermediary Goal 3

The third intermediary goal was for the mother and grandmother to support Tywan's participation in drug court. Under the "Advances in Treatment" heading, the therapist documented that Tywan and his grandmother attended drug court and reported on his drug test results and progress. Drug court attendance would be a weekly intermediary goal for Tywan and his caregivers.

Intermediary Goal 4

To address the fit factor of deviant peer association, Tywan needed to first develop involvement in prosocial activities. To start this process, his prosocial interests were surveyed by the therapist. His interest in running had been identified during the strengths assessment, but this activity met only once per week in the neighborhood, and it was too late to join the track team at school. As shown under the "Advances" heading, however, Tywan also expressed interest in karate. The therapist knew that karate lessons were given at the community center once per week, and weekend tournaments were occasionally held. Furthermore, Tywan's prosocial cousin was enrolled in this activity. Thus, the goal for the next week was to enroll Tywan in the neighborhood karate class and running club. This intermediary goal also addresses overarching goals 2 and 3.

Overarching Goal 2

Tywan will follow rules at home, as evidenced by parent and grandparent report.

Intermediary Goal 5

During the previous weeks, the treatment team had identified the development of increased structure in the home as an important intermediary goal. Ms. Echo wanted her son to follow the rules, but parental expectations were vague. As the therapist worked to help the mother identify rules and link consequences to them, Ms. Echo began to feel overwhelmed, and the therapist learned that the lack of family structure was driven largely by maternal cocaine abuse. Such abuse needed to be addressed effectively before Ms. Echo could implement a discipline system at home. However, the children needed structure and discipline immediately. Help was recruited from the grandmother until Ms. Echo had the personal capacity to monitor and structure her children by herself. Hence, a new intermediary goal was set for the mother and grandmother to jointly determine the monitoring needs of the children after school and to put a plan in place with Grandmother in charge.

Under the heading "How has your assessment of the fit changed . . . ?" in Figure 6.3, an additional fit factor for Tywan's drug use, Mom's drug use, was noted. Treatment for maternal cocaine use was added as a goal, and intervention protocols similar to those for Tywan were developed for treating Ms. Echo.

Step 6. Intervention Development

Interventions are applied to the fit factors that contribute to the target behavior. Although extensive efforts are made to implement interventions through the primary caregivers, this is not always possible. In the case of Tywan, low monitoring and minimal structure at home were primary fit factors driving his drug use. Unfortunately, however, the mother's drug use was a major barrier to the development and implementation of effective monitoring and discipline practices. Until her drug use was reduced, Ms. Echo was not going to be able to implement a discipline system. When parents are not ready to engage in more formal treatment interventions, other practical solutions might have to be put in place for the safety of children. Here, Grandmother stepped in to help monitor the children until Ms. Echo was prepared. This support from the grandmother was crucial to buying the time needed for the other interventions to take effect.

As listed at the end of this chapter, several empirically supported interventions were used to achieve the overarching goals in Tywan's case. This section focuses on three of them, provided in the areas of peer association, family cohesion, and substance abuse.

Changing Peer Affiliations

When association and friendship with deviant peers contributes to a youth's problem behavior, the therapist and family must determine ways to decrease negative peer affiliation and increase relations with prosocial peers. As with all interventions, the therapist and caregivers should help the youth understand the rationale for treatment decisions. For example, the caregivers and therapist might talk with the youth about his or her current peer choices and whether those peers are helping or hurting him or her in the quest to stay out of trouble. During these conversations, care should be taken not to put down the peers. The youth most likely hangs out with these individuals because he or she has fun with them and likes them. Putdowns will place the youth on the defensive with the peers and less aligned with the parent. Most likely the youth will not be amenable to the idea of giving up time with close friends, even if they increase his or her own risk of trouble. Hence, parents must be ready to stand strong against the youth's complaints or even extreme behavior (e.g., running away). Changing negative peer associations is one of the most challenging clinical tasks that will be faced.

Some of the basic procedures for parents to implement toward the goal of breaking deviant peer association follow (Henggeler, Schoenwald, Rowland, & Cunningham, 2002).

- *Monitoring.* Know where the youth is at all times. If there have been few rules in the home, parents will have to start from scratch with regard to monitoring, and the youth can be expected to resist such monitoring with all his or her might. The therapist can help the parent understand the basics of monitoring, such as the youth asking permission to go out, the parent setting rules regarding where the youth can go after school, and the youth leaving notes regarding his or her whereabouts and calling the parent when he or she arrives at the designated destination. Being monitored can be very difficult and embarrassing for a youth who is accustomed to running the streets and leading an adult-like lifestyle. Hence, the youth might also be given strategies for saving face with his or her peers. For example, the teenager can tell the "boys on the corner" that "I can't hang out because I got a judge up in my business." Even the youngest deviant peer understands this rationale. When all peers are deviant and part of a cohesive group in a neighborhood, the parent will have to get the youth out of the neighborhood during times when close supervision is not possible. School-based after-school programs, recreational activities, or even a job will be important in redirecting the youth's energy and attention away from deviant peers.
- *Contact.* Get to know the youth's friends and their parents. When the MST team is working in an individual neighborhood, the deviant peers are likely well known to the parent and might even be cousins or MST clients. When peers are familiar to parents, their problem behavior might not feel quite so deviant because the parents have seen their strengths as well. Therefore, the parent might need a special understanding of how this deviant peer is impacting her or his child. Often neighbors or relatives can help the parent appreciate that continued association with problematic friends is not helping the child achieve the goals of treatment. Parents of fellow deviant peers might also cooperate in keeping their children apart.
- *Consequences.* Apply serious negative consequences when the youth breaks the rules and spends time with deviant peers. Parents might set rules, and the youth might scoff at them. The best possible lesson for a youth to learn about breaking rules is that the parent will provide significant consequences for such behavior. The consequences will need to be strong (i.e., impact resources and privileges that are highly valued) to break deviant peer associations. In addition, rewards should be in place to reinforce

prosocial peer contact. When youth are enrolled in drug court, they will receive sanctions and rewards from the court as well as from caregivers.

• *Activities.* Involve the youth in structured, supervised, and prosocial activities in which he or she is interested. Activities might be within or outside the neighborhood and include sports, music, art, recreation, or academics. The youth should identify areas of interest and have the capacity to build a reasonable level of competence in the activity. Interest and competency increase the chances that the activity will be sustained.

Increasing Family Cohesion and Positive Relations

Low family cohesion and lack of emotional support are risk factors for many problems experienced by children and adolescents. Typically, families are low on cohesion when they cannot ask each other for help, do not do activities together, are closer to people outside the family than inside, and do not spend free time together (Olson, 1986). As with all MST intervention targets, the therapist and family will need to understand the fit of the low cohesion within each particular context. For example, low family cohesion might be due to weak emotional bonds, little time left in the day after school and work, poor communication skills, limited knowledge of positive parenting, or developmental changes in the child. The following are tips for increasing family cohesion.

• *Strengthen the emotional bond between parent and child.* When a child has been in trouble with the law or consistently experienced behavioral problems, such problems can bring about and sustain negative parent–child interactions. In addition, the parent might be so stressed from personal problems or work that positive interactions are difficult to initiate. Moreover, parents who are not strongly bonded with their children are less likely to carry out interventions that reward them. An emotional bond is demonstrated through how people talk with each other and treat each other, and whether they spend time together. Activities and skills that strengthen the parent–child bond include learning positive communication skills (see Chapter 5), teaching the parent and child how to have "heart-to-heart" talks without resorting to negative communication, greeting each other when coming together, recognizing positive things about each other, using praise liberally with a youth, engaging in enjoyable activities that both people like, and accomplishing a goal together. As the family and therapist determine activities that the family can do together, the therapist must be open to those that fit within the culture of the family (e.g., church activities for the family who attends church) and community (see Chapter 8).

• *Increase family time together.* As children develop, they normally increase time with peers and decrease time with parents. Thus, interventions to increase family time should take this developmental norm into account. Parents might need help to realize that consuming their child's time is not the point of the intervention and might actually work against them. Family time, however, can be built into the everyday routine. For example, family members might eat breakfast and dinner together and have a family ritual at bedtime. Family time can also be increased through special events that become rituals such as eating out together once a week, attending church services together, holding family meetings, or participating in other activities that the members enjoy (e.g., fishing, playing basketball, playing board games or cards).

• *Increase reliance on each other.* In families where cohesion is low, relying on each other for help is uncommon. Although family members might be available for each other during times of crisis, everyday problems might not get addressed adequately. When problems that feel serious are minimized (e.g., You are just a child, how can you be stressed?), family members might stop asking each other for help. To build reliance on each other requires strong communication without minimization and skill in problem solving (see Chapter 5). Parents and their children need to learn to listen to each other, take each other's feelings seriously, and assist with brainstorming solutions.

Substance Abuse

As noted earlier in this chapter, standard MST interventions to improve parental monitoring, remove youth from drug-using peer groups, and so forth have earned MST important recognition in the field of substance abuse treatment. Recently, however, these basic protocols have been enhanced to achieve even better outcomes for substance-abusing adolescents. The enhancements integrate key components of the contingency management (Donohue & Azrin, 2001) and community reinforcement (Budney & Higgins, 1998) approaches to treating substance abuse and dependence. These components add a specific focus on substance use per se that complements the standard MST emphasis on changing risk factors in the social ecology. These enhancements as integrated into MST treatment for youth substance abuse are specified in a treatment manual (Cunningham et al., 2003) that includes several basic features.

• *Contingency management.* The contingency management system includes the development of a contract and setting up a reward system. First, the youth and his or her family complete a contract that explains the three-level reward system and frequent monitoring of substance use through urine drug screens. At Level I, a youth starts out with 50 points in a "checking account" that is worth the equivalent of $50. Each week that his or her urine drug screens are clean, the youth keeps the points. Each week that a screen is dirty, the youth loses points. At the end of the first month, the youth may use points to purchase desired and approved items off a reward menu. After eight consecutive weeks of clean screens, the youth moves into Level II. Here, a youth can earn bonus points for clean screens and, with sustained abstinence, advance to Level III. Level III focuses on maintaining abstinence using naturally occurring consequences.

• *Functional analysis of drug use.* Throughout treatment, functional analyses are used to identify cues and triggers for drug use as well as for abstinence. Cues and triggers can be people, places, or events that lead to the initiation of substance use. Also, the functional analysis identifies positive and negative consequences of substance use to determine the contributing factors. When a youth uses a substance, the detailed analysis of use identifies the antecedents–behaviors–consequences of that use. That is, triggers of the use, thoughts and feelings, how the use occurred, and positive and negative consequences are delineated. This information is used to facilitate the design of self-management planning and drug-refusal training interventions.

• *Self-Management Planning.* A self-management plan uses specific strategies to manage drug-use triggers. Budney and Higgins (1998) have identified three ways to manage triggers including (1) avoid triggers, (2) rearrange the environment, and (3) make a new plan (e.g., different skills, social support). For example, when a youth identifies certain people as triggers for drug use, a plan is made to avoid socializing with them. Also, any drug paraphernalia that has been in the possession of the youth will need to be removed.

• *Drug-refusal training.* Given that drug use relapse most often occurs in social situations (Budney & Higgins, 1998), drug-refusal training aims to develop the youth's capacity to manage social situations that trigger drug use. The training includes instruction in social skills relevant to refusing drugs, accompanied by in-session practice. For example, the youth may decide to tell drug-using friends that he or she wants to play more basketball and can't use because it hurts the game.

Step 7. Intervention Implementation

As discussed earlier, several features of interventions should be taken into account as they are implemented to achieve the intermediary goals, which, in turn, are needed to achieve the overarching goals (see Figure 6.3).

1. Determine the target behavior and define it well. All treatment participants (e.g., youth, caregivers) and collaborators (e.g., neighbor, teacher) should have the same definition of the target behaviors.

2. Measure the target behaviors to determine their frequency, intensity, and duration. Measurement can be through daily logs kept by family members, behavior checklists, or biological indices. When outcomes are measured by self-reports, multiple respondents should be assessed to determine the convergence of their perspectives. For example, Tywan's association with deviant peers was measured by his mother and grandmother's report of days he missed curfew and teacher reports based on observations in school. The validity of urine drug screens to measure drug use, however, is high as long as specimen collection protocols are followed (see Cunningham et al., 2003).

3. Apply the intervention. Figure 6.3 lists the intermediary goals, which indicate how the interventions are being applied. Note that these goals are stated using relatively simple and straightforward language.

4. Advances and barriers to lack of progress are assessed weekly, and any new information regarding the fit of factors influencing the overarching goals is integrated into the case materials. The advances and barriers are shown in Figure 6.3 and should provide the treatment team with a weekly snapshot of therapeutic progress.

Step 8. Assessment of Advances and Barriers to Intervention Effectiveness and New Fit Factors

The therapist reports advances related to each intermediary goal to the supervisor and MST consultant each week. The therapist might also note the fit of the advance (i.e., what caused the advance). This information is recorded on the weekly summary sheet (Figure 6.3). In addition, if the intervention is not working, the therapist attempts to identify the barriers to progress, and the team might hypothesize additional barriers. Interventions are then altered or redesigned to overcome these barriers. Thus, additional fit circles might be brought to supervision or refined in supervision so that interventions can proceed in a successful manner. For example, a new fit factor for Tywan's drug use was the discovery of his mother's cocaine abuse. This new information required the team to develop alternative plans to improve monitoring of Tywan and to provide substance abuse treatment for Ms. Echo. The MST process continues around the steps of the do-loop until the overarching goals are met.

Treatment Strategies for the Case of Tywan Echo

The figures and tables presented for Tywan illustrate the process early in the case and show how fit factors were prioritized. The MST analytical process and treatment, however, are continuous processes. Interventions for reducing negative peer affiliations, increasing family cohesion, and implementing a focused substance abuse intervention were described earlier. Over the course of treatment for Tywan and his family, however, a relatively broad array of additional interventions was delivered as well. The following interventions were provided to Tywan and his family.

For Low School Performance

- Strategies to increase parental monitoring
- Strategies with the mother to break Tywan's link with deviant peers
- Strategies to improve the relationship between Tywan's mother and the school
- Training to improve parental control techniques
- Strategies to increase involvement in school sports and foster Tywan's relations with his school counselor

For Drug Use

- Contingency management and the community reinforcement to target substance use by Tywan and his mother
- Interventions to increase family cohesion
- Strategies to increase parental monitoring
- Strategies with the mother to break Tywan's link with deviant peers
- Training to improve parental control techniques
- Strategies to increase involvement in karate and running in the neighborhood

For Not Following Rules

- Contingency management and the community reinforcement to target substance use by Tywan and his mother
- Interventions to increase family cohesion, including beginning to write to dad and involving Rocky in activities and treatment
- Strategies to increase parental monitoring
- Strategies with the mother to break Tywan's link with deviant peers
- Training to improve parental control techniques
- Strategies to increase involvement in karate and running in the neighborhood

Through the implementation of multiple interventions addressing risk and protective factors across multiple systems, Tywan and his mother reduced their cocaine and marijuana use, and Tywan improved his grades. The family reported becoming closer, and Ms. Echo developed more effective disciplinary practices. Tywan completed drug court successfully.

CONCLUSION

In this chapter, an MST case focusing on youth substance abuse was presented. As shown through this case, factors from multiple systems drive substance use in youth; thus, interventions will need to relate to these multiple systems such as peer association, family functioning, parental monitoring and discipline, and school performance. Importantly, specific evidence-based strategies to reduce substance abuse were applied within the context of the MST analytic process.

CHAPTER 7

The MST Approach for Reducing School Problems and School Expulsion

Success in school is a major life task for children that influences almost all aspects of their lives as adults—their future occupation, income, access to health care, spouse, friends, home, recreational opportunities, and longevity. Unfortunately, attaining academic success is very challenging for many children. When a youth is struggling with academics, has been retained in the same grade, and is much older than classmates, school can be very painful. In addition, youth struggling with behavioral disorders or issues such as depression, abuse, or violence in the home often experience problems concentrating and getting along with others. These problems can further interfere with school performance.

Society's heightened concern with school violence, unfortunately, compounds the academic challenges for youth with behavior problems. Many school districts have instituted zero tolerance policies, whereby youth can be expelled for many behaviors that would have resulted in trips to the principal's office or parent–teacher conferences in past decades. Indeed, some professionals believe that such punitive policies are primarily intended to reduce stress on school personnel by eliminating the need to address the learning and behavioral needs of the highest risk youth. Instead, these expelled youth return to their neighborhoods, often to homes that lack supervision because the caregivers are working during the day. Few of these youth receive any meaningful educational substitute, and most have increased opportunity to get into more trouble in their neighborhoods. Interventions are sorely needed to keep youth in school and learning, and schools need community support to educate our youth.

The goals of this chapter are:

1. To present evidence that MST facilitates educational attainments and reduces youth school problems in the context of a neighborhood project
2. To demonstrate the application of MST for school-related problems via a case example

THE EVIDENCE THAT MST WORKS FOR REDUCING YOUTH SCHOOL PROBLEMS

In contrast with extensive research documenting MST effects on youth antisocial behavior, evaluations of the effects of MST on school-related outcomes are more limited. In a study of MST with substance-abusing juvenile offenders noted earlier (Henggeler, Pickrel, & Brondino, 1999), youth assigned to the MST condition significantly increased school attendance at posttreatment in comparison with youth receiving usual community services, and these gains were maintained at a 6-month follow-up (Brown, Henggeler, Schoenwald, Brondino, & Pickrel, 1999). Similarly, in the trial of MST as an alternative to emergency psychiatric hospitalization (Henggeler, Rowland, et al., 1999), MST was more effective than hospitalization at promoting children's attendance in regular school environments (i.e., not special education classrooms or residential settings). Together, these findings support the capacity of MST to influence an important precursor to successful school performance, that is, attendance at school.

Though not a controlled trial, the Neighborhood Solutions Project provides additional support for the ability of MST and associated interventions to improve the school-related functioning of adolescents presenting serious clinical problems. Union Heights residents had serious concerns about the school-related problems their youth were experiencing. Suspension and expulsion rates for neighborhood youth were high, and many children wandered the streets by day because they had either been put out of school or attendance was not being enforced. For example, during a routine survey of neighborhood homes, neighborhood leaders discovered two youth, ages 9 and 11 years, at home alone on a weekday. The children had decided that they would not attend school that year, so they just stayed home. The neighborhood leaders made a mental note for a future referral.

WHAT THE NEIGHBORHOOD SOLUTIONS PROJECT ADDED TO TRADITIONAL MST

Referral Process

Referrals for school-related problems came primarily from teachers and administrators rather than from families or neighborhood leaders. In each of the six schools that served children in Union Heights, neighborhood leaders and project staff met with key professionals at that school. The primary purpose of the meetings was to inform these professionals that the Neighborhood Solutions Project was available to take referrals of youth from Union Heights. Specifically, the project aimed to curb the high rate of expulsion of neighborhood children by providing schools with resources to help manage these children's behavior problems. Teachers generally knew where their students lived, so making an appropriate referral through the project paging system or directly to the project director was not difficult. As the project progressed, referrals for academic or attendance problems began to come directly from parents to the project director. Youth with acute problems were generally identified through the early response system described next.

Early Response System

The early response system became the hallmark of the project's school interventions. School administrators and teachers determined that they would like to reach an MST team member quickly for children who were escalating toward a crisis. When a teacher indicated that a student was beginning to escalate with a behavioral or emotional problem, the school paged the team and made an immediate referral. The challenge for the team was to locate the parent and drive to the school as soon as possible to address the problem. This system was extremely effective at deescalating crises. Rather than having contentious relations with school personnel, the MST team helped caregivers to support the efforts of teachers and others to maintain classroom order. Implementation of this system often made the difference between whether a child was sent home for a half a day to cool down or was arrested.

Engagement

Considerable efforts were needed to develop more collaborative relations between families and school personnel. Parents often felt frustrated because the only contact they had with the school was negative. In addition, parents who had struggled with school themselves faced bad memories or feelings of intimidation when attending school meetings. To overcome these issues, a tremendous amount of support and advocacy was needed from the project team to engage the parent with the school.

The neighborhood also facilitated engagement of families and schools by becoming involved with the schools and showing support of the families. For example, during teacher appreciation week, schools that worked closely with the team received food prepared by community members. The neighborhood recognized teachers on major holidays with treats or small gifts. Principals were invited to the community center for a reception or tour. Principals and other school personnel received fliers inviting them to neighborhood events. The neighborhood leaders got to know the school leaders and, in doing so, the schools became more engaged with the MST team.

Neighborhood Intervention Support

A network of people and resources located directly in the neighborhood was activated to provide a variety of support for the children's educational efforts. For example, when a neighborhood youth had an expulsion hearing, the team could count on attendance by a room full of neighbors as a show of support for the parent and youth. When a child was struggling academically, homework help and tutoring were available at the community center. Older teens were available to help younger children with homework. The Center enabled youth to earn funds for the Black College Tour by helping children with academics. For some youth, high school was not the most appropriate option, and they were encouraged to complete a GED at the center's program at no cost. In addition, job-related education was available at the center. For example, the Tools for Success program discussed in Chapter 8 offered teens training in preemployment skills.

Outcomes for Referred Youth

After the early response system was put in place, teachers, principals, and parents began to refer youth to the project. Sixteen youth were referred for MST intervention. Thirteen were at the brink of expulsion due to school violence (e.g., death threats, destroying others' personal property), and three were referred for various behavioral and academic problems. Using school-based interventions described in the MST treatment manuals (Henggeler et al., 1998, 2002) and protocols developed especially for the Neighborhood Solutions Project, only 1 of the 16 referred youth were subsequently expelled! This student was rapidly enrolled in an alternative school program and was able to continue academic progress. Furthermore, youth in the NS-school group (expulsion risk group) showed significant or near significant reductions in self-reports of minor assault, self-reported crime against persons, and school delinquency. Project staff learned a crucial fact: With considerable advocacy from parents, neighborhood leaders, and professional staff, school administrators could demonstrate great flexibility in addressing the needs of children presenting serious behavior problems. Thus, even in a system with a zero tolerance policy for school violence, problems can be resolved if parents and neighborhood leaders provide intensive support for their children and the professionals charged with educating them.

CASE APPLICATION OF MST

The fictionalized case example presents a youth at risk of expulsion. Note that the MST analytical process, the do-loop shown in Figure 3.2 (Chapter 3, p. 48), is followed through the various steps.

Step 1. Referral Behavior

Ronquetta Sweetgrass, a 12-year-old female, was referred to the clinical team by her middle school teacher (see Figure 7.1). Ronquetta had excessive school absences and missed the first 6 weeks of school. Moreover, she put forth little effort in school and was failing all subjects. The teacher reported that Ronquetta was moody, often lethargic, and often brought candy to class. School personnel worried that she was having health problems or was not being fed at home. On the day of the referral, Ronquetta had attended school, refused to work, and munched on candy belligerently. When the teacher tried to get her back on task, Ronquetta stated in a loud voice, "Leave me alone you crackhead, or I'm gonna stick you." The teacher called the law enforcement officer assigned to the school and was prepared to have Ronquetta arrested. The officer was unable to reach the parent and with the teacher decided to page the neighborhood's MST team.

Step 2. Desired Outcomes of Key Participants

The desired outcomes are gathered by interviewing each key participant in the youth's social network. In this case, getting to the school rapidly to prevent Ronquetta's arrest was of urgent importance. Hence, the therapist contacted Ronquetta's mother while driving to the school, and she arranged for a neighbor to pick her up from work. The parent needed to sign the consent to treat form and appropriate release of information forms before interventions could begin. The desired outcomes could then be elicited from the teacher and parent.

Genogram

The genogram (McGoldrick & Gerson, 1985) is drawn to document the family context and give an overview of the extended family. As shown in Figure 7.1, Ronquetta lives with her 26-year-old mother and 51-year-old grandmother. The whereabouts of Ronquetta's father are unknown. Ms. Sweetgrass has experienced several losses, including the deaths of her father, brother, and sister. Her younger sister is away from home attending college.

Family: _Sweetgrass_ _____   Therapist: _Hackemann_ _____   Date: _10/21/03_ _____

Genogram

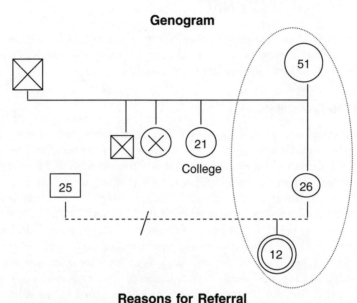

Reasons for Referral

1. Excessive school absences
2. Failing all work when present
3. School's concerns that youth may have health problems

Initial Goals/Desired Outcome

Participant	Goal
Ronquetta	Go to school and pass my classes Get my blood sugar under control
Grandmother	Ronquetta to attend school and pass her classes Ronquetta to check her blood sugar and take her medication Ronquetta's Mama to calm her nerves
Mother	Ronquetta to pass in school and stop staying home
CPS Worker	Ronquetta to attend school, pass her classes, and get her diabetes under control Ms. Sweetgrass to deal with her anxiety
Teacher	Ronquetta to attend school and get her health problems taken care of
MST Therapist	Ronquetta to attend school, improve her grades and get her blood sugar level consistently below 200 Ms. Sweetgrass to decrease anxiety

FIGURE 7.1. Initial contact information.

Intake

For school-related cases, the initial interview and assessment are conducted individually and in depth with the caregiver, child, and teachers. During these interviews, the therapist obtains mental health, social, and educational histories, and observes important aspects of the participants' interpersonal relations. The teacher is asked to identify the contexts in which the problems are occurring (e.g., lunchroom, English class), characteristics of those contexts (e.g., structured or not), the youth's interactions with other students, and information regarding the youth's attendance and grades. The parent, child, and teacher might also be asked to complete standardized measures to obtain a baseline index of symptoms or functioning. During the intake with Ronquetta and her mother, the therapist discovered that both were struggling with adherence to a diabetes regimen. This fact was unknown to the school, although they suspected some kind of health problem.

Strengths and Needs

A crucial step in the assessment process is for each participant to report on the strengths and needs of each system. Figure 7.2 shows the strengths and needs in each of the systems related to Ronquetta and her family. Multiple strengths were identified. Ronquetta wants to manage her diabetes better and improve her attendance and performance in school. In addition, several teachers are very concerned about Ronquetta, and the school nurse is available three times a week to help monitor her health. With regard to the family, Ronquetta has a supportive mother and grandmother, and the family is emotionally close. Ronquetta has an excellent role model in an aunt who is attending college. In the community, Ronquetta has several positive peers, she is interested in double Dutch jump roping and dancing, and the neighborhood has activities that can help with health and wellness. In addition, Ronquetta lives two blocks from a health center that has many patients with diabetes.

On the weaknesses side, Ronquetta is experiencing consistently high blood sugar levels and has poor management of her diabetes. Her health problems have contributed to excessive school absences and low performance, and she is at risk of being referred to juvenile court. Within the family, Ms. Sweetgrass is also having difficulty managing her own diabetes and reports high levels of anxiety and depression related to grief over the losses in her life. Little support is being provided to help either Ms. Sweetgrass or Ronquetta manage their diabetes. The school has minimal understanding of Ronquetta's health status and, since the principal threatened to have Ronquetta sent to juvenile justice due to the absences, the school–parent relationship is strained. Although Ronquetta's neighborhood peers are positive, they do not understand her diabetes and share candy with her after

Family: Sweetgrass   Therapist: Hackemann   Date: 10/21/03

Systemic Strengths	Systemic Weaknesses/Needs
Individual	
A desire to improve in school	Excessive school absences
A desire to control diabetes	Low academic performance
Enjoys double Dutch jump roping and dancing	Type 1 diabetic with consistently high blood sugar
	At risk for juvenile court referral and expulsion
Family	
Supportive mom and grandmother	Mom highly anxious
Aunt in college	Mom's own poor care of diabetes
Close family relations	Depression over multiple losses
	Poor support of diabetes care in the family
School	
School nurse available 3x week	Low understanding of health status
Interested teachers	Negative interaction with assistant principal
	Threats to make report to child protective services and juvenile court
Peers	
Group of positive peers in neighborhood who participate in activities	Peers don't understand her diabetes and eat a lot of candy with her
Community	
Access to physical activities	"Candy lady" lives next door
Health center in neighborhood	High prevalence of diabetes in neighborhood

FIGURE 7.2. Strengths and needs summary.

school. Ronquetta and her friends purchase candy from the neighborhood "candy lady," who is also unaware of Ronquetta's diabetes. Finally, the diabetes rates in the neighborhood are high.

Initial Goals

As each participant is interviewed, he or she is asked to give desired goals, which are recorded on the Initial Contact Information form (see Figure

7.1). The desired outcomes of each participant are combined to delineate the overarching goals.

Step 3. Overarching Goals

In Ronquetta's case, the key participants identified overarching goals pertaining to management of diabetes, school attendance and performance, and the mother's anxiety (see Figure 7.3). With these goals in mind, the therapist and family members agreed on several criteria that would indicate successful therapeutic outcomes. These criteria included a 50% increase in school attendance, a grade-point average of at least a C, average blood sugar levels of less than 200 mg/dl for mother and daughter, and a reduction of the mother's anxiety out of the clinical range as measured by a validated self-report instrument. As noted in the preceding chapters, additional overarching goals can be set during the course of treatment as new information becomes available. It is important to note that prior to work on a medical overarching goal, the therapist, child, and parent should talk with the physician or nurse practitioner who is overseeing the treatment.

Step 4. MST Conceptualization of Fit

Fit factors for each of the systems are considered (see Figure 7.4). In Ronquetta's case, the key problems were low school performance, elevated blood sugar levels, and her mother's high anxiety. To determine fit, the therapist brainstormed potential factors that she observed when conducting the intake and strengths and needs assessments. Drafts of fit circles were brought to supervision for the team to review, and those fit factors backed by evidence (therapist observation or that of another participant) were noted.

Low School Performance

Several factors seemed to be contributing to Ronquetta's difficulties in school. Individual factors included excessive absences, consistently elevated blood sugar levels, and depression over the deaths of several relatives. The excessive absences had put Ronquetta behind in her work. She felt fatigued and unmotivated due to the depression and elevated blood sugar levels, which made it hard to focus on her work. Since the school was unaware of her health status, they made no accommodations in her educational environment. The poor relationship between Ms. Sweetgrass and the school made developing a warm relationship with the teacher difficult for Ronquetta. Family factors included the mother's high level of anxiety,

Family: _Sweetgrass_ _____   Therapist: _Hackemann_ ____   Date: _10/21/03_ ____

Weekly Review

Overarching/Primary MST Goals
1. Ronquetta and Ms. Sweetgrass will stabilize blood sugar levels and maintain average levels, as evidenced by blood sugar levels < 200 across 6 weeks.
2. Ms. Sweetgrass will reduce anxiety based on self report.
3. Ronquetta will increase school attendance by 50%.
4. Ronquetta will improve grades to at least a C average.

Previous Intermediary Goals	Met	Partially	Not
1. Grandma, Mom, Ronquetta, and neighborhood nurse will meet to lay out a plan for diabetes care for Ronquetta and Mom.	x		
2. Mom and Grandma will set up reward system for Ronquetta for diabetes care.		x	
3. Mom will identify fit factors for low diabetes care.	x		

Barriers to Intermediary Goals
Family could not identify rewards

Advances in Treatment*
1. Family set up a plan for taking blood sugar levels daily.
3. Mom identified lack of knowledge and anxiety.

How has your assessment of the fit changed with new information/interventions?
Mom revealed she was raped 2 years ago with severe physical force and injuries, and felt she would die. Assessment indicates she has PTSD; this is a stronger source of anxiety than all the losses.

New Intermediary Goals for Next Week
1. Nurse, Mom, and grandmother will record successes with taking daily blood sugar levels
2. Mom will talk with the candy lady about selling Ronquetta sugar-free candy.
3. Mom and Ronquetta will meet with peers about alternate snacks.
4. Neighborhood nurse will help family identify rewards that have worked with other families.
5. Mom will complete a trauma assessment to obtain baseline measures prior to beginning work on PTSD.

FIGURE 7.3. Weekly review for MST supervision and consultation. *Numbers correspond to those of previous intermediary goals above.

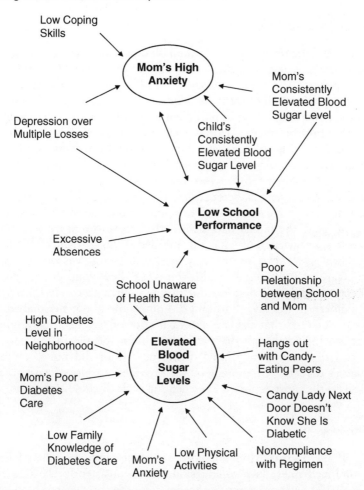

FIGURE 7.4. Fit circles for Ronquetta.

which led her to have little patience with her daughter and made her inaccessible for helping with schoolwork. In addition, the mother's elevated blood sugar levels left her too fatigued to help with her daughter's school problems. The therapist reported evidence for all of these factors except depression over multiple losses. Further investigation with Ronquetta revealed that she felt sad sometimes and missed her grandfather but mostly she was worried that her mom would die because she did not take her insulin like she should.

Elevated Blood Sugar Level

The individual factor related to elevated blood sugar levels was noncompliance with diabetic regimen. Ronquetta did not check her blood sugar level as recommended and her participation in physical activities was low. Although the physician had recommended exercise and activities were available in the community, lack of participation in the activities contributed to Ronquetta's noncompliance. Family factors included Mom's difficulty with anxiety, Mom's own poor diabetes care, and low knowledge in the family about diabetes care. Mom's anxiety left her unable to deal with her daughter's problems. She felt too "stressed out" most of the time to attend to her own and her daughter's diabetes regimen. Not attending to her own diabetes needs set a negative example in the family and made Ms. Sweetgrass feel worse. Although the family had dealt with diabetes for several years, they still had low knowledge of what they needed to do to reduce blood sugar and function in a more healthy way. A school factor was that the school was unaware of Ronquetta's health status, so they could not support her care. A peer factor was that Ronquetta hung out with candy-eating peers. Other children in the neighborhood did not know about her diabetes and did not understand that she could not eat a lot of sweets. Finally, community factors included high diabetes level among people in the neighborhood, and that the "candy lady" living next door did not know about Ronquetta's diabetes. Unknowingly, she provided a route of easy access to sweets. The therapist reported evidence for each of these fit factors.

High Anxiety

Individual factors for Mom included the depression she often felt over losses of loved ones, low coping skills, and consistently elevated blood sugar levels. The depression may also be related to the elevated blood sugar levels, and the combination leaves Ms. Sweetgrass worried and anxious about her health and family. Her low coping skills make anxiety reduction difficult and immobilize her from acting. Family factors included Ronquetta's elevated blood sugar levels and Ronquetta's low school performance. Mom was highly anxious about her daughter's health status and stressed over the calls from the school. The therapist had evidence for each of these factors, but she felt that there was "something more to the picture" that she hoped to learn with continued engagement.

After determining fit factors for which evidence is clear, the next step is to prioritize them for intervention. Again, priority is given to factors that (1) are the most proximal or immediate cause of the problem, (2) are the most powerful or consistently connected, (3) occur in the present, (4) are important to the participants, (5) need to be resolved in order to address other factors, (6) are known correlates of the problems based on research, and (7) have practical solutions. Based on these criteria, priorities were placed on two factors: Ronquetta and her mother's low adherence to the diabetes treatment needs (i.e., insulin adjustment based on blood sugar testing, eating schedule and types of foods consumed, and exercise) and Mom's anxiety. Although Mom's anxiety was a key problem for which the team needed to understand the fit, it also was a fit factor for the low diabetes adherence, which could prove life threatening.

Step 5. Intermediary Goals

Figure 7.3 shows the Weekly Review sheet taken from week 3 of treatment with Ronquetta and her family. Intermediary goals linked directly to the overarching goals and initially addressed the fit factors of the mother and daughter's low medical compliance and maternal anxiety.

Overarching Goal 1

Ronquetta and Ms. Sweetgrass will stabilize blood sugar levels and maintain average levels, as evidenced by blood sugar levels < 200 across 6 weeks.

Intermediary Goal 1

In light of the pervasive effects (e.g., on school performance and emotional affect) and health-threatening nature of the consistently high blood sugar levels experienced by Ronquetta and her mother, they, along with her grandmother, were scheduled to meet with the nurse practitioner at the neighborhood health clinic to make plans for diabetes care. The therapist would also participate in the appointment to help reinforce the health plan. Under the "Advances in Treatment" heading, note that the family met with the nurse and set up a care plan that would involve checking blood sugar levels multiple times daily and changes in diet.

Intermediary Goal 2

A review of the literature on diabetes regimen adherence (Lemanek, Kamps, & Chung, 2001) indicated that behavioral procedures are empirically supported. Hence, a system was developed where Ronquetta could earn rewards for monitoring her blood glucose levels frequently and adjusting her insulin dosages appropriately. For the prior 2 weeks, her blood sugar levels had been between 350 and 380 mg/dl, and these scores served as the baseline. The intermediary goal of implementing a behavioral plan was partially met in that procedures were set in place for Ronquetta to track her blood sugar levels more effectively. Family members, however, did not come up with ideas for rewards because Ronquetta only wanted candy as a reward, and eating candy was one of the primary problems in controlling her blood sugar levels (see "Barriers to Intermediary Goals" heading). To move past this barrier, the family was scheduled to meet with the neighborhood nurse practitioner again (see "New Intermediary Goals") and obtain additional recommendations. Moreover, because candy was such a strongly desired snack, the family set a new intermediary goal to recruit the neighborhood "candy lady" and Ronquetta's friends to support her treatment adherence. Specifically, these peers were asked to share other types of snacks after school, which the family provided, and the "candy lady" was asked to sell sugar-free candies.

Overarching Goal 2

Ms. Sweetgrass will reduce anxiety based on self-report.

Intermediary Goal 3

The team needed a better understanding of the factors that contributed to the mother's elevated blood sugar (overarching goal 1) and anxiety. She met with the therapist and reconfirmed that her almost continuous state of anxiety and depression made it very difficult to care for herself as needed. Moreover, a negative cycle was created where the anxiety and depression contributed to poor diabetes care, and the resulting high blood sugar levels led to increased anxiety and depression. However, an additional fit factor was identified. Ms. Sweetgrass disclosed that she had been raped 2 years ago, and continued to experience anxiety-arousing thoughts and memories of this victimization. Further discussion indicated that she evidenced most of the symptoms of posttraumatic stress disorder (PTSD). She had been using grief over the deaths in her family as an explanation for her anxiety and depression because she was ashamed of the rape. She had certainly felt sadness and loss over the deaths of her father and siblings, but had some resolution on those. Hence, a new intermediary goal was set to complete a trauma assessment and obtain a baseline level of PTSD symptoms.

Step 6. Intervention Development

Interventions are applied to the key fit factors that contribute to the target behavior. In Ronquetta's case, empirically supported interventions were provided in several areas, as described later. In this section, overviews of four of the interventions are presented. These pertain to low adherence to the diabetes treatment regimen, maternal depression, maternal PTSD, and poor parent–school relations.

Increasing Adherence to the Diabetes Treatment Regimen

The primary goal of treatment for diabetes is to maintain blood sugar levels within the normal range, and this level of metabolic control promotes normal growth and activities and helps to prevent complications such as amputations and blindness (Johnson, 1995). The regimen for diabetes includes monitoring blood sugar levels and adjusting medication, dietary adherence, and exercise.

• *Monitoring.* Monitoring of blood glucose levels should be jointly determined by the patient and health care provider assisting the person with diabetes management, and is usually recommended at least three times a day (American Diabetes Association, 2003). Recommended blood glucose levels are between 90 and 130 mg/dl fasting, before meals and at bedtime, with peak after-meal glucose less than 180 mg/dl (American Diabetes Association, 2003). Monitoring of blood glucose levels is usually conducted before meals and bedtime. Also, monitoring 2 hours after a meal is used to determine peak blood sugar control after eating and to determine if carbohydrate intake and medications are balanced (American Diabetes Association, 2003). Reagent strips and meters give a reading of blood sugar level. Also, glucose meters may store readings for future reference. In addition, for people with Type 1 diabetes, urine is monitored for ketones during acute illness or stress or when blood glucose levels are greater than 300 mg/dl or when any symptoms of ketoacidosis such as nausea, vomiting, or abdominal pain are present (American Diabetes Association, 2003).

For Type 1 diabetes, subcutaneous injections of insulin are required to regulate blood glucose levels, whereas people with Type 2 diabetes may or may not need insulin. Insulin is a hormone that is essential for glucose metabolism. Without insulin, glucose will accumulate in the bloodstream. The body will draw on other sources of energy, and this eventually leads to death (Rovet & Fernandes, 1999). Therefore, taking insulin and regulating it is vital to survival. Insulin can be of animal or human origin and is either short-acting or intermediate-acting. Insulin is usually administered by injection (shots) in multiple daily doses. The doses will need to be adjusted based on the interaction of diet, exercise, illness, and stress (Johnson, 1995). The blood glucose level gives an understanding of how the dose must be adjusted.

Interventions related to monitoring must involve daily monitoring of blood glucose levels and taking insulin. The parent or other adults in the child's ecology will need to manage the child's care at home. Furthermore, when fully informed, school personnel can also assist with monitoring of children's status. Finger sticks and daily injections can be stressful, and many children and adults are avoidant. Behavioral strategies can be put in place in the home, and include implementing a behavioral contract (Ellis et al., 2003) and daily recording of the levels on a monitoring sheet (see Figure 7.5). Graphing daily levels give clients an opportunity to see how often they are out of range. The behavioral contract includes a reward system to reinforce taking blood sugar levels and/or keeping levels within the normal range. Parents will need to assure that the child keeps all endocrine appointments. Sharing the blood sugar level graph with the physician provides information on patient status and can be reinforcing for the child if he or she is improving.

• *Dietary adherence.* Diet guidelines have been published for individuals with diabetes. Suggested are three meals and up to three snacks daily that include foods from each food group or at least contain carbohydrates, proteins, and fats in proportion to recommended levels. Individuals should limit sweets, whole milk, fried foods, and salty foods to help control blood glucose, fats, and blood pressure. Diet education should come under the direction of the individual's physician or nurse. Dieticians can work with families to design a diabetes meal plan that outlines how much and what kind of foods to eat for meals and snacks. The American Diabetes Association website outlines evidence-based nutrition principles (*www.diabetes.org*). For the child to adhere to a diabetes meal plan, the parents will need to be in charge of meal and snack planning and provide access to appropriate foods. The dietician may help parents incorporate limited sweets into a healthy eating plan. Furthermore, if there is a "candy lady" in the neighborhood (as they are found in most inner-city neighborhoods), she will need to be a part of the snack plan.

• *Exercise and physical activity.* Individuals with diabetes should follow a regimen of exercise. When the individual is not experiencing complications and when blood sugar control is good, most types of exercise can be performed. Prior to starting an exercise program, the individual must seek recommendations from his or her physician regarding what activities are recommended and which ones should be avoided (*www.diabetes.org*). Physical activities should ideally be planned for times when insulin levels are lowest. Also, it is important to monitor blood sugar levels prior to exercise and have additional carbohydrate foods if blood sugar level is below recommendations. For children to adhere to an exercise regimen, parents should find activities that interest the child and provide social support from positive peers. In the case of Ronquetta, Ms. Sweetgrass found two activities of interest that took place in the community center. Ronquetta favored activities with known peers.

# BLOOD SUGAR LEVELS (BSL)
NORMAL = 90–180

NAME _____   MONTH _____

SUN	MON	TUE	WED	THURS	FRI	SAT

FIGURE 7.5. Diabetes monitoring form.

• *Reducing depression.* Clinical depression can contribute to medical noncompliance and reduce one's capacity to parent effectively. Prior to beginning psychosocial treatment, the client reporting depression should have a thorough physical examination to ensure that the depression is not related to a medical disorder. Cognitive and cognitive-behavioral treatments (CBT) have been empirically supported for treating depression (Hollon & Beck, 1994; Leahy & Holland, 2000). Cognitive therapies follow the assumption that depressed people view themselves negatively and have maladaptive beliefs about situations. The maladaptive beliefs result in negative emotions. Therefore, changes in thinking must occur to decrease depression. CBT follows the same premise but also adds an action-oriented component. A brief overview of the components of depression treatment is provided.

• *Monitoring.* Daily monitoring includes keeping track of thoughts, feelings, behaviors, and consequences related to an event that spirals one toward depression. In effect, the individual conducts a functional analysis of each event that seems to lead to feelings of depression. Such monitoring informs the client and therapist of the sequence of events that intensify depression, the relationship of thinking to feelings, and thinking errors in need of change. This information provides the bases for intervention planning.

• *Identifying and managing thinking errors.* Thinking errors refer to the beliefs an individual holds that reflect exaggerations or distortions that maintain depression. For example, thinking errors might include negative mind reading, ignoring the positive, magnifying the intensity of an event, overgeneralizing, or personalizing. As a "scientist team," the therapist and client work together to investigate possible thinking errors. A good place to start is with automatic thoughts, those that pop into your head. Examples of parental thinking errors found in automatic thought when a child performs poorly in school are the following: "She did not do her homework just to get at me" and "She is going to fail just to hurt me." These thoughts would bring about negative emotions toward the child. To challenge thinking errors, the therapist guides the client through several questions.

1. What is the evidence that this explanation is correct?
2. What evidence suggests that this explanation is not correct?
3. Is there an alternative explanation for your child not doing her homework?
4. Are other motives possible?

• *Diversion strategies.* Diversion strategies are used to manage thinking errors. An example is thought stopping. In a situation where a thinking error occurs, individuals would tell themselves to STOP, then they would substitute a rational and correct belief for the irrational one. For example, "She needs extra help to pass since she may not be understanding the work" replaces "she is going to fail just to hurt me." A second strategy is to reframe the negative view of the situation by labeling it as neutral or positive. For example, disappointment over a child's grades could be reframed as an opportunity to spend more time together since the child will be working longer on homework.

• *Increasing activities.* Increasing involvement in pleasurable events or activities will also help decrease depression (Lewinsohn & Gotlib, 1995). When individuals are depressed, thinking of enjoyable activities is a challenge at best. The individual and others in his or her social network should be asked to recall activities that used to be enjoyable. To help the depressed individual get back into these activities; the therapist or others might need to accompany him or her to the activity and address maladaptive thoughts that emerge during participation. Alternatively, role play during treatment sessions might help prepare the individual to use social skills in activities that require uncomfortable interactions with others.

Reducing Symptoms of PTSD

Anxiety disorders such as PTSD can be major barriers to managing stress and carrying out the tasks necessary to parent children. If the parent is suicidal, safety measures should be immediately put in place (e.g., enlisting the help of other adults for monitoring, hospitalization in the case of significant suicidal intent). For parents who are more stable, empirically supported interventions for PTSD or victimization-related anxiety can begin immediately. In addition, psychiatric consultation might be helpful, to consider the use of evidence-based pharmacological treatment as an adjunct to psychosocial intervention.

Treatment for PTSD is supported by a wealth of research. The reader is referred to several texts for a comprehensive review of treatment techniques for these problems (Follette, Ruzek, & Abueg, 1998; Meichenbaum, 1994; Resick & Schnicke, 1992). Common components of CBT for PTSD and anxiety include systematic desensitization, flooding, prolonged exposure, and cognitive processing. The manuals cited above provide in-depth discussions of PTSD treatment. Here, the basic components of these cognitive and cognitive-behavioral treatments are outlined.

• *Systematic desensitization.* The first step in implementing systematic desensitization techniques is to develop a graduated hierarchy of anxiety-provoking scenes related to the anxiety-producing problem. The first scene should elicit minimal anxiety. Subsequent scenes are rank-ordered by the amount of anxiety they provoke. The second step involves helping the client establish a deeply relaxed state, typically using techniques such as deep muscle relaxation and imagery. Once the relaxed state is established, the client is asked to imagine each of the scenes in the hierarchy, starting with the least anxiety-producing scene. The anxiety-provoking scene is paired with the relaxation repeatedly until the scene no longer elicits anxiety. Then the next scene is introduced, and the same procedure is followed. This pattern continues until the scenes no longer elicit anxiety.

• *Flooding.* Flooding techniques can also be used after the therapist and client have developed a hierarchy of anxiety-provoking scenes from the anxiety-producing events (e.g., sexual assault). As in systematic desensitization, scenes are rank ordered from lowest to highest in terms of producing anxiety. Next, the client is asked to imagine all aspects of the trauma and is directed to the highest anxiety-provoking scene as quickly as possible. Unlike systematic desensitization, with flooding there is no attempt to minimize anxiety at the beginning of exposure or to gradually increase the client's ability to tolerate the anxiety. Rather, the fear response is maintained at a moderate level of anxiety from the start, until it subsides. Flooding has not been proven superior to systematic desensitization in reducing symptoms of PTSD (Meadows & Foa, 1998).

• *Prolonged exposure (PE).* Prolonged exposure is more widely used than systematic desensitization. This is likely due to findings that longer exposure is more effective than short exposure in decreasing anxiety, and that actual (in vivo) stimuli bring about greater change in symptoms than imagined stimuli (Meadows & Foa, 1998). Prolonged exposure has been shown to be a superior treatment for PTSD in rape victims (Foa, Rothbaum, Riggs, & Murdock, 1991). The first step of prolonged exposure involves developing a hierarchy of anxiety-provoking scenes from least to most anxiety-producing. Exposure sessions begin with the scene that is least anxiety-producing (so here it differs from flooding). The exposure can be imagined (e.g., reliving trauma memories) or in vivo (e.g., a feared situation is confronted). The higher anxiety-producing scenes are described repeatedly over several sessions until habituation is achieved. Sessions generally last from 1 to 2 hours.

• *Cognitive restructuring.* Three steps are involved in cognitive restructuring: (1) identifying dysfunctional thoughts, (2) evaluating the validity of the thoughts and challenging those that are thinking errors, and (3) replacing dysfunctional thoughts with more helpful ones. For example, a dysfunctional thought is "I was raped because I had on a thin shirt." Evaluating this thought will help the client to see that rape does not happen because of the clothing one wears. A more helpful thought might be "I did not cause this rape to happen; the person who did it committed a crime."

• *Cognitive processing therapy (CPT).* CPT combines exposure and cognitive therapy and is empirically supported for the treatment of rape victims (Resick & Schnicke, 1992, 1993). The treatment follows the assumption that when individuals experience a traumatic event, their basic beliefs about the world are shattered. Therefore, changing the meaning given to the event is important to moving forward. When an individual's core beliefs are inconsistent with information from a traumatic event, two processes might occur that are either adaptive or maladaptive. When the process is maladaptive, the individual might accommodate or assimilate. Accommodation refers to altering preexisting core beliefs unrealistically in order to make sense of the traumatic event (e.g., from "the world is a safe place" to "there is no safety in the world"). Assimilation refers to distorting aspects of the traumatic event to be consistent with prior beliefs (e.g., "the world is a safe place," so "this must not have really been a rape"). The goal of CPT is to provide corrective information and experiences regarding the faulty thinking and intense feelings that often can occur as a result of a traumatic event. For example, CPT would help the client view a sexual assault as an indication that there are people in the world who commit violent crime rather than the entire world being an unsafe place. Thus, treatment techniques help the individual face the trauma for what it was and integrate it.

Over 12 treatment sessions, the major components of CPT are the following:

1. Exploring what it means to have had the traumatic experience and the individual's beliefs about safety in the world and what caused the event.
2. Understanding the relationship between cognitions, feelings, and behavior. Clients are taught to see the connection between thinking and feeling and the impact of thinking and feeling on behavior.
3. Exposure through writing about the traumatic event and reading this material repeatedly. As clients write about the event, feelings, thoughts, and sensory details should be included.
4. Challenging thinking such as "stuck points" involving beliefs prior to the victimization that do not match with beliefs resulting from the victimization (e.g., "the world is safe" versus "the world is dangerous" and having difficulty seeing evidence of safety). The concept of faulty thinking patterns is presented. Clients are taught to identify maladaptive thoughts and then are given a list of questions to ask themselves to challenge those beliefs.
5. Challenging thinking about five areas—safety, trust, power, intimacy, and self-worth. These five themes are discussed and analyzed. Clients are asked to examine how prior positive beliefs in these areas are disrupted and how prior negative beliefs are sup-

ported. Suggestions for resolution of maladaptive beliefs in these areas are included.

Improving Parent–School Relations

Parents might avoid contact with schools due to factors such as past negative interactions, feeling intimidated, or having a low educational background. Several strategies can be used to improve this important relationship.

- A good assessment of the fit of poor relations is the first order of business in understanding why the parent avoids the school.
- Help parents understand that they have a more powerful effect on achievement than does the teacher (Rodick & Henggeler, 1980).
- Be present to advocate for and support the parent in all school meetings and to teach the parent to be assertive. For example, when the parent is talking and teachers in the meeting begin to talk privately, show the parent how to stop the meeting and ask to have the floor.
- Prepare the parent for school meetings by role-playing conversations that the parent wants to have but might feel too intimidated to act upon.
- NEVER engage in parent bashing with the school or school bashing with the parent.
- Speak positively of the parent to the school. Highlight to the parent the strengths of the school that you observed during meetings.
- When designing an intervention, create a collaborative situation for the parent and school. For example, the school might keep a daily report card for behavior and send it to the parent, who rewards successes and disciplines poor behavior.
- Monitor the success of interventions and planned communications.

When conflict between the parent and school is intense or both parties feel the situation is beyond repair, the best solution might be to move the child to a different school. If a move is not possible, the therapist will need to empathize with both sides, but also show that he or she is not willing to give up on the youth or the goals of treatment. The therapist must stand his or her ground on appropriate decisions regarding what the child needs. The therapist should also guide the parent and school in defining common goals for the best interest of the child. If the therapist does not have the power needed to facilitate these aims, an unbiased individual within the school system might be recruited to help.

Steps 7 and 8. Intervention Implementation and Evaluation

Intervention implementation follows the basic steps described in the corresponding sections of the previous two chapters and depicted in the do-loop: targeting the behavior, implementing the intervention, evaluating the outcomes, redesigning the intervention to address barriers to desired outcomes, implementing the modified intervention, evaluating outcomes, and so forth, until the goals are achieved. Again, fit circles are revised to incorporate advances in understanding the fit factors. In Ronquetta's case, her mother's sexual assault was a powerful fit factor, and understanding the new information enabled the team to help the mother resolve a serious problem that also impacted her health and her daughter's functioning.

Treatment Strategies
for the Case of Ronquetta Sweetgrass

Over the course of treatment with Ronquetta and her family, the following interventions were implemented at various points in time.

For Maternal Anxiety and PTSD

- Prolonged exposure
- Cognitive restructuring

For Maternal Depression

- Cognitive and CBT techniques
- Strategies to increase activities

For Ronquetta's Poor School Performance

- Meetings to make school personnel aware of Ronquetta's health status and needs for adaptation in the classroom
- Strategies to improve the relationship and communication between mother and school personnel
- Development of an incentive system to promote school attendance

For Noncompliance
with the Diabetes Treatment Adherence Regimen

- Reward system to increase monitoring of blood sugar levels
- Instruction on diet and health given by the neighborhood nurse

- Meeting with peers and the "candy lady" to obtain their support in changing Ronquetta's snacking habits
- Ronquetta joined other girls at the community center each afternoon for double Dutch and participated in competitions
- Ronquetta joined Djole, the neighborhood's West African dance company

Through the multiple interventions addressing multiple systems and using the strengths of the community, Ronquetta and her mother increasingly adhered to the key features of their diabetes management—checking blood sugar levels frequently and adjusting their insulin accordingly, selecting and eating appropriate foods on schedule, and exercising. Ms. Sweetgrass markedly reduced her anxiety over the rape, and Ronquetta's school attendance and performance improved.

CONCLUSION

In this chapter, an MST case focusing on youth school problems was presented. Consistent with social-ecological models of behavior, the school problem was influenced by characteristics of several systems in the young lady's life. In addition, what appeared to be primarily a school-based problem was largely due to a poorly controlled chronic illness. Nevertheless, MST principles and the analytic process still applied.

CHAPTER 8

Neighborhood-Designed Prevention Activities for Promoting Health and Wellness

One of the single most important ways to combat neighborhood violence is to provide children with regular, violence-free, well-structured, and supervised prosocial activities that do not exclude children with learning or behavior problems. Such activities not only attract children away from the streets and provide constructive outlets, but also can foster a sense of cohesion and ownership in a neighborhood. Recreational activities are recognized as one influential component of a comprehensive program to address youth delinquency (Howell, 2003; Lovell & Pope, 1993). This chapter describes four initiatives implemented in the Neighborhood Solutions Project and factors to consider for successful implementation. Activities were designed by neighborhood leaders and residents in conjunction with professional staff, an important consideration. The chapter goals are:

1. To discuss the importance of violence-free youth activities
2. To describe how to design activities that fit the culture and interest of a neighborhood
3. To explain strategies for getting youth and families involved in activities
4. To discuss the importance of using volunteerism in community activities
5. To describe activities within the Neighborhood Solutions Project Education Initiative
6. To describe activities within the Fitness and Recreation Initiative
7. To describe activities within the Family and Community Cohesion Initiative
8. To describe activities within the Entrepreneurial and Job Initiative.

WHY IMPLEMENT VIOLENCE-FREE YOUTH ACTIVITIES?

Research on youth violence and delinquency reveals that after-school hours and weekends are the highest risk times for the commission of crimes by juveniles (Henggeler et al., 1998). Typically these times are relatively unstructured and supervision might be low, especially in families where parents work. Adults are working more hours now than ever before, leaving unsupervised children vulnerable to the influence of the streets. An alternative to unstructured activities is to provide well-monitored violence-free activities for children directly in the neighborhood where they live. Neighborhood-based activities remove barriers to access, such as lack of transportation, and increase the likelihood that children living within the neighborhood will be involved in safe, constructive activities at high-risk times. A secondary benefit of neighborhood-based activities is the increased opportunity for participating children to connect with successful adults. Often, youth will interact with adults who run the activities, and mentorships can be formed.

Achievement and social forms of leisure and recreational activities are important to youth growth and development. Achievement leisure activities include those that provide challenge and require commitment, such as sports and artistic performance. Social leisure activities provide peer interaction and tend to foster competency in social relations and social skills. These types of activities contribute to personal growth and development as well as children's well-being. On the other hand, time-out leisure activities, such as listening to music or watching television, occupy children's free time. These types of activities are socially isolating and have been negatively associated with mental health outcomes (Passmore, 1998). Farnworth (1999), for example, reported that young offenders engaged in time-out leisure activities for 30% more time than did nonoffenders.

In the Neighborhood Solutions Project, neighborhood residents were clear at the start that they wanted to increase the availability of prosocial activities in the neighborhood. These individuals, who knew the children best, reasoned that an increase in prosocial activities would direct their children away from drugs and crime. In the words of one community leader, "The 45 minutes they are playing basketball is 45 minutes they are not selling drugs." Moreover, the residents believed that an increase in activities would promote community cohesion, foster a sense of volunteerism in the youth, and, if some of the activities addressed academics, would contribute to the children's success in school.

Although the neighborhood was providing some activities through the Gethsemani Community Center, their resources were low in terms of staff and equipment. The city Recreation Department provided some resources, but those pertained primarily to team sports geared toward younger children, and most of the activities appealed to only a small segment of the children in the neighborhood. Moreover, many of the available activities took place outside the neighborhood. Even though Union Heights had a high crime rate, the children felt safer in this familiar environment than when venturing outside the bounds of their community. Furthermore, lack of transportation prevented many children from participating in city Recreation Department sports, and activities outside the neighborhood did little to foster cohesion or ownership of these activities by the neighborhood.

The neighborhood residents desired health- and wellness-promoting activities that could be implemented within the bounds of the neighborhood. Moreover, as described later, many of the most appealing activities were outside the domain of a typical city recreation department. Hence, neighborhood leadership and many residents became closely involved in the design and implementation of these new activities.

DESIGNING ACTIVITIES THAT FIT THE CULTURE AND INTEREST OF A NEIGHBORHOOD

Activities implemented within a neighborhood must make sense to the residents of the community. That is, the activities must be consistent with the culture and interests of the people living in the neighborhood and not feel "foreign" (Lovell & Pope, 1993). Each neighborhood and culture has its own preferences for types of music, movies, food, and other activities; and these might seem unusual to people from other communities. Thus, "canned," or "one size fits all," activity programs may not be accepted or supported by neighborhood residents. In the Neighborhood Solutions Project all activities were either the ideas of community members or revised and approved by the community if they were an idea of project staff.

A structured process was used to facilitate the development and implementation of desired neighborhood activities. One morning each week, "activity rounds" were held, and the entire community was invited to attend. The structure of the meetings followed the MST supervision format. Keeping our sights on the overarching goals (i.e., crime reduction, drug-use reduction, and academic success), current activities, accomplishments, and weekly intermediary goals pertaining to these activities were reviewed. Barriers to meeting the goals were identified, and strategies for overcoming these barriers were developed. Often visitors would come to the meeting and agree to help with or direct an activity. The activity rounds provided an excellent opportunity to brainstorm ideas for activities, gain community support, and learn about the talents that various residents could contribute. The strengths of people in the community could come to light during these meetings, and an activity could be designed that built on those strengths.

For example, in activity rounds a mother–daughter tea was placed on the list of possible activities. Several women in the community were skilled and enthusiastic cooks. Hence, the tea was structured around these interests and talents.

In the context of an activity, many more skills and values can be taught and practiced than might be apparent. For example, in addition to the values of teamwork, sportsmanship, and hard work that pertained to players in a summer basketball league, the league provided opportunities for other neighborhood children to learn the values of respect for property and volunteerism. During the summer basketball league children were offered the opportunity to earn a "Chilly Bear" for picking up trash to keep the court and park area clean. If a child picked up 20 pieces of trash, showed the trash to a project staff member or neighborhood leader, and put it in the trash can, he or she would receive a certificate that could be redeemed by one of the community leaders for a Chilly Bear—frozen Kool-Aid in a paper cup. The grounds were kept immaculate during the Chilly Bear Incentive Program. Similarly, older teens were taught to keep the score books for the games and to run the clock. Thus, the teens basically ran the league, which gave them a sense of ownership and skills that could land a job with the Recreation Department in future summers. In effect, the community desired activities that could have primary and secondary goals as well as teach the children what was valued in their neighborhood.

GETTING YOUTH AND FAMILIES INVOLVED IN NEIGHBORHOOD ACTIVITIES

Even when neighborhood residents truly desire an increase in activities, barriers can remain to people attending them. Providing activities directly in the neighborhood eliminates the barrier of lack of transportation, but individuals might be unable or reluctant to attend for other reasons. Some of these reasons include work schedules, not being used to being on time for structured activities (e.g., the start of a sports event), being afraid to try unfamiliar things, and low awareness of activities.

Signing Up Children

In today's fast-paced world, finding time to devote to neighborhood activities is difficult for almost all parents, but particularly for single parents who might be working multiple jobs to make ends meet. For these parents, neighborhood activities are often considered a luxury. Rare is the boss that allows employees to take off weekly for their children's basketball games. Often it is easier for children to attend activities with peers, siblings, or extended family than with parents. Out of respect for busy, working parents, and in line with MST principles, some activities must be held at times that are convenient for parents—during the evening and on weekends. In addition, in standard recreation programs, parents must sign up their children during the Recreation Department's office hours, which do not typically correspond to a parent's time away from work. To address this barrier the Neighborhood Solutions Project activity director, Paul Campbell, developed a sign-up strategy based on "outreach." The project staff contacted parents directly, met them in the streets outside traditional office hours, and in some cases visited the parents on the job or other places to get children signed up for activities. Because many of the activities were under the umbrella of the city Recreation Department, parents had to sign up their children on Recreation Department forms and present a birth certificate. The parent had to be witnessed signing the form for liability reasons and to assure us that the parents knew their children were participating. The outreach also gave project staff an opportunity to get to know the parents and work toward getting them to attend the events. Although labor intensive, the outreach strategy was extremely effective at increasing the number of children participating in structured and prosocial neighborhood activities.

Increasing Attendance

When children are not accustomed to attending structured activities in their neighborhood, free time is spent in unstructured activities. Therefore, when signed up for structured activities, the children are not necessarily accustomed to the expectations of being on time, keeping commitments, or attending an event because others are counting on them. In Neighborhood Solutions Project activities, failure to show up for an event was not easily accepted. Project staff and neighborhood leaders joined together and were vigilant about following up with children who did not show. We would go to their house, tell them they made a commitment and were expected to follow through, and walk them to the activity. Unless there was a family emergency, the child was grounded, or the parent did not want the child to attend, project staff did not take "no" for an answer. If the child was not home, the consequence was sitting out and observing during the next activity and apologizing to peer participants. The children rapidly learned they had to either follow through on commitments or answer to the Neighborhood Solutions Project staff *and* their community leaders. Pursuing such a strategy was labor intensive at first. Once the standard was learned, however, and the children understood that irresponsible behavior would not be accepted, the increase in activity attendance rates was dramatic. In addition to holding children to the follow-through standard, it was vital that project staff and community leaders also lived up to their commitments. That is, project staff had to show that they would stay the entire time for a scheduled activity, even if turnout was low. Doing this, modeled for the children the behavior we were trying to teach.

Increasing Efforts

In addition to fitting the culture of the community, the activities must be those that children will actually try. The wisdom in the community taught us that children would often avoid activities they could not do well, especially ones that are unfamiliar. In the words of one leader, "No one wants to go into something feeling like a fool." To encourage the children to try new activities, project staff focused on those that were of high interest to the youth and that almost anyone could do. Furthermore, the activities were usually not restricted by age, to children with certain skills, or to those without disabilities. Everyone was included, and when the whole community was brought together the children felt supported in trying new activities. In addition, the activity director often worked with children individually to increase a skill if that was a barrier to participation. Providing a variety of activities allowed children with different interests to get involved with something they liked.

Strategies for increasing efforts often involved successive approximations—taking things that anyone can do and building an activity around them. Then, in little spurts, new behaviors are introduced that eventually lead to the desired outcome. For example, most children can eat. Even when a child cannot play basketball, he or she can eat. Therefore, a prosocial activity can be built around cooking or having a meal, and no one has to feel inadequate in this skill. Then, the new, unfamiliar activities are introduced in small snippets. For example, none of the children were interested in soccer because they did not know how to play. Project staff held brief sessions to expose the neighborhood children to soccer. During these 20–30 minute sessions, the children would practice kicking a ball to each other, and then the group had snacks, which everyone could eat. This series of activities eventually led to an informal game. The unfamiliar became familiar without pushing the issue of learning something new.

Increasing Awareness

Awareness of upcoming neighborhood activities is often low because they are announced primarily by word of mouth. In the Neighborhood Solutions Project, at the advice of community leaders, activities were publicized through a variety of methods. First, bright, large-print, easy-to-read fliers were designed and placed in high-traffic areas of restaurants and businesses. Second, one of the community leaders built a community bulletin board that was placed in a central location. Fliers were regularly posted on the board. Third, person-to-person communication about community activities was provided through informal contacts by project staff and others, and street captains from the neighborhood council would leave fliers at each home in their area.

In addition, generating positive publicity about neighborhood activities through the print and electronic media became an important focus of activity-awareness efforts. For multiple reasons the neighborhood had a bad reputation. It seemed as if every time a significant crime was committed, the media were called, and the negative event was broadcast across the entire Charleston area. For the general public, the name of the neighborhood was associated with crime and fear. Early in the project, getting the media to publicize a positive event was virtually impossible. To change this tendency, project staff and neighborhood leaders decided to focus on developing relationships with individual journalists at the local newspaper, writers for small community papers, newscasters at local stations, and DJs at local black radio stations. To initiate these relationships, people in the community who had any kind of media connection were contacted to help us get a foot in the door and meet persons in the media. Stories were told of what the Neighborhood Solutions Project was trying to accomplish, reporters were invited to events, and press releases were faxed to television and radio stations prior to an event. The main goal of the activity-awareness campaign was to get people out to the activities, but a secondary goal was to change public perception about the neighborhood. We wanted the public to be inundated with news about the positive events that were happening in Union Heights. By and large, the strategy was successful. At one event, a reporter remarked to Dr. Swenson that 3 years earlier no one could have gotten her to come into Union Heights, even at 4 o'clock in the afternoon, because of fear of being victimized. But on this day she felt comfortable and was delighted to report the story. Another reporter, a local runner, even helped project staff form the neighborhood girls' running team.

USING COMMUNITY SERVICE AS AN ACTIVITY

Community service can be a valuable activity within itself or a way for youth to earn special privileges. Participation in community youth service can reduce violence among youth (O'Donnell et al., 1999) by providing opportunities to practice communication, decision making, and self-management skills. In addition, through community service, youth can begin to form mentoring relationships with successful adults. Community service can also be used to promote responsibility. For example, youth in the Neighborhood Solutions Project were encouraged to participate in the

Black College Tour conducted annually by the local YMCA. This trip involved traveling with a large group to visit universities in several states and taking side trips to theme parks. In light of the $575 cost per youth for the trip, the neighborhood leaders worked to obtain donations for youth. The leaders then provided community service opportunities that enabled the youth to "earn" the donated funds. Thus, the service activity experiences were not only inherently helpful (e.g., gaining experience in health care and research settings), but provided an opportunity to earn an experience that might have lifelong benefits.

According to community leaders, involving youth in volunteer activities promotes ownership of the services and plants seeds of what can be accomplished in their own neighborhood. The children desire activities, so neighborhood residents arrange for the children to become part of the process. Children who volunteer give to their community and, at the same time, learn new skills such as planning and managing money and time. The community, in turn, assures that youth who volunteer are recognized and appreciated. So, in effect, everyone benefits in one way or another.

In the Union Heights community, volunteering among older youth has been such an important part of well-being activities that it has become the norm. An entire generation of younger children now assumes that they will volunteer like their older brothers, sisters, and cousins, and that helping out is the way things are done in their community. The volunteer and community responsibility torch gets passed. The drug-dealing and crime torch does not.

VIOLENCE-FREE ACTIVITIES: THE FOUR INITIATIVES

The four health and well-being initiatives implemented in the Neighborhood Solutions Project are described next. The overarching purpose of these initiatives is to provide an alternative to crime and substance abuse for neighborhood youth and to prevent younger children from adopting criminal and drug-use lifestyles. Descriptions of these initiatives include many examples of what worked and is valued in the Union Heights community.

The Education Initiative

The purpose of the Education Initiative, which includes programs for children and adults, is to improve reading, math, and writing skills as well as to foster a love of learning. This initiative is vital to the Union Heights community, as statistics show that only 25% of residents graduated from high school, and only 30% of neighborhood children meet minimum standards for reading. The major activities within this initiative are outlined, although, as interests change, new activities are developed to promote academic learning among residents.

The Rainbow Reading Room

The community center in Union Heights is located in an old church. In the past, the majority of the building was occupied by a private daycare center. During the beginning of the Neighborhood Solutions Project the daycare center moved, which freed up space. A reading and learning center was started in one of the rooms with books that were donated to the community center from the local library and other sources. Prior to moving the books in, the community refurbished the room. Originally, the walls were hot pink, and the floor was covered with a tile that was cracking. The children who come to the center and some of the youth being treated by therapists from the Neighborhood Solutions Project got together with the staff and designed the new reading room. Local businesses were contacted for donations of materials. The youth painted the walls Carolina Blue, and one of the therapists painted clouds. Carpet was purchased at cost and installed professionally by a carpet layer in the community. As word got out about the work, people from the community dropped by to put their touch on the room. Hot air balloons and birds were painted on the walls. A huge rainbow was painted, and a mother in the community made curtains. One day, project staff walked into the room and noticed that one of the adults in the community had painted a fighter jet named H-Town (the neighborhood's nickname) on the wall. The jet was patrolling the community for safety. Three round tables were purchased at a school district auction, and the Weed and Seed program donated shelves. After the Rainbow Reading Room was opened, the center was enrolled in the Reading Is Fundamental program. This program enabled books to be given to the children to carry home and own. Currently, the room is used primarily for reading and special programs. Books are also on the shelves for adults. Some children use the room for completing homework, as it is generally a quiet area. The Rainbow Reading Room is an example of a true community collaborative effort and a show of neighborhoodwide support for reading.

Computer Lab

A second room in the old daycare was converted into a computer lab. A man from the community with carpentry skills built a wall-to-wall table on which computers and printers are placed. The children and community leaders painted the room. Computers and software were purchased through a Weed and Seed grant, the city of North Charleston, the Neighborhood Solutions Project grant, and whatever other donations could be tapped. In addition, grant funds were obtained to provide Internet access so that neighborhood children could do their homework research at the center. The computer lab provides the perfect space for a computer skills class, which is taught to adults. Neighborhood children have come to expect their community to provide the latest in technology to support their schoolwork.

Daily Homework Help

Each day after school until 4:30, the center becomes a place to do homework. If a child has no homework, he or she must engage in some kind of academic work. No computer games are played, and any work on the computer must be academic in nature. The center staff provides assistance, and when the homework is completed, checked, and corrected, students earn a ticket that can be traded for a healthy snack.

H-Town Readers

The H-Town Readers program was developed to provide an incentive for children in grades 1–12 to read for pleasure. A business donated funds to purchase a CD-ROM from the Accelerated Reader Program, and a book list was developed. A local librarian works with project staff to gather listed books from libraries across the county. She literally checks out the books to the center so that volumes are readily available to the children there. Children and their parents or caregivers must sign a brief contract enrolling in the program. The contract assures us that parents know their children are participating. A large poster-size board with names of all enrollees is posted in a visible place in the center.

To jumpstart the reading program, the center arranged for all children who read a certain number of books within a designated time to earn a computer. A group of used computers was purchased for a nominal price ($10-$15 each) from a local business. To determine the current reading level of the students so that appropriate book selections could be made, project staff conducted a brief screening using the Wide Range Achievement Test III (WRAT-III; Wilkinson, 1993). Based on the results, youth were directed toward an appropriate reading list. They picked out a book, and after finishing the book, they answered test questions from the Accelerated Reader software on the computer. If the child answered 80% of the questions correctly, he or she was considered to have read and comprehended the book and received credit for it on the board. If the child did not pass 80% of the questions, he or she read the book a second time and retook the test or selected another book to read.

Unfortunately, many of the children were unable to read at their current grade level, and some of the high school students were reading at elementary levels. To save the children from embarrassment if their reading level was far behind, the grade levels of the books were not listed. Rather, a coding system was used. Furthermore, high school students who were reading on an elementary school level were asked to help the first graders with their reading, and these books counted toward their total. This strategy saved the older students from embarrassment, reinforced volunteerism, and gave them a sense of connection with younger children in the community. H-Town Readers has gone over well. When the program is in session children and teenagers occupy every available space in the chairs and on the floors of the center. The youth are reading!

The Great Math Challenge

To increase the children's skills in math, the Great Math Challenge was developed and implemented. Through a school district grant, a part-time teacher was hired to conduct a brief math screening using the WRAT-III, and to provide math worksheets that are similar to those used at school. This program is in session twice a week. A large poster-size board is strategically placed in the community center, with names of all who sign up. The children complete their math worksheets with help from the math teacher, and she records the number of sheets completed at each session. In addition, the teacher works with the children to assure that they are continuing to increase the difficulty level of their worksheets, so that new skills are learned. Prizes are awarded according to the number of sheets completed. Examples of prizes and number of worksheets required are (1) bicycle = 200 sheets; (2) boom box = 150 sheets; (3) small television = 150 sheets; (4) 2-way radio = 75 sheets; (5) large doll and outfit = 50 sheets; and (6) modeling clay set = 30 sheets. The first year that this program was implemented, we learned that the children would not work intensively for small prizes. They wanted bigger prizes and liked saving up points for them. Project staff and neighborhood leaders responded to their request.

Spelling Bee

An annual neighborhood spelling bee was initiated to increase the children's spelling skills. Spelling lists are retrieved from the Internet and made available for practice for children who want to participate. Local celebrities come to call the bee, and via small grants every child who participates earns a prize. Those who do not win first, second, or third place for their age group earn a trip to the center candy store worth about $2. Winners in each age category earn gift certificates to the mall. Some of the children who have participated in the neighborhood spelling bee have gone on to enter the citywide competition.

Soul Bowl

To increase general knowledge, an annual knowledge bowl, named by the children in the community as the Soul Bowl, is held. Children who enter are placed by the Center director on teams of up to five members of varying grades and skill levels. Questions and answers are made available for the teams to hold practice sessions. The knowledge categories include geography, science, history, music, and history of the neighborhood. Local celebrities come to read the questions, and every child on each team earns a prize recommended by the children before the contest. Each child on the first-, second-, and third-place teams earns a gift certificate to the mall of the same value as those of his or her teammates.

Writing Contests

To practice writing, poetry writing contests are held for high school students and essay contests are held for younger students. High school students are given a specified period of time to write a poem on a topic selected by center staff and delivered to the youth in a sealed envelope. Examples of topics have been "Grandma's Hands" and "My Life as a Puppy." The poems of the winners are prepared in calligraphy, framed, and hung on display in the center. For contestants in middle and elementary school, a poster of a child sitting on a basketball was displayed for 1 week, and each student wrote a short story about the child in the picture. Judges are teachers from local schools and universities, and they select the top three poems and stories. Winners earn gift certificates to the mall.

Storytelling

The Storytelling Troupe of Charleston occasionally conducts a storytelling session in the Rainbow Reading Room. Especially interesting are stories, using parts of the Gullah language, about the African slaves who came to the Charleston area. Keeping storytelling alive is akin to honoring the children's cultural heritage and the richness it brought to American life. Storytelling has sparked the interest of children in being creative and even in writing stories they make up.

The Black College Tour

The local YMCA conducts an annual weeklong tour of historically black colleges along the East coast and in the South. The tour is by bus, and each student has to pay about $575. The tour was viewed by neighborhood leaders and project staff as an excellent opportunity for high school sophomores and juniors in the neighborhood. However, it has come to be an important opportunity for middle school students who are looking for a future direction. Adolescents in the neighborhood rarely attended college and almost never talked about college. The tour had the potential to help these students realize that college, and its attendant economic opportunities, might be possible after graduating from high school.

A significant barrier to going on the tour, however, was coming up with the money. Many of the students' families do not have extra cash after covering living expenses. To address this challenge, project staff and community leaders developed strategies to both raise the funds and promote youth responsibility and ownership. Businesses and churches were approached for donations that would cover the majority of the costs. Families had to contribute a down payment to show commitment. Then, the youth could only access the donations by working for them. Youth were placed in libraries, and at the center to help children with homework; they cleaned the Center and surrounding grounds; and they volunteered in a variety of capacities around the community. Youth earned $6 an hour and had to complete a specified number of hours to earn the required sum.

Each year the number of youth from the neighborhood going on the tour has increased. Even middle-schoolers are now sitting around talking not about whether they will go to college but about *which* college they might attend and how they might obtain scholarships, grants, and financial aid. The number of youth in the neighborhood who attend college has increased.

GED Classes

For adults and older youth who did not complete high school, General Equivalency Diploma (GED) classes are offered periodically. During the most recent classes, a teacher from a local literacy group came twice a week at no cost and worked with youth and adults who wanted to complete the GED. The classes were offered in the center, which removed barriers to lack of transportation.

The Fitness and Recreation Initiative

The primary purpose of the Fitness and Recreation Initiative is to provide convenient and enjoyable prosocial activities for area youth. A second aim is to improve physical fitness within the community. Rates of hypertension and diabetes are high in Union Heights, and fitness and recreation supported by the community could help battle these common medical conditions.

A Fitness Center and Weight Room

A third room in the old daycare was converted into a fitness center and weight room open to adults and adolescents over the age of 14 years. To renovate this room, the youth painted the walls, the city installed the same flooring as used in a local ice hockey rink (very durable), and a glass company donated wall-sized mirrors for two walls at opposing ends of the room. A fitness center in the city was closing, and grant funds were used to purchase their weight machines. In addition, a community leader donated a treadmill and stationary bike. The fitness center is used mainly by adults in the community.

Summer Basketball League

The summer basketball league was formed in response to a request by the children and teens. Basketball leagues were not available to the older teens, and leagues for younger children were often restricted to those with strong skills who also had transportation. During the first summer of the project, youth were transported to community game sites using a van that belonged to a woman in the neighborhood. Although the neighborhood team was relatively successful in traveling around the city, several limitations concerned project staff and neighborhood leaders. Drug use was evident on several occasions, and the older youth had difficulty distinguishing between hard play and physical aggression (i.e., there were frequent fights). This is not how residents wanted their neighborhood to be represented. Moreover, few people from the neighborhood could come to watch an off-site game due to lack of transportation. Hence, a different approach to summer basketball was needed.

The Union Heights summer league was formed during the second summer. Rather than loading neighborhood children in a van and taking them to play in another neighborhood, 350 children were registered to play in Union Heights. A massive outreach effort was conducted to sign up children for the league. Anyone could play; no one was excluded. Considerable effort was put forth to find coaches. Some coaches in the outside community came with a team, and other coaches were recruited. In many cases, older teens in the neighborhood came forward to coach the younger children. A time clock was borrowed from the city Recreation Department, and scorebooks were obtained. Volunteers learned to keep time and to score the games. Again, many youth in the community came forward and helped out. As a result, they learned skills that would enable them to obtain part-time work in other basketball leagues. Officers from the local community-policing unit worked on a holiday and built benches for the teams. A local business donated shorts for the league, as many children did not have the required regulation shorts (i.e., no zippers, buttons, or pockets). The city put up lights on the covered court so that games could be played in the evenings. As the league progressed and the neighborhood took ownership, many people came out to watch. One evening when the center director was out of town, a group from outside the community came in and began to start trouble. The drug dealers stepped forward, advised the group that we don't do that in "our" community and certainly not in "our" league and that it would be best for them to leave. The outside group left, and the problem was averted. The city Recreation Department provided referees, and the referees spread the word that this neighborhood league was one of the best-run leagues in the city and that violence was not tolerated.

Volleyball

One of the parents in the community was skilled at volleyball and wanted to teach the children to play. Building on her strength, a sand court was constructed. A leader in the community donated a lot, another leader cleared the lot, and a local company donated the sand. Balls and a net were donated as well. The children have had a beach volleyball court in the heart of the community and an interested parent who volunteers her time to teach an unfamiliar sport.

Girls' Running Team

The children in the neighborhood asked for gender-divided running groups. One of the Neighborhood Solutions Project staff was a trained runner, and she agreed to begin a weekly meeting with the girls. A neighborhood leader charted a 1-mile course in the neighborhood, as the girls stated they preferred to run on the local streets. Next, project staff assembled a group of local women runners to act as a Board, give suggestions for a curriculum, and actually complete a Saturday run with the girls once a month. The women runners also helped the team obtain running shoes from area runners so that the risk of injury would be minimized.

Prior to forming the team, an outreach effort was conducted to sign up school-age girls. Graduate students from the Medical University of South Carolina nursing program assisted with physical examinations to identify any problems that might interfere with safe participation. Finally, the girls running team began to meet weekly at the community center. The first 20 minutes of the meeting were devoted to pertinent topics such as nutrition, preventing injuries, proper shoes and clothing, proper hydration, and safety. After the talk, team members completed a brief hand weight workout (two hand weights at 3–5 pounds each) and then followed the 1-mile course. Initially the girls would walk–run the course, but eventually worked up to running only.

As the girls ran through the neighborhood, residents cheered them on and neighborhood women began to ask what they were doing. As a result, a group of women who were elders in the community began to join the group. The elders walked at the back of the group, but began to count on making that 1-mile walk once a week. Interestingly, a subgroup of the women began to walk the course on additional days. Thus, in the context of the running group, relations were developed between the young girls in the community and the older women. In addition, this activity contributes to positive health practices among the older women, some of whom have diabetes and hypertension.

As the girls' running team matured, several of the young ladies decided to run in the annual 10 kilometer Charleston Bridge Run, which attracts about 30,000 participants from around the world. The team began training toward this goal. Six girls and one of the community leaders completed the 10K course over the bridges. Despite complaints about the distance and discomfort, and fear of falling through the grates in the bridge, these girls achieved a significant goal that most youth their age cannot accomplish. Some of these girls have gone on to run other races (shorter ones) and to win in their age division.

Boys' Running Club

The boys in the neighborhood, feeling that it was grossly unfair that they did not have a running group, demanded inclusion. However, they did not want to run with the girls, did not want to be on a running team, and did not want to run in the neighborhood. The boys wanted to form a running "club" that was structured differently. Center leaders searched for someone to lead this club and found Mike Aiken, a runner on the College of Charleston cross-country team. Mike agreed to run with the boys and mentor them as long as the center would transport the boys to a local park that had a running trail. Transportation was arranged. It even turned out that several of the boys were not aware of their own speed (i.e., 6-minute mile at a leisurely pace).

The boys were interested in competing in running events. Local race organizers were very positive about the Union Heights running club and waived the race fees for club members. One of the young men, nicknamed "Cheerio," was a fast runner and trained to compete in the annual bridge run. He worked at a local fastfood restaurant. Project staff called the corporate office, which agreed to sponsor Cheerio's participation in the run. Their donations enabled this young man to go to a local running store and purchase appropriate shoes, clothing, and a gear bag. Although he was not able to quite keep up with the runners from Kenya, Cheerio completed the race with an excellent time. He has run other races in the area, winning in his age division.

African Dance and Drumming

Early in the Neighborhood Solutions Project, the project was given complimentary tickets by the city Arts office to attend a performance of the Adande Dance Company, a local, professional adult African dance and drumming company. A group of youth was taken to the performance, and the attendees were so energized that they decided that they must have African dance in their community. In addition to the joy of dancing, the activity has the advantages of exercise and teaching the children about their cultural heritage. In light of the high cost of dance and drumming lessons, project staff sought small grants to bring Adande into the community and began to cultivate a relationship with Jesse Thrower, director of Adande. Soon, grant funds were received from a local youth organization and used to purchase 6 weeks of lessons and a few djembe drums. The lessons were held in the auditorium of the community center. When the drumbeats started, neighborhood people would flock to see what was going on. Although they were a bit distracting, residents were encouraged to walk through the auditorium for the first couple of months, to garner interest and support.

During rehearsals the children initially needed considerable supervision by adults from the center and neighborhood. Arguing and fighting were common, and chaos generally prevailed. Many of the behavioral problems seemed to stem from having a large group of children in one room and their embarrassment at not knowing the drumbeats or dances. Furthermore, the children were exhausted after 5-10 minutes of dancing because their fitness levels were so low. Many of the participants ate fried food prior to the lessons and developed stomachaches after intensive activity. Mr. Thrower began to talk with the children about how long it took him to learn the beats and dances, and he encouraged them to understand that these skills would take time to learn. In addition, the adult supervisors became stricter and had misbehaving children sit quietly and observe instead of participating. Project staff also had weekly conversations with the children about "performance nutrition" and helped them figure out the kinds of snacks they should eat before class. In addition, children walking around before class with pig's feet or a fried pork chop were made to put the food away until after class. As the children became competent and saw that rules were being enforced, the behavior problems improved and eating habits before class changed. Additional grant funds were obtained to extend the lessons and, 4 years later, the lessons have turned into rehearsals as the neighborhood children now comprise the Djole Dance Company (pronounced Jolay). The dance company has performed at major arts events in Charleston, opening two city festivals in 2003, and meeting dancers and drummers from all over the world. For example, during Charleston's annual Spoleto International Arts Festival, Djole was invited to participate in a private rehearsal with a company from West Africa. The children were patient, watched, learned, and played the beats taught them by the drummers. At the end of this rehearsal, the neighborhood children asked if they could teach "the boys from Africa" a few beats. Fortunately, the master drummers from Africa humbly accepted instruction from 10-year-olds.

During these past 5 years the children's pride in their work has skyrocketed. Children who used to spend after-school hours watching TV or carrying drugs for the dealers on the corner now practice drumming and dance moves after homework is done. Three of the young ladies in Djole have now danced with Adande, the adult professional company. Regarding fitness, the children can dance and drum for 1½-hour periods and only stop because the rehearsal ends. This one activity has been able to address fitness, cultural heritage, nutrition, commitment, professional behavior, and geography. Many of the children had never been to downtown Charleston, a 5½-mile trip from Union Heights, or seen the ocean. Through Djole, they have traveled across coastal South Carolina and have viewed the ocean from several vantage points. Through their travels and national and international contacts, the neighborhood children have come to see themselves as citizens of the world.

Girl Scouts and Boy Scouts

From time to time, a Girl Scout and Boy Scout troop will be activated at the community center. The troops meet weekly, and the leaders are generally from outside the community. Participants have traditionally engaged in crafts and neighborhood beautification activities, which the children enjoy.

The Cooking Club

The Cooking Club, which meets monthly, was developed by neighborhood residents to educate the children about nutritional needs. Funds to purchase food are provided by the local Clemson University Extension Office, and cooking and serving instruction is provided by volunteer students from a local school for the culinary arts (chef school). Working in small groups with the culinary students, children learn about nutrition in the healthy foods they are preparing. After the food is prepared, club members sit down to a well-prepared meal served on china.

The Family and Neighborhood Cohesion Initiative

The goal of the Family and Neighborhood Cohesion Initiative is to increase cohesion within and among families in the neighborhood. This initiative is supported by several special events that take place on an annual basis.

Sons of Union Heights Breakfast

This breakfast provides an opportunity for the men and boys of the neighborhood to get to know each other better and reflects an effort by the men to initiate informal mentoring relationships. The breakfast is held either in the community center or on a vacant lot in the community. The community leaders cook and the police officers serve the breakfast.

Mother–Son Dinner

The mother–son dinner honors the relationship between mothers and their sons. Mother is not necessarily defined in a biological sense—grandmothers, female neighbors, aunts, or family friends can be included. Given that many single mothers live in the community, the dinner is intended to pay tribute to their hard work in raising their boys. The general structure of the dinner, catered by residents of the community, includes a poetry reading, a talk about mothers and sons from a guest speaker, singing, dinner, small gifts, and mother–son dancing.

Father–Daughter Dinner

An annual dinner is catered to honor the relationship between daughters and their fathers. This dinner was the original creation of Dyshell Williams, one of the elementary school-age young ladies in the community. She felt it was unfair to have a mother–son dinner without honoring fathers and their daughters. Fatherhood is not necessarily defined biologically, but pertains to the nurturing relationship that an adult male has with a young lady. Thus, grandfathers, uncles, stepfathers, and family friends have been included. Young men from the community escort the girls to the dinner, serve the food, and clean up. Because this is a special event, the young men dress in tuxedos donated from a local formal wear shop. The dinner includes a poetry reading, words about fathers and daughters from a guest speaker, singing, a meal, and small gifts. At the end of the dinner, photographs are taken of each father–daughter pair and given as mementos. This event is a prime example of one activity leading to another and sparking creativity in the children.

Mardi Gras Parade

In light of the fact that the director of the Neighborhood Solutions Project is a Louisiana native, the community was interested in learning about Mardi Gras. This desire led to an annual Mardi Gras Parade. Initially, neighborhood residents were curious but a bit reluctant to pursue a Mardi Gras celebration because it was assumed to include exposure of the body. Now, however, everybody has a different knowledge and experience of Mardi Gras. As stated by one community leader, "If you can't go to Mardi Gras, bring Mardi Gras here."

Prior to the parade, several children work with center staff to stuff bags with beads, doubloons, candy, and trinkets. Facts about Louisiana and Mardi Gras are posted around the center. A poster board is placed in the main area of the Center where anyone who wants to "give up something for Lent" can sign up to do so and receive support around this personal goal. A Mardi Gras Queen is named from one of the elders in the community. The police are contacted 2 months before the parade to assure that the streets will be blocked off during parade time. Bands from local middle schools, local dance groups and dance lines, and the media are invited. Press releases are sent out as well. On Mardi Gras day, right after school, the children assemble at the center and give out bags to everyone there. The Queen is placed in a convertible at the front of the parade, just behind the police. All participants—including bands, dance groups, children on bikes, and anyone who wants to join—begin the parade. The parade winds through the neighborhood, and paraders not playing an instrument throw beads and trinkets to the bystanders in their yards or on the street. At the end of the parade, Mardi Gras music is played for dancing in the street. Next, the children assemble outside to break open a Mardi Gras piñata, and the stragglers get an opportunity to try a piece of King Cake. In addition to being an entertaining event, the celebration of Mardi Gras has helped us teach about another culture, history, and geography.

Principal's Reception

Near the beginning of the school year, a reception is held honoring the principals of the six schools the neighborhood children attend. This reception is designed to foster positive relationships between families and the schools and to help principals have a positive perception of the neighborhood.

Caroling

Each year before Christmas, youth gather at the center to walk around the community and sing Christmas carols. This activity is especially valued by the elders in the community and is viewed as a gift from the children to them.

Beat Down in H-Town

This annual basketball game between neighborhood teens and community police officers was intended to change neighborhood perceptions of the police and to strengthen the relationship between the police and the community. The game is well advertised, and friendly competitive "trash talk" is exchanged (e.g., "I hope you officers don't try to cheat cause it's the only way you'll win") during the weeks prior to the game. The city provides referees, and the game is held on a court behind the center. This event has been invaluable to improving police and youth relations. Some of the known drug dealers even play because they want the police to see them as people and not criminals.

Bicycle Rodeo

The annual bicycle rodeo is a joint effort of the community policing team and the Clemson University Extension Service. This event occurs on a Saturday, and the main goal is to teach bicycle safety. Children not only learn about safety, but also can have their bikes inspected. In addition, a bicycle is usually given away as a prize.

The Coca Cola Jam

Once a year the local office of Coca-Cola sponsors a talent show directly in the community. The top three winners receive prizes.

The Miss Union Heights Talent Pageant

The talent pageant is held annually when sufficient numbers of girls are interested. The purpose of the pageant is to recognize teen females who would like to represent the community. Girls meet with center staff on a regular basis for several months before the pageant to plan their clothing and talent event. Guest speakers come to the meetings to discuss tips for hair, skin, nutrition, social poise, and social skills. The contest is held in a local auditorium outside the community. Each year that the pageant has been held, the local YMCA has provided full or partial scholarships for the top three winners to attend the Black College Tour.

Mother–Daughter Tea

The teens that enter the talent pageant participate in a tea with their mothers or mother figures. The mother–daughter team must select and research facts about a specific country. On the day of the tea, mother and daughter prepare food common to that country and dress in clothing that illustrates what is worn there. They prepare a table and judges taste the food and judge the display. Afterwards, neighborhood residents are invited to sample food at each table.

Contestants' Candlelight Dinner

The community decided to treat pageant participants to a candlelight dinner. This is an important function because the children have not had the experience of eating at a fine restaurant with tablecloths and candles. Restaurants in downtown Charleston were contacted, and one agreed to host the girls at a nominal fee. The restaurant also agreed to prepare food that the girls would recognize. Next, a local funeral home agreed to donate use of a limousine. In addition to wanting the girls to feel special, we knew that the only time they had ever ridden in a limousine was during a funeral of a family member. On the night of the dinner, the limousine driver picked up the young ladies at their homes and transported them to the restaurant. Community leaders met them there and presented a red rose to each girl as she got out of the limousine. A picture was taken with each girl holding her rose and standing in front of the limousine. After dinner, the young ladies were returned to their homes. The candlelight dinner has become a much-anticipated part of the talent pageant.

Haunted House

The children in the community decided that they wanted to turn the center into a haunted house at Halloween. The haunted house is now a Halloween mainstay in the neighborhood and is staffed by the teenagers. At the time of the first haunted house it was quite ironic that teens who had been involved in crime were now receiving our blessing to scare younger children by stabbing at the air with plastic knives, operating fake chainsaws, and yelling and screaming with blood on their hands and face. Each year the haunted house is different, depending on the ideas of the teenagers running it. This event is the premier volunteer job of the year, and children talk about it all year long. The cost of entrance to the haunted house is one can of food, which is later given to families in the community who are in need.

Summer Day Program

Each summer when school is out, the City Recreation Department holds a daily program from 9:00 A.M. to 5:00 P.M. Parents can bring their children in for the entire summer at a cost of less than $50. To supplement funds from the city, the community obtained donations and grant support to provide additional educational activities. Education is a daily focus of the program, as neighborhood leaders, parents, and Center staff want the children to sustain academic skills during the summer.

Senior Appreciation Dinner

An annual senior dinner is held to show gratitude to community elders for their many contributions to the neighborhood. Male teens in the neighborhood dress in tuxedos (donated locally), escort the seniors to their tables, serve their meals, and clear the settings. As such, a secondary goal of the appreciation dinner is to change the perception some seniors have of many young males in the community. It is indeed heartwarming to overhear seniors who had wanted a particular young man locked up say, "What a nice young man."

Neighborhood Family and Friends Day

A communitywide family and friends day is held at the beginning of the summer. The teens in the community make and sell T-shirts. Leaders in the community prepare and serve food donated by local businesses.

The Heights

Several elementary, middle, and high school students decided that they wanted to write and present a play about Union Heights and the positive things that happened in their community. Veronica Gilliard, a local actress involved in drama programs in the schools, worked with the children to write the play. The children worked with Ms. Gilliard for months to learn their lines and practice their acting. Several adults from the community also were in the play. *The Heights* told a story of youth at a community center who lost a peer to violence. The play showed the process the children went through to cope with the loss and the inspirations that led community leaders and citizens to confront the drug problems in the neighborhood. *The Heights* was presented to the greater North Charleston Community at a local auditorium. Admission was free as a gift from the children to the community.

The Entrepreneurial and Job Initiative

The goal of the Entrepreneurial and Job Initiative is to prepare youth for the working world and to assist adults in career development. A standard component of clinical interventions implemented in the Neighborhood Solutions Project is to help problem youth find employment to support their movement toward prosocial activities. The community wanted programming for these youth as well as for youth who are too young to secure jobs and for unemployed young adults who needed improved job-seeking skills. The following activities addressed these aims.

The H-Town Youth Cooperative

This cooperative includes any youth who lives in the neighborhood and wants to be a part of a money-making venture. In general, the youth decide on prices for their goods that will cover the cost of materials, contribute a small sum toward the cooperative for operating expenses, and return a profit. The specifics of the business are detailed in an in-house manual (Taylor & Swenson, 2001). The funding for the cooperative started with a small grant aimed at making ceramics. Youth are responsible for all aspects of making ceramic figures, from pouring the mold to painting the finished product. The center already had a kiln, and this is used to fire the figures. Youth are responsible for marketing and selling their products.

Although the ceramic business was relatively successful, the youth realized that they could make T-shirts, tote bags, and hats much more quickly and profitably. Hat and T-shirt heat presses were purchased using grant funds from the local Weed and Seed program. Youth make pictures with a digital camera and put these photos on T-shirts to sell. One group of young men, for example, decided to design and sell T-shirts at a local child abuse conference to obtain money for the college tour. They used computer programs to make a design relevant to child abuse and sold over $300 worth of T-shirts to conference participants. Youth have also made original T-shirt designs for church functions and family reunions.

Men of Distinction

Following the first Senior Appreciation Dinner, a group of teen males decided that they wanted to provide various services, paid and volunteer, to groups and individuals in the community. These services have primarily revolved around serving meals at moderately formal banquets.

Tools for Success

Community leaders determined that teens and young adults could benefit from a job-training program. Ms. Toby Smith developed the curriculum for the program, named "Tools for Success," and a Weed and Seed grant covered the costs. The program is designed for youth 14–16 years of age and 17–21 years of age. The classes are taught separately to these two age groups by adults inside and outside the community. The objective of the 12-week program, held at the center, is to equip participants with basic skills to obtain a first job or to advance in their current positions. Class topics include phone etiquette, references, résumé writing, filling out applications, posture, hygiene, necessary identification, how to interview, work ethic, work behaviors, and goal setting. The classes combine videotaped role play, instruction, a skills inventory assessment, and team building exercises. Local employers give weekly talks to provide insight into marketplace trends. The program has been open to communities within the Weed and Seed area, and transportation and child care are available for participants.

Youth Job Fair

The center occasionally hosts a youth job fair. Local businesses and agencies involved in hiring youth are contacted, and each business sets up a table and gives away information and prizes. Youth have an opportunity to fill out job applications and interview with business representatives. Barriers to transportation are removed because the fair is in the community.

Music Studio

The youth in the community decided that they wanted a music studio in which to write and record their own beats. These youth wrote a successful grant application, and the funding was used to purchase recording equipment. Although this activity is leisure oriented, considerable skill is required to use the equipment. Moreover, the potential for an entrepreneurial venture is enhanced by this studio.

CONCLUSION

This chapter provided examples of activities that community residents can implement to support the academic, social, and economic success of their children. The more effort a community puts into its children, the greater is the return. Through the activities implemented by the Neighborhood Solutions Project, many positive changes in the youth have become evident. We have seen:

1. An increase in activities in the neighborhood
2. An increase in participation and community involvement
   a. Basketball League with at least 350 youth participating
   b. Community and family cohesion activities attended by 100–400 residents (varied by activity)
   c. At least 60 children attending homework and academic programs daily.
3. An increase in involvement by parents in activities
4. An increase in interest in academics and college
   a. During the initial trial of H-Town Readers, 340 books were read and 17 youth earned computers
   b. A 50% increase in youth participating in the Black College Tour
   c. An increase in the number of youth attending college
5. Development of the Djole Dance Company, a youth African drumming and dance company. This company has now performed at arts festivals and for local events.
6. Changes to resources in the neighborhood
   a. The covered basketball court was lighted to support evening games.
   b. The basketball court was resurfaced with a more professional surface.
   c. A sand volleyball court was built in the neighborhood.
   d. The old daycare was renovated by neighborhood residents to provide recreation and academic programming.
7. A youth cooperative was developed as a way for children to earn money and learn business skills.
8. An increase in volunteerism among the youth was observed.

Additional outcomes will be realized in the future because neighborhood residents have learned how to sustain the activities presented in this chapter. The methods used for building sustainability are discussed in Chapter 11. In closing, we cannot overstate the importance of developing constructive activities to help keep neighborhood children off the streets and on pathways to success. In developing these activities, providing time, structure, monitoring, and emotional support is much more important than the simple provision of building space and various types of equipment.

CHAPTER 9

Neighborhood-Based Health Services

with CAROLYN HOLBROOK JENKINS

To improve the health of a neighborhood or community, many broad social, economic, political and ecological forces that affect the health status of
populations must be addressed (Anderson & McFarlane, 1996; Guide to
Community Preventive Services, 2003; Institute of Medicine, 2002). One of
the best ways to address the general health of neighborhood residents is
to develop, implement, and maintain community-oriented primary care
(COPC) and integrate this care with other population-based health care
services. COPC combines primary care, public health, and epidemiology to
systematically identify and address the health problems of a defined population (American Public Health Association, 1998). When COPC is united
with strong community engagement and support (e.g., Kretzmann &
McKnight, 1993), the resulting neighborhood-based health services have an
increased likelihood of improving and sustaining the health of neighborhood residents.

The goals of this chapter are:

Carolyn Holbrook Jenkins, DrPH, RD, CDE, RN, BC, is an Associate Professor at the
Medical University of South Carolina and principal investigator on a REACH 2010 grant. She
received her Doctor of Public Health degree from the University of South Carolina. For 20
years, Dr. Jenkins has worked with communities to improve health outcomes related to
diabetes and its complications. Her work focuses on reducing racial disparities and creating
effective academic–community partnerships.

1. To define neighborhood-based primary care health services
2. To present steps to implement neighborhood-based primary care health services
3. To review methods for financing neighborhood-based primary care health services
4. To explore the principles of health outreach with families
5. To discuss how neighborhood-based primary care health services fit into health promotion and prevention
6. To discuss how primary care health providers can work with an MST team to improve outcomes for youth and their families

NEIGHBORHOOD-BASED PRIMARY CARE HEALTH SERVICES

Neighborhood-based health services were once a rarity, especially in diverse neighborhoods. Health care was traditionally equated with illness care and gradually moved from a generalist practitioner model to the specialized model in practice today. Typically, community members did not seek care until they were ill and, until recently, little emphasis was placed on preventive care for chronic diseases. During the 21st century, however, health professionals have been challenged to aim for wellness in communities rather than trying to fill hospital beds (O'Neil & the Pew Health Professions Commission, 1998). Likewise, the U.S. Preventive Services Task Force (1996) has emphasized prevention with regard to illness care and has presented evidence-based recommendations to improve health outcomes. As health care costs escalate, economically challenged communities must take more active roles in securing preventive health care, disease management, and illness care for their constituents. Currently, with the exception of emergency health services, access to health care is not a right for all citizens, but a privilege. Nevertheless, a proactive community that uses its assets can do much to assure access to high-quality and culturally appropriate health and illness care for its members.

Consistent with this vision, the World Health Organization (1978, p. 1) has articulated the ideal features of neighborhood-based primary health care.

> Essential health care based on practical, scientifically sound, and socially acceptable methods and technology made universally accessible to individuals and families in the community by means acceptable to them and at a cost that the community and the country can afford to maintain at every stage of their development in a spirit of self-reliance and self-determination.

Approaching this ideal is the overarching goal of the neighborhood health care initiative discussed in this chapter.

STEPS FOR IMPLEMENTING NEIGHBORHOOD-BASED PRIMARY CARE HEALTH SERVICES

Although several approaches can be used to establish neighborhood-based primary care health services, all include the following fundamental components.

- Committed individuals who are community champions, providers, and stakeholders for health services and primary care—persons who get the daily tasks completed and who can support the development of services and care
- Resources that support community involvement in health care
- Principles that guide effective community-driven partnerships for health services
- Processes that can provide an organized approach to accomplishing results
- Methods for sustainability of services

As described later, these components were integrated into the steps taken to develop and implement the neighborhood-based primary health care project in the Charleston area.

Step 1. Meeting with Neighborhood Leaders

In 1995, representatives of the City of Charleston and the College of Nursing at the Medical University of South Carolina (MUSC) collaborated with Charleston's Enterprise Community and residents to explore health issues for several neighborhoods. An Enterprise Community is a selected geographical area that has been designated by the U.S. Department of Housing and Urban Development(HUD)to receive funding for improvements. The designation incorporates community and economic development initiatives targeted to communities with higher levels of unemployment, underemployment, and poverty. The community implements a plan with specific strategies/activities to encourage economic opportunities for community residents, community-based partnerships for improvements and for sustainable community development, and a community-developed strategic vision for improvement. In December 1994, 65 urban sites received Enterprise designation and funding over a 10-year period. Recently, Charleston (and many of the other original Enterprise communities) was designated as a "Renewal Community" by HUD and currently receives special tax incentive packages but no additional grant funding, as designated in the original Enterprise Community designation (Health & Urban Development, 2003).

Members of each of the public sector groups met with the leaders and residents of various neighborhoods to discuss health issues and to link residents with community members working to improve health within the neighborhoods. To begin building the partnership, letters were sent to neighborhood association presidents to explore ways that MUSC nursing faculty and students could work on health projects within the neighborhoods.

The Union Heights community in North Charleston was one of the first to respond to the nursing initiative. Ms. Ida Taylor called to invite the nursing group to a health fair and to encourage them to volunteer with the youth and older adult programs at the Gethsemani Community Center. We asked about ways the community wanted to learn about health, and several health-screening activities were identified for the fair. On the day of the health fair, Mr. Roscoe Mitchell, president of the neighborhood association, set up a meeting to discuss health issues within the community. Mr. Mitchell, Ms. Taylor, Ms. Bessie Salisbury, and Ms. Rosa Benekin emerged from that meeting as the neighborhood champions. Under their guidance, the nursing group continued to meet with neighborhood representatives at the community center. Mr. Mitchell brought neighborhood leaders, and the nursing group brought a representative from the city of Charleston who had worked with the neighborhood and with MUSC nursing faculty to develop the health component of the Enterprise Health Program. Instead of taking "canned" programs to communities, our goals were to work in partnership with neighborhood associations to improve health within Charleston's Enterprise Community and to develop health programs that empowered the community to take leadership in designing and implementing their own programs.

During the first meeting, for example, the neighborhood leaders discussed multiple health issues and brainstormed ways that we could work together to address priority issues. Attendees were most concerned about the lack of affordable access to health care, especially for the older residents of the neighborhood. Thus, their dream was a "doctor's office or clinic within the community" that would provide affordable health care for all, and especially for older adults who had no way to travel to a doctor's office without their children taking a full day off from work! During the meeting, the key roles of the nursing group were to listen as community members shared information about health and health issues and to identify and focus on community strengths. We left the meeting agreeing to explore the possibility of pursuing the residents' dream of building a health care facility in their neighborhood. Health activities that could be provided on a regular schedule were also identified as priorities, and joint responsibilities were specified to accomplish these goals. The nursing group was invited to attend the next Neighborhood Association meeting to learn more about the health concerns of the neighborhood residents.

Step 2. Meeting with the Whole Neighborhood

The nursing group attended the next evening meeting of the Neighborhood Association on the advice of the neighborhood leaders. At that meeting, it was learned that many residents had high blood pressure and diabetes and wanted more information about how to live with these problems. For example, one woman shared that she was supposed to take five pills and insulin shots each day, but was not able to administer the injections by herself. Based on a telephone survey, the diabetes rate in the neighborhood was 13%, and the hypertension rate was 40% among adolescents over age 16 and adults. Another resident described her family's concerns about the environmental pollutants in the community. At the conclusion of the meeting it was agreed that a nurse would teach community members more about high blood pressure, diabetes, and how to manage these conditions. In addition, a decision was made to explore the environmental concerns within the neighborhood.

Step 3. Assessing Needs

Following the Neighborhood Association meeting, another meeting was scheduled with a small group of key leaders and interested residents to plan the health education programs, screening programs, and ongoing care that would be available within the community. During this meeting, the community leaders again emphasized their desire for ongoing health services and primary care. To determine what type of care was needed in the community, several other discussion groups (i.e., focus groups) were conducted with members of the community, and neighborhood leaders were interviewed to determine the answers to the following questions:

1. What are the most important health issues or concerns in your family?
2. What might be done to help address these concerns?
3. For which health issues or concerns do you currently lack sufficient resources?
4. What are the most important health issues or concerns of your neighbors and what changes might help address these concerns?
5. What "things" happen in your neighborhood that affect the health of your neighbors?
6. What "things" happen outside your neighborhood that affect its health?

7. What health-related activities in your neighborhood do you most enjoy?
8. What health-related activities outside your neighborhood do you most enjoy?
9. What health related activities do you want to see improved, or done differently?
10. What health related activities do you want to see added?

Hypertension and diabetes were the leading health concerns identified by this assessment. Residents expressed needs for accessing primary and episodic care, screening for disease (e.g., cancer), and receiving preventive health information (e.g., healthy eating, weight management, physical activity, environmental concerns about lead and other contaminants). Later, as community trust increased with the MUSC representatives, community-based services for substance abuse and mental health issues were identified as health concerns as well.

Step 4. Implementation

Following the assessment, nursing instructors and their students, community leaders, and volunteers collaborated to provide health activities in local community and senior centers, schools, churches, and during home visits to families. Soon thereafter, students and faculty from pharmacy, medicine, health administration, dentistry, and public health joined the nursing faculty and students. An interdisciplinary nurse-led team of nurses, pharmacists, a physician, a health administrator, a nutritionist, and a community volunteer set up weekly walk-in clinics at community centers in five neighborhoods, including Union Heights. In addition, home visits to families that were unable to come to neighborhood clinic sites were available, and the community volunteer served as the contact person for these home visits. Family home visits and the clinics offered health checks (e.g., weight, blood pressure, blood glucose and A1c, and lipid and microalbumin screening), health counseling, medication review and teaching, and linkage to primary and specialized care (i.e., home health, medical specialist care, mental health, vocational rehabilitation, or social services) as indicated. More than 1,000 clients used the services regularly over a 5-year period.

FROM DREAM TO REALITY: A NEIGHBORHOOD-BASED HEALTH CENTER

As noted earlier, Union Heights residents desired a health center in their neighborhood. To move from dream to reality, the nursing group in conjunction with neighborhood leaders began to generate support for a community center for primary care through informal discussions with leaders in local city government, MUSC providers, and other stakeholders. For example, North Charleston Mayor Keith Summey identified individuals within his staff who had the expertise to move the project forward. Similarly, Mr. David Rivers at MUSC emerged as a local champion and contributed expertise in tapping into University resources and government agencies to support the development of the Health Center. The city of Charleston's Enterprise Advisory Board joined the efforts, and these groups brought in regional and national government representatives to help build additional support.

The planning process for the health center was finally formalized with the formation of a Board to move the project forward. The Board was comprised of members from city governments (Charleston and North Charleston), MUSC (including a representative from each college), stakeholders and champions from the community, and local groups and individuals that supported the development of the center. Although several attempts were made to implement bylaws for the Board, the group as a whole decided that a less formal structure was preferred. As time progressed, the advantages and disadvantages of this decision became evident. Some members wanted the group to serve as a Board of Directors, while others preferred the role of an Advisory Board. Bylaws could have clarified the decision, but later, as leaders changed, the Board was named the Enterprise Health Center Advisory Board.

In spite of great support for the development of the health center, many logistical problems emerged along the way. For example, several "false starts" were experienced after an agreed site for the health center was identified. Just prior to signing the lease on the building, local government supporters placed several stipulations on the length of the lease, and the owners of the building decided that they could not make a long-term commitment to the health center. Although this site was lost, several supporters and the community and University champions continued to pursue the goal of establishing a health center for primary care within the community. Later in the summer of 1997, a family from the community donated a site. Mr. Paul Donado and the staff of the City of North Charleston Board of Public Works, in collaboration with the MUSC champions, started the initial planning for a new building on this site. The University, city of Charleston, and city of North Charleston donated funding for the building, and a grant for center operations was obtained from the Healthy South Carolina Initiative at MUSC. In September 1999, local politicians and leaders lifted shovels for the groundbreaking ceremony for the Health Opportunity Center. In spring 2000, the city of North Charleston completed the construction of the building shell, but during winter 2001, another snag delayed construction. Those several months were called the "winter of our discontent," but "hope springs eternal" and again the project was on track for completion in spring 2001. Then on October 6, 2001, Mr. Roscoe Mitchell died, and the greatest champion of the health center was lost. The center, however, was finished, and primary care services commenced in the Enterprise Health Center, housed in the O. Roscoe Mitchell Building, on November 5, 2001, with a focus on diabetes and hypertension—the two health concerns that had been identified as priorities through focus groups and interviews with community residents.

The Enterprise Health Center enrolled more than 2,000 families between November 1, 2001, and November 1, 2003. The Center provides primary care; pharmacy services; a diabetes education program recognized by the American Diabetes Association; community outreach for diabetes through REACH 2010, Charleston and Georgetown Diabetes Coalition; and mammograms through the Hollings Cancer Center Mobile Unit, MUSC. Patient feedback has been positive, and the census continues to grow. Ms. Bernadette Pinkney, a family nurse practitioner and faculty member in MUSC's College of Nursing, provides primary care.

METHODS FOR FINANCING NEIGHBORHOOD-BASED PRIMARY CARE HEALTH SERVICES

Once the Health Center was in operation, the challenge became sustainability of funding. For a health clinic in an economically disadvantaged neighborhood, sustainability of funding is a challenge that requires continued teamwork by health care professionals, neighborhood champions, neighborhood residents, and members of the Advisory Board. Although a lower cost model of services using volunteer health providers and volunteers from the community was initially considered, stakeholders eventually decided to maintain the Enterprise Health Center with blended funding. Thus, the health center became a federally qualified health center site by affiliating with one of the local community health centers. This decision provided enhanced reimbursement for services and allowed the center to offer a sliding fee scale. Currently, the health center continues its relationship with the Franklin C. Fetter Family Health Center, which provides administrative oversight, financial and billing services, and assistance with quality-improvement processes. In addition, foundation and government support, grants, and donations from businesses have been acquired to maintain the quality and quantity of services.

HEALTH OUTREACH WITH FAMILIES

Health outreach is an integral part of improving neighborhood health through community-oriented primary care. Outreach helps to link services with individuals, families, and groups that might be overwhelmed with other priorities or unable to travel to health care facilities or activities.

The National Community Care Network (CCN) Demonstration Program provides an excellent framework for improving the health of populations through outreach and partnerships. CCN publications (Health Research and Educational Trust, 2002) include step-by-step plans with many examples of health outreach and partnership building. The CCN vision encourages communities to (1) return patients and communities to the center of health care delivery; (2) include those populations that are now outside the system of care by virtue of poverty, culture, or language barriers; (3) emphasize prevention; (4) make the health system more understandable and user-friendly; (5) continually improve the continuity and quality of health services; and (6) ensure that resources are allocated and used so that health is maximized and costs are constrained. Building a partnership with the community requires that outreach staff take the time to learn about the community and their health practices as well as to develop relationships with community leaders.

The Hypertension and Diabetes Management and Education Program is an excellent example of health outreach. As a component of the city of Charleston's Enterprise Program funded by the HUD, a partnership was built between the College of Nursing at MUSC and 15 inner-city neighborhoods (about 24,000 residents) to identify local health priorities. The group formulated a community profile from available epidemiological data and health statistics, including data from the Census Bureau, vital statistics related to birth and death rates from the South Carolina Department of Health and Environmental Control, hospital and emergency visit data from the South Carolina Office of Research and Statistics, and other existing data sets such as school absences and community survey results. The group worked with leaders from each of the neighborhoods to host group discussions and focus groups with community residents.

In the North Charleston community, the public health efforts began with health outreach. After several meetings to discuss health issues in the community, attendance at Neighborhood Association meetings, discussions and focus groups with community members, participation in health fairs, and tutoring of youth at the community center, health outreach efforts were organized into ongoing community activities and a regular schedule was developed. The services were offered by Ms. Lisa Kozlowski and included informal consultation with any resident who had health-related questions or wanted his or her blood pressure or blood glucose checked. Neighborhood residents were greeted by a community leader and were introduced to the nurse. The nurse performed the health counseling, recorded the results for the clients, and, as needed, referred the client to a primary care provider. National guidelines for screening and referral were implemented in the community sites, and participants were educated about "knowing their numbers" for control of diabetes and hypertension. A client-held "mini-record" was used so that clients could share their results with their primary care providers.

Neighborhood residents who were unable to attend outreach health activities at the community health center because of illness could request a home visit by the nurse. The home visits often led to referrals to primary care and on several occasions to the emergency room of the local hospital. The nurses also participated in ongoing community events, celebrations, and meetings. One of the keys to program success and to increased neighborhood participation in health screenings and education was the integration of the health activities into ongoing neighborhood activities. Another key was the assurance that personal health information would remain confidential. A frequently heard comment was "I do not want everybody to know my business." Although many residents openly shared their successes and challenges with managing their health problems, others did not. Privacy of medical records and information must be guaranteed.

For communities that have identified health outreach priorities, finding the health professionals or programs that demonstrate cultural competence while meeting community needs can also be challenging. One strategy for identifying health outreach resources is to contact local organizations that link people with appropriate service agencies. Some examples of resource agencies include the United Way and volunteer organizations such as the American Cancer Society, American Heart Association, or American Diabetes Association. These organizations offer information as well as referrals to local hospitals and health care facilities that may have outreach programs, public health departments, and colleges and universities that offer educational opportunities. Some communities have established the "211" telephone number (or similar numbers, such as New York City's 311) for information and referral services, just as many communities use "911" for reporting and obtaining assistance for emergencies. Linking with academic institutions and health professional instructors and students can be a cost-effective method of improving community health. Moreover, the community members can play a major role in educating future health professionals to work more effectively with communities and families.

In summary, several points are important to remember in engaging community members in health outreach efforts.

- The groundwork must be carefully laid to develop an effective program and gain the trust of neighborhood residents. Agendas cannot be forced on residents, and professionals must work in partnership with the community to develop and implement programs.

• All personal health information is confidential. Confidentiality of personal health information is the law, and all program participants must be assured that the health outreach program is doing everything within its power to treat information confidentially. Release of information or discussion of information with others outside the outreach program requires written permission of the participant or legal guardian.

• Professionals are "guests" in the community and should behave accordingly.

• Rather than make assumptions about health needs based on other communities, professionals should stop and ask about community norms and preferences.

• Goals and resources for health outreach must be aligned with community needs.

• Printed materials that list contact names and numbers as well as services can be helpful, but are no substitute for personal contact in the community.

• Providing small activities that can be easily accomplished (e.g., health screening booth at a health fair) provide excellent first steps in building positive relationships and community support.

• Even very troubled neighborhoods with few resources can quickly detect insincere people, so effective listening and clear communications are very important to building and maintaining trust throughout all phases of the health outreach efforts.

THE ROLE OF NEIGHBORHOOD-BASED CARE IN PREVENTION

Preventing illness, reducing risky behaviors, and optimizing health are goals of Healthy People 2010 (U.S. Department of Health and Human Services, 2000). The leading health indicators for Healthy People 2010 are focused on the following:

• Physical activity
• Obesity
• Tobacco use
• Substance abuse
• Responsible sexual behavior
• Mental health
• Injury and violence
• Environmental quality
• Immunization
• Access to health care

The majority of these indicators are most important to the prevention of illness. To lead healthier lives, citizens must eat healthier, consume fewer calories (for most), become involved in more physical activity, maintain or attain healthier body weights, and reduce tobacco and drug use. In addition, environmental conditions must be improved in homes, neighborhoods, and surrounding areas. Thus, nutritional and physical activity programs as well as tobacco and drug abuse prevention programs should be public health priorities. These healthy living goals are more easily accomplished when individuals are supported by their social networks.

In the development of preventive programs, neighborhood residents might identify priorities for promoting healthier lifestyles, or health professionals might recognize particular health risks based on epidemiological data. In either case, neighborhood ownership and leadership are essential for the success of wellness programs. Examples of prevention programs established in Union Heights included walking and physical activity groups, healthy shopping and cooking activities, home safety fairs, and weight control classes based on building healthy living skills.

COLLABORATION OF PRIMARY HEALTH PROVIDERS WITH AN MST TEAM

From one author's view (*CHJ*), MST is consistent with the traditional community health nursing model of caring for individuals, families, and communities with a clearly defined therapeutic intervention that spans multiple systems. Thus, primary health care providers who truly focus on family and community-oriented care and the role of community systems in addressing health issues can be true partners with MST therapists in working with families. At-risk youth need routine primary care, screening, and early intervention for health risks, especially for health issues that can affect school performance and interactions with parents, siblings, and community members. Parents, families, teachers, and therapists need primary care providers to support their intervention efforts, and the primary care provider needs the MST therapist for families and children who are struggling with social and physical health challenges. Additionally, MST is currently being examined as one method for addressing and managing individuals with chronic health problems, such as diabetes, more effectively (Ellis, Naar-King, Frey, Rowland, & Greger, 2003). Thus, integrated community-oriented primary care and MST are a natural fit.

The MST team, the health team, and the community of Union Heights often worked together on projects related to health promotion, disease prevention, and disease management issues. The health team conducted the physical exams for the girls' and boys' running teams, collaborated on disease prevention activities, and made home visits when the MST team identified residents needing disease management or illness care. The key to healthier communities is collaboration and building community capacity for health improvements, as well as building trust while working in a true partnership with the community. The partnership in Union Heights has truly been a positive learning experience for our health team, students at the university, and community members.

CONCLUSION

The key to developing neighborhood-based health services in economically challenged neighborhoods is building effective partnerships with neighborhood residents, as well as funders, and maintaining and nourishing the relationships over time. Developing trust while providing services leads to higher utilization of services needed by the residents. Maintaining adequate financial supports for these health services and primary care is an ongoing challenge, especially when residents are uninsured or underinsured. Community ownership/input and participation by community members, as well as community responsiveness by health care providers are ingredients for success.

CHAPTER 10

Neighborhood-Based Law Enforcement

with DAVID LAURIE, DONALD WARD, and HARRY M. ROPER

Addressing crime in a neighborhood requires that all the "fingers on the glove" be present. Prosocial activities, educational support, clinical treatment, and medical care are only part of the solution. Neighborhood-friendly law enforcement services are essential to suppressing crime, solving crime-related problems, and promoting crime prevention. This chapter focuses on community policing as one critical part of an overall plan for changing troubled neighborhoods. The goals of the chapter are

---

David Laurie is a Corporal with the North Charleston Police Department and currently serves as the crime prevention officer for the City of North Charleston. He was a community police officer during Neighborhood Solutions and has been an officer for 26 years. Corporal Laurie is also a member of several state and national crime prevention associations and a 24-year Navy veteran. He has received a number of awards for his work in law enforcement and his military service.

Donald Ward is an Officer with the North Charleston Police Department and was a community police officer during Neighborhood Solutions. He has been a police officer for 25 years and has also worked as a detective and with undercover narcotics. Officer Ward is a Marine veteran and a member of several professional law enforcement associations, and has received a number of awards and commendations for his work in law enforcement.

Harry M. Roper is a Sergeant for the North Charleston Police Department and currently works in the Office of Professional Standards. He was a community police officer during Neighborhood Solutions and has been an officer for 15 years. Sgt. Roper is a Mason and a Sir Knight of the Knights of Pythagoras, where he mentors youth. He has received many awards and commendations for exemplary service as a police officer, most notably from crime victims and their families.

1. To discuss changes in law enforcement that led to community policing
2. To present characteristics of community policing
3. To describe steps to implementing a community-policing program
4. To discuss the Police and Community Team (PACTeam), a community-policing team that worked with the Neighborhood Solutions Project
5. To discuss how community-policing officers can work with an MST team to improve youth outcomes

CHANGES IN LAW ENFORCEMENT
THAT LED TO COMMUNITY POLICING

Since police were first introduced into municipalities in the 1840s, the methods that police use to control crime have gone through several transitions. Kelling and Moore (1988) place the history of policing into three eras: (1) political, (2) reform, and (3) community policing. During the political era, from the 1840s to the early 20th century, the police had very close ties with politicians and depended on them for their resources. Moreover, officers had a wide range of responsibilities, providing services ranging from crime control to solving social problems. Technology was limited, so officers relied on neighborhood residents to support their efforts. The "cop on the beat" was a common method of providing services.

As law enforcement moved toward greater proficiency, the FBI became the model of police professionalism. Management was centralized and officers were assigned to shifts that rotated around multiple locations. The move away from the "cop on the beat," however, tended to isolate officers from the communities that they served. Moreover, the dominant perspective was that the officers knew best how to solve crime and, consequently, did not need community interference. The relationship with communities became "us versus them." Advances in technology also contributed to breaking the link between police and the community that they served. With the increased use of patrol cars, officers on foot became virtually obsolete. Likewise, the 911 call system came into place during the 1970s, and this system demanded that officers respond to calls immediately. A quick response to all calls replaced taking time to implement strategies for prevention. Services became more reactive than proactive.

As urban communities began to experience increases in crime and disorder, especially drug and gang activity, government and law enforcement officials began to question the effectiveness of their strategies for addressing current problems. Interest increased in gaining the support of community residents in keeping their neighborhoods safe (Bureau of Justice Assistance, 1994). This change in emphasis led to the community-policing movement, which began in 1982 and was fully developed by 1988 (Kelling & Moore, 1988). This movement reflected a shift toward more direct involvement of citizens in reporting crimes and helping the police to address the problem of crime (Thurman, Giacomazzi, & Bogen, 1993).

CHARACTERISTICS OF COMMUNITY POLICING

Community policing is a philosophy of policing that focuses on the development of supportive relationships with community residents and proactive problem solving. The overriding goal of community policing is to "reduce crime and disorder by carefully examining the characteristics of problems in neighborhoods and then applying appropriate problem-solving remedies" (Bureau of Justice Assistance, 1994, p. 13). Although there is variation in practice, several goals and characteristics are common to all community-policing programs (Adams, Rohe, & Arcury, 2002).

1. Taking a proactive stance—problem solving before a crime is committed rather than reacting after a crime has been committed
2. Maintaining involvement with the community
3. Assigning officers to a particular geographical area
4. Decentralizing administrative control with more participatory management
5. Greater use of foot patrols
6. Using a variety of resources to achieve crime reduction (e.g., housing, recreation)
7. Increasing officer discretion in arrest (Hahn, 1998; Rosenbaum & Lurigio, 1994).

With community policing, the role and responsibility of the individual officer is greatly expanded, and increased independence and the wise use of discretion in decision making is needed. Through a true community-policing program, the officer becomes a valued member of the neighborhood, and adversarial relationships change to collaborative relationships. Crime occurs within a social context, and community policing allows the officer to be an agent of change in that context. Table 10.1 presents a more thorough list of differences between traditional and community policing (Brown, 2002).

TABLE 10.1. Differences Between Traditional and Community Policing

Traditional Policing	Community Policing
Police are reactive.	Police are proactive.
Community involvement is low.	Community involvement is high.
Recruitment is based on a spirit of adventure.	Recruitment is based on a spirit of adventure.
Officers are not expected to do creative problem solving.	Officers' major role is problem solving.
Training relates to law enforcement role of police.	Training relates to community relations, problem solving, community dynamics, and prevention.
Management is authoritarian, centralized.	Management is participatory, decentralized.
Supervision is control oriented.	Supervision promotes skills needed to problem solve.
Officers have little discretion in practice.	Officers have broad discretion.
Performance evaluation is based on activities.	Performance evaluation is based on outcomes.
Police departments are entities unto themselves.	Police departments are closely joined with the community.

RESEARCH ON COMMUNITY POLICING

Research on policing that was conducted during the 1970s showed that some traditional techniques were not effective. For example, in the Kansas City Preventive Patrol Experiment, Kelling and colleagues (Kelling, Pate, Dieckman, & Brown, 1974) concluded that neither random patrolling nor rapid response was effective at reducing crime. Other studies pointed toward community policing as a promising alternative.

The first empirical study of community policing was conducted with the San Diego Police Department (Boydstun & Sherry, 1975). Findings showed that increased officer interaction with community residents was associated with improved attitudes of officers toward their job and the community. The officers also found that getting to know residents helped them obtain information on criminal activity. Officers involved in community policing have higher job satisfaction and better relations with coworkers and citizens (Lurigio & Rosenbaum, 1994), and report that their work is more important, rewarding, and less frustrating (Wycoff, 1988). Furthermore, officers who practice community policing report improved attitudes toward community residents as they get to know them (McElroy, Cosgrove, & Sadd, 1993).

Other studies have helped refine components of community policing. For example, the Newark Foot Patrol Experiment (Kelling, 1981) showed that foot patrols were effective at creating more positive attitudes among community members toward police. In addition, foot patrols brought a greater feeling of safety to residents and increased job satisfaction among officers (Kelling, 1988). Likewise, research on community policing strategies such as door-to-door contacts, intensive enforcement plus community involvement, and community organizing has supported the effectiveness of these strategies for reducing fear of and improving relations with the police (Rosenbaum & Lurigio, 1994).

Pertinent to the Neighborhood Solutions Project, community-supported strategies seem especially important for managing interactions between the police and juveniles in high-crime neighborhoods. Early studies indicate that younger people hold relatively negative attitudes toward traditional law enforcement (Decker, 1981; Smith & Hawkins, 1973), and these are likely perpetuated by negative contacts with the police (Woodbury, 1972). Findings from a neighborhood safety survey conducted with 968 high school students in Chicago (Wisby, 1995) indicated that 84% reported being treated disrespectfully or witnessing other people being treated with disrespect by the police. Further, 71% of the adolescents reported having been stopped by the police and 22% reported physical abuse (e.g., slapped, guns put to their head) by the police. In a study assessing police misconduct and use of force toward youth, staff at the Institute for Violence Reduction at the University of Connecticut interviewed 132 youth who were identified as having had confrontations with the police during the past 2 years (Borrero, 2001). These youth reported that 39% of the incidents involved physical use of force, 24% verbal harassment, 3% sexual contact, and 34% other harassment (e.g., theft of property, intimidation). Of the incidents involving physical force, 46% entailed being punched, kicked, slapped, hit, or thrown down; and 13% resulted in injuries such as broken teeth, cuts, and black eyes. If these experiences are at all representative of those encountered by adolescents in Union Heights, the potential value of a community-policing program cannot be overestimated.

IMPLEMENTING COMMUNITY POLICING

Currently, community policing and traditional policing are both in widespread practice across the United States, often in the same department. Many law enforcement professionals view community policing as a return to some of the original policing practices as well as a way to challenge ineffective practices that have been a way of life for decades (Hahn, 1998). Clearly, the shift to community policing takes a major philosophical change. Even today, when community policing is fairly commonplace, implementation requires overcoming barriers to a new way of thinking and working. As such, several steps are fundamental to implementing a community-policing program: (1) obtaining buy-in from stakeholders—from the top official to the rank and file; (2) changing management styles to become more participatory; (3) adequately defining "community"; (4) developing a community partnership; and (5) implementing problem-solving strategies.

Obtaining Buy-In from Stakeholders

The implementation of a community-policing program requires major changes in many aspects of a department's functioning and requires buy-in at every level, from the mayor's office to the patrol officer. A community cannot be approached to begin a community-policing program if the city government and police department are not on board. Thus, in the early stages of developing a community-policing initiative, the chief executives (e.g., mayor, police chief) must clearly appreciate the rationale and characteristics of community policing and explain these to all concerned constituents, including city political leaders, leaders in the target neighborhoods, and the community at large. Successful collaboration between police and other key systems (e.g., government, neighborhood, agencies, businesses) will require ongoing communication and opportunities for mutual feedback. Similarly, implementation of community policing should move at a reasoned pace, with careful planning and coordination between the police and community stakeholders.

Obtaining officer buy-in for shifting to community policing can also be challenging, as major changes in the way a job is conducted are stressful for most individuals. Although officers might be apprehensive about such changes, trust in their supervisors and fellow officers can go a long way toward securing support for the development of the program. Dicker (1998), for example, showed that officers who viewed themselves as part of the organizational culture and trusted their supervisors were less resistant toward community policing. Nevertheless, in light of the challenges in changing over to community policing, this law enforcement model is sometimes implemented initially within special units or in specific districts. For example, a certain district might use officers on bikes to fight crime, but not other components of community policing.

As the community-policing program begins, the model's philosophy and strategies should be taught to officers throughout the department, even those not assigned to the target communities. Officers in traditional contexts might have erroneous conceptions of the roles of their community-policing counterparts. For example, community-policing officers who work with citizens to problem solve might not be viewed as "real police" because their emphasis is not strictly on law enforcement. Later, when crime rates begin to decrease due to community-policing efforts, all officers in the department should be informed of the success of this more comprehensive approach to crime reduction. Officers must know that they are making a difference in the lives of citizens and that a community-policing program is not just for public relations purposes.

Changing Management Style

Community-policing programs usually embrace a participatory management style or total quality management (TQM; Hahn, 1998). This management style is distinguished by participation from employees at all levels, teamwork, an emphasis on consumer satisfaction, and a focus on meeting goals rather than meeting quotas. Citizens, for example, are viewed as customers. As such, officers must prioritize the crimes that are of highest interest to the community. Such flexibility in prioritizing, however, requires officer autonomy in identifying problems in the community and setting solutions into action. Officer autonomy and discretion are fostered in community policing by shifting the management structure from top-down to bottom-up decision making. Here, officers are provided the flexibility to handle problems as they arise and to participate in community events that serve the greater mission of reducing crime. New programs are adopted with input from the officers who will be doing the work. Job satisfaction is enhanced through policies that promote employee (i.e., officer) independence and accountability (Lurigio & Skogan, 1994). Importantly, teamwork around program development gives officers a sense of ownership in new programs.

These changes in management style suggest that recruiters should consider the personal characteristics of officers who might be eligible for community-policing positions. For example, officers who believe in citizen involvement and have been involved in volunteerism and human services activities are more likely to respond favorably to community policing. Similarly, officers who respect diversity and have skills in communication, negotiation, and mediation are likely good matches with community-policing initiatives.

Defining Community

In community-policing programs, officers are assigned long-term to specific geographical areas that should follow the natural borders of a neighborhood. At the time of the Neighborhood Solutions Project, the community-policing unit was assigned to a neighborhood that was specifically identified by the city of North Charleston. The population of the area was roughly 2,500 persons.

Although schools and churches are sometimes outside the lines of a neighborhood, they are still important parts of the lives of the residents. Thus, for example, school leadership should be involved in community-policing efforts, and some of the programs implemented by officers should take place in the schools. At a time when the Care Bears toys were popular, one of the authors of this chapter was involved in a police-sponsored "We care" program in an elementary school. In this program, students who wrote essays about a solution to a local problem were allowed to carry a Care Bear throughout the day. Although the school was outside the confines of the neighborhood that the officer patrolled, this program helped him build relationships with the neighborhood children. Similarly, churches play a central role in the day-to-day lives of many communities, and community-policing officers should take the time to get to know ministers and seek collaboration from church members in solving problems.

Developing a Community Partnership

The key to developing a partnership with neighborhood residents is to build trust. Unfortunately, however, persons in many minority neighborhoods view the police with great suspicion and resent the air of authority and superiority conveyed by some officers. To counter this perception, officers must get to know the neighborhood leaders and treat all persons from the community with the utmost respect. Likewise, officers must be willing to learn and understand the desires of neighborhood residents concerning crime reduction. The community-policing program enables officers to attain such understanding by attending community meetings, interacting with residents informally, and walking the neighborhood on foot patrol. Thus, with sufficient time, officers can develop collaborative relationships with residents and come to understand the characteristics, strengths, and problems in a community. This understanding and the opportunity for personal contact and involvement provided by community-policing provide the context for developing community improvement and crime reduction projects.

Implementing Problem Solving

Problem-oriented policing, a concept developed by Goldstein (1990), entails identifying specific problems in a community, analyzing the determinants of those problems, examining a variety of potential solutions, and implementing solutions in conjunction with community residents. The underlying theory of problem-oriented policing is that problems are multi-determined by factors associated with the individuals involved (e.g., offenders), the social setting, the physical environment, and the way these factors come together to create trouble (e.g., dilapidated home provides a setting for a group of teens to hang out and drink). The problems will continue as long as the conditions supporting them persist (Eck & Spelman, 1987). To truly understand the underlying determinants of problems, officers must develop extensive knowledge of the community. This knowledge can then serve as the basis for designing strategies to overcome the particular problems by addressing the underlying factors.

A method of problem-oriented policing that has some evidence of effectiveness is termed "hot spots" policing (Sherman, 1992). Here, police focus intensive attention on a particular area that is high in criminal activity. Hot spots policing has been successful at reducing incidents of stranger violence (Sherman & Weisburd, 1995).

THE PACTEAM

The community-policing program in Union Heights was called the PACTeam (Police and Community Team) and included three officers. The PACTeam's goals were to (1) reduce the number of calls for law enforcement service by 50%, and (2) improve the "quality of life" of the citizens by using problem-solving policing. Because the three PACTeam officers are authors of this chapter, the remainder of the chapter is written in first person plural.

Preparation for Implementation

The PACTeam was started due to interest by the police chief. This Union Heights team was one of three community policing units developed in North Charleston. We received initial training on concepts of community policing by an officer in our jurisdiction. Later, however, the Internet was used to study other successful community-policing programs and to gain ideas that could be tailored to the PACTeam. In particular, we modeled ourselves after the successful community-policing programs that applied the "broken windows theory." James Q. Wilson and George Kelling (1982) published a now-famous article in the *Atlantic Monthly*. This article referred to the "broken windows theory," which proposes that minor forms of disorder (e.g., broken windows, loitering, graffiti) left untended lead to serious crime. This theory led to what became known as "broken windows policing." That is, minor disorder became targeted as a strategy to prevent greater crimes.

Zero-Tolerance Policing

After increasing our knowledge and formulating the foundation of our approach, we started targeting minor disorder through zero tolerance. In zero-tolerance policing, laws are strictly enforced and suspicious people are stopped and questioned, which increases the opportunity to find fugitives. An example of zero-tolerance policing is the targeted approach to crime control used in New York City. From 1993 to 1997, murder and non-negligent homicides dropped 60.2%, forcible rape decreased 12.4%, robbery dropped 48.4%, and burglary was reduced by 45.7%. The mayor's office credited the police department for this crime decrease; the zero-tolerance policy was a primary strategy the department used.

Please note that zero-tolerance policing is not the same as zero-tolerance practices in schools. The former has been associated with reductions in crime, and in the case of the Neighborhood Solutions Project was used short-term with follow-up by community policing. Zero tolerance for misbehavior at school, however, is associated with greater numbers of youth being removed from school and is often applied to youth who are not committing crimes at school. Expulsion and suspension can have detrimental effects because youth may be at home and in the neighborhood unsupervised, which places them at higher risk for committing crimes. Further, youth removed from school are less likely to learn, as instruction time is reduced. Educational progress is an important predictor of favorable long-term adjustment in our society.

When we came into the community that was the target of the Neighborhood Solutions Project, it was battling high crime rates. Drug use, drug selling and violence were commonplace. Some of the neighborhood residents, especially the elderly, were afraid to come out of their homes. People who stayed inside might see crimes occur through their window, but they would not give the police information because they were afraid of retaliation and did not trust the police. The situation was "us versus them." Thus, to meet the PACTeam's goals, it was important to get the community to support the program. To build buy-in, we had to show residents that we had a stake in the community, needed their help to reduce crime, and were going to help them reclaim the streets.

In our case, the zero-tolerance strategy was intended to clearly demonstrate that we were serious about addressing crime in the neighborhood and were going to do so with a high level of professionalism. The philosophy was that people in the neighborhood had to see that we were not going to put up with the run of the mill criminal behavior, and that we were going to take a stand and do our job no matter what. The residents and crime perpetrators came to understand our level of commitment. Importantly, zero tolerance eliminated the vast majority of the visible crime, got every-one's attention, and won confidence with the elders in the community. Zero tolerance was practiced for 6 months, and after that we were able to use more discretion in arrest.

Partnership Building and Problem Solving

After the zero-tolerance period, we began to intensify our work on develop-ing community relations, getting to know people, and problem solving. Recognizing that one of the PACTeam's goals was to improve the quality of life in the community, we operated under the assumption that we could not compound the problem by locking up large numbers of residents. All law violators did not need to go to jail. Rather, the "90/10 rule" was applied. That is, 90% of the people are good, law-abiding citizens and 10% are causing trouble. Therefore, everyone cannot be treated like a criminal. This concept has to be communicated to new officers to prevent stereotyping of neighborhood residents. Whereas traditional policing focuses almost exclu-sively on the 10%, community policing also addresses ways to make life better for the 90% of law-abiding citizens.

The participatory management style that is part of community-policing provided us with the latitude needed to improve the quality of life for law-abiding citizens. In particular, we had free rein to find solutions to problems and implement those solutions. To identify relevant problems, we met with community leaders and went door to door to survey neighbor-hood residents regarding goals that they wanted us to address. These face-to-face contacts allowed us to meet residents and to discover and target ma-jor complaints. Based on these surveys and our own experiences in the community, we each picked a specific problem-solving project to address each month to improve the quality of life for residents.

Examples of problem solving activities included the following:

1. At the end of each week a knock-and-talk was conducted to reex-amine all the calls for services in the neighborhood and determine whether anything further could be done to alleviate the problem. We practiced "getting back" to people and following through on solutions.
2. We identified families that did not have electricity or water and helped them get these services resumed or find other shelter.
3. We conducted lighting surveys to deter crime that was being com-mitted in darker areas. This also helped us find out where the hid-ing spots were.
4. We worked with the neighborhood to get abandoned houses torn down that were the site of drug activity and prostitution.

After building trust that we would follow through on solving problems, residents began to come to us with requests for help. We would discuss the problem, examine various solutions, and try the solution that made the most sense. People in the neighborhood began to flag us down on the streets to talk or give information regarding criminal activity. Once we started the community-policing approach, going to work became much more enjoyable.

Recommendations Based on Lessons Learned

Based on our work together in the Union Heights neighborhood for several years and after observing the success of community policing, we have created a set of recommendations for fellow officers working with neighborhoods in the community-policing model. We sincerely believe that these recommendations will help officers build collaborative relations with people in the neighborhood and, thereby, impact criminal activity favorably.

1. Remember that 90% of the people are generally law abiding, so don't treat everyone like a criminal.

2. Get the visible crime taken care of and out of the way. The older residents of the neighborhood were afraid to talk to the police for fear of retribution by the drug dealers. The zero-tolerance practice helped decrease fear among the elderly, and having the officers around on a regular basis facilitated the development of trust. Older residents who are home all day are the eyes and ears of the community and can help solve and prevent crimes. However, they must feel that they can help without being in danger.

3. Take a subtle approach when talking with residents about crime, and don't let everyone know or see you talking to that resident. As the police begin to develop relationships with people in a neighborhood and those residents begin to give information on crimes, the officers must make sure that divulging that information does not place the resident's safety at risk. Going door-to-door and talking with many people can help disguise the identity of those who gave the information.

4. Get rid of visible eyesores. For example, taking down abandoned properties where drug dealers and drug users hang out helps with safety by eliminating hiding places. In addition, removing abandoned buildings makes the community look better and reduces related health risks. The people in the community must come together to accomplish goals such as this.

5. Don't be afraid to get your hands dirty. Raking leaves and picking up trash helps the neighborhood understand that you are there to do more than harm. You are there to help improve the attractiveness of the neighborhood and increase the quality of life of its residents.

6. Partner with code enforcement from the city government. Such partnerships help in tracking down owners of abandoned properties and going through the steps necessary to clean up the area. Code enforcement has a set of effective procedures that officers can put in motion.

7. Attend community events and drop by during off hours. Attending community events gives the residents an opportunity to interact with the police around something other than crime. In the Neighborhood Solutions Project, the PACTeam members were a regular part of many prosocial events. For example, we attended father–son breakfasts that were held in the streets or at the community center, and we served the individuals attending. The breakfast gave community leaders and residents an opportunity to tease that our mission had changed from "to serve and protect" to "to serve grits and protect." The fact that residents could tease and have fun with us showed a development of trust in the relationship. The more we became a focal part of the community, the greater the cooperation we received from residents interested in preventing crime. The officers in the PACTeam also helped with community tasks during their time off. For example, two officers volunteered their time on July 4th to build benches for the basketball court. The residents saw the officers working on a holiday and never forgot this sign of commitment to the neighborhood. At a later date, when the police chief was going to move one of those officers out of the community, the residents pulled together, wrote a letter, and signed a petition to keep him in the neighborhood. This action was successful, and the officer was able to stay.

8. Talk with the children and youth, give them the time of day, and have fun with them. Even the youngest children who experience a positive relationship with an officer do not forget how they were treated. This interaction may influence future relations with the police and the citizens' willingness to help prevent crime in the neighborhood.

9. Treat people as people, even if they have a criminal history. Doing this helps them see that you can be trusted not to harm them. An example occurred one evening when a PACTeam officer stopped a man in the neighborhood driving with an outdated license. This gentleman had a prior conviction and had served time in jail. Using discretion, the officer made the decision not to arrest the man, but instructed him on handling the problem. This interaction changed the gentleman's relationship with the police, and later he provided valuable information that helped the police close down some drug dealings. Adults do not forget how they are treated. People who were once part of the problem can become part of the solution.

10. Develop a working relationship with community leaders. In some cases residents will not feel that they can go directly to the police with information pertaining to criminal activity. However, residents can tell com-

munity leaders, and the leaders can pass the information to the officers. The leadership in the community was critical in giving the PACTeam the support we needed to accomplish our and the community's goals.

11. Look for small acts of kindness to build trust and relations. For example, stopping to help an older woman take a bag of groceries into her house costs an officer 3 minutes and gains trust and support.

12. Get out of your car. If you drive through a neighborhood, do so with the windows down. Always speak with people. Much of the work of community policing is done on foot or bicycle.

13. Develop good communication skills because they are essential to community policing. Good communication is perhaps the most potent weapon that you can have to reduce crime. Several resources are available to help with communication, but our favorite is a book titled *Verbal Judo*. This book was written by George Thompson (Thompson & Jenkins, 1994), an English professor who became a police officer and realized he did not know how to communicate with people on the street. He tested out techniques and organized them into a book that describes how to talk citizens out of conflictual situations without escalating the crisis.

14. Be a good role model, and watch your appearance and language. Officers set an example by their own behavior. Many "street cops" may be accustomed to using strong language and do so automatically without understanding the impact on children. An example occurred one day when children were playing ball in the middle of a neighborhood street. A police car turned a corner and had to stop for the children. The officers in the car were part of drug enforcement and were not with the PACTeam. An officer yelled, "You f***ing children need to get out of the street." Four years later those children continue to view that incident as a sign that the police who come into their neighborhood do not care about the people who live there. The children, however, do make the distinction between outside police and the PACTeam. In addition to not using derogatory language, officers need to show respect for property. For example, officers who smoke should not throw butts on the ground.

15. Get past the stereotypes of a neighborhood. Even neighborhoods that have high rates of criminal behavior include many law-abiding citizens. Stereotypes drift away as officers learn the culture of the neighborhood, forge relations with neighborhood residents, and engage in collaborative projects.

Officer Commitment and Community Appreciation

Working as part of a community-policing team requires commitment that can extend to off-hours. Although some officers might not be willing to work off-hours without overtime pay, they should understand that this extra work provides important advantages. As residents see the officers' commitment and come to like and trust them, the job gets easier, satisfaction should be higher, and officers will likely perceive their jobs as safer. On the other hand, communities should appreciate the extra efforts donated by the police and realize that officers value any level of recognition of their work and commitment. For example, receiving a small plaque of recognition can go a long way toward building positive relations between the police and the community.

WORKING WITH AN MST TEAM

When the MST team first came into the neighborhood, we did not know their purpose. We did not set out to work in a neighborhood that had an MST program in place. This opportunity was serendipitous. When we saw their work, however, we felt it made the whole package complete. All the parts were working together like a fine-tuned machine. One evening, for example, the MST team was contacted about a young man who was standing on the corner and could have been arrested for loitering. We were concerned that he was involved in drug activity. He told us that he was receiving treatment with the Neighborhood Solutions Project. We paged the project director, who paged the therapist, who called the family. Within an hour the therapist was holding a session with the young man and his family. He went on to improve in school, worked out problems in his life, and is on the college track. He might have followed a different trajectory had we arrested him that evening instead of solving the problem.

In addition to working directly with the therapists to solve youth problems, we collaborated in the development and implementation of youth activities. The community and MST team put the activities together, and we participated to strengthen our relationship with the community. The activities provided excellent opportunities to talk with and get to know the youth. For example, during activities or on the basketball court, the police and youth came together—the us versus them was gone.

In sum, having professionals available to work therapeutically with troubled children can be extremely helpful to community-policing efforts. Such availability can mean the difference between arresting those youth versus allowing them to return to caregiver supervision. With MST, the therapist is available 24 hours a day, 7 days a week. With the community-policing team having that same availability, we can manage problems together to prevent crimes.

CONCLUSION

During our time in the Union Heights neighborhood, calls for police service were reduced by about 80%. Indeed, as the Neighborhood Solutions Project was drawing to a close, crime was virtually nonexistent in the neighborhood. In fact, crime was so low that our department could not justify continuing a community-policing team in the neighborhood. The neighborhood was ready to take over with external police support.

Looking back to the broken windows theory, graffiti was not totally eliminated, but, interestingly, the graffiti changed. Early in the Neighborhood Solutions Project, we recall meeting the MST team and Ida Taylor (Center Director) at the community center. The words "Die Ida" were spray-painted all over the center. She had called the police to remove drug dealers from outside the center the previous day. Today, the graffiti does not have a tone of violence, drugs, or death threats. Today, graffiti in the neighborhood is either someone's initials or "H-Town Till We Die." As H-Town is the community's nickname, the slogan is a sign of solidarity, neighborhood cohesion, and pride.

As all the accomplishments in Union Heights are considered, we see a neighborhood that went from dire straits to a very low crime rate. We see a place where the elders in the community get out and walk and are highly visible—a place where the community haggles over which grants to go after rather than how to get the drug dealers off the corner. Such substantial accomplishments took a well-functioning community-policing team working in concert with the people of the neighborhood, health programs, and the MST team. Together, these are the fingers on the glove, and it takes the whole glove to change a troubled neighborhood.

PART III

Attaining and Sustaining Neighborhood-Based Programs

Methods for funding MST programs and other neighborhood-based programming are covered in Chapter 11. Steps for turning a neighborhood association into a business are described, as this important process is directly related to the sustainability of programming.

Chapter 12 is presented in a question-and-answer format designed to cover key points in implementation of a neighborhood project. Finally, the Neighborhood Solutions Project story ends with words describing the experiences of youth, parents, neighborhood leaders and residents, teachers, principals, and policymakers.

CHAPTER 11

Funding Clinical Services and Neighborhood-Based Programs

with MARSHALL E. SWENSON and TOBY SMITH

Communities and their leaders frequently identify potential solutions to problems only to find that properly financing those solutions or sustaining currently funded programs is very difficult. Rapidly changing governmental priorities often make former funding alternatives disappear. Strategies that work in other states might not even exist locally. These and other challenges make the development of a single funding strategy that works everywhere impossible. This chapter focuses on the basic elements involved in developing and implementing a financing plan that fits the individual needs of a community, regardless of location or time. As specific examples, funding strategies for MST clinical services and neighborhood-based interventions that promote health and fitness are addressed. The chapter goals are

Marshall E. Swenson, MSW, MBA, received his MSW in clinical social work from the University of Arkansas at Little Rock and his MBA from Centenary College. He is Vice President for Program Development for Multisystemic Therapy Services and a Clinical Instructor at the Medical University of South Carolina, Department of Psychiatry and Behavioral Sciences. He has also worked in the development of a variety of school and community programs.

Toby Smith is a graduate of the University of South Carolina, where she earned a BA in Government and International Studies. She did graduate work at the American University in Washington, DC, and is a graduate of the Women's Executive Leadership Program. Miss Smith is a senior certified grants specialist and provides consulting services to nonprofit organizations. She is currently Vice President of funding for the Greater YWCA of Charleston.

1. To present methods to help community leaders identify and select the funding sources that are currently available and best meet their needs
2. To describe the major components found in most funding proposals
3. To detail the step-by-step process used to develop and implement a sound financial strategy
4. To present ways to build a neighborhood association
5. To discuss steps for turning a neighborhood association into a business in order to sustain neighborhood-based programs

FUNDING AN MST PROGRAM

Identifying and Selecting Funding Sources

MST program developers must consider two components in the area of finance: start-up and long-term funding. Grant funding often provides start-up money to pay for personnel and overhead expenses until a source of recurring funding begins the cash flow. Grant funds are typically found through government or foundation sources. To sustain programs in the long run, however, a recurring source of funding is needed. Such funding is typically found through state and federal programs such as Medicaid. The elements presented here apply to both the start-up as well as ongoing funding, although the sources of these funds may differ.

How to Find Available Funding

When determining what funds may be available for a given project, it is helpful to investigate how similar programs are funded in or near the targeted community or within the state. Representatives of social service agencies, public agencies, and identified stakeholders can often provide ideas and paths to follow for grant support. Grant funding to start MST projects has come from such sources as the federal Safe Schools initiative (U.S. Department of Education) to reduce behavior problems in schools, the Substance Abuse and Mental Health Services Administration (SAMHSA) (U.S. Department of Health and Human Services) to reduce substance abuse, and from major foundations such as the Robert Wood Johnson Foundation. In today's Internet world, typing the word "grants" in a search engine will lead to sites like *www.grants.gov*, where numerous grants for many uses are listed. Keep in mind, however, that grants only provide a short-term solution for start-up financing. Most grants have a maximum life of about 3 years.

Acquiring resources from state-level organizations such as Medicaid, and departments of mental health, juvenile justice, and social services will likely be required to sustain financing. These are the agencies that typically pick up the cost of the current array of services targeting the needs of communities, families, and youth. These therapeutic services are often both costly and ineffective at solving the problems of serious antisocial behavior in youths and their families, thus making programs like MST attractive alternatives. Some states already have funding structures in place for sustainable funding of MST, but many do not. Local political representatives might provide needed support when seeking the best contact persons in state agencies. Agency representatives can provide information about funding structures successfully used within the state, but also might reveal current efforts to develop those structures if they are not yet in place. Short-term grant funding might provide enough money to demonstrate program success to key stakeholders sufficient to affect state-level policy initiatives regarding program finance.

Specific Steps to Selecting a Funding Source

After completing the investigation of all available funding sources, applicants must determine which sources have missions most compatible with their needs.

- Foundation centers, computerized databases, publications, and public libraries are some of the resources available to assist the funding search.
- Do not limit the funding search to one source.
- Look for a match between the goals of the project and those of the funding organization. Pinpoint specific funding priorities and preferences.
- Make direct contact with funders who support similar projects.
- Request proposal guidelines and a list of projects previously funded. In some cases, an annual report may reveal the priorities of a given funding source.
- Inquire about the maximum amount of funding available. Inquire about the average size and funding range of previous awards.
- Determine if the funding levels of the grants are appropriate for the project. Inquire if there is a funding floor or ceiling (i.e., a minimum or maximum amount of dollars that can be requested).
- Find out if the funder knows of other grant or recurring funding sources appropriate to the project.

If the funding source provides annual recurring funding, the standards under which the funding operates will need to be ascertained. Include the requirements of the standards in the funding proposal to assure compatibility with the funding source. Also, determine the method of payment and the expected time between billing and receipt of cash reimbursement.

Grants can potentially provide a methodology to manage the cash flow during the period between initial billing and the flow of funds from the recurring funding source. For example, one program secured a small, short-term federal grant that allowed the purchase of equipment, renting of facilities and hiring of staff. The program immediately started billing for services. There was about a 4- to 6-month gap between billing and reliable cash flow from billing, so by the time the small grant ended, cash flow from billing supported the ongoing program expenses.

For each funding source, identify the primary contact person, who is a resource to guide the applicant through the process of applying for that funding. Some contacts are willing to provide technical assistance while others are not, so ask. Determine if the contact person would be willing to review and provide feedback on drafts of the proposal. Inquire about how the final proposals are reviewed, and how the funding decisions are made. Often different portions of a proposal carry different weights when being reviewed for funding. Keep in mind that some grant programs might expect matching funds or in-kind funds. If so, find out how the funding source defines each of these.

Hint: Often, persons reviewing proposals for funding have to review countless numbers of proposals for one grant. Help them decide in your favor by making the proposal well organized, easy to read, complete with attention to specifications, concise, and persuasive. Make sure that questions asked by the funding source are answered. Avoid using jargon or big words in an attempt to impress, as these might slow down the reading process and frustrate the reviewer. Finally, attend to the appearance (e.g., professional-looking colorful binder with tabs) to invite a reviewer to select yours over another proposal of equal merit.

Components of Funding Proposals

Most proposals written to finance a program contain similar components. The following list introduces these components with a brief explanation. A grant writer can often develop the proposal components for one funding source, and cut and paste the same elements into another proposal with minimal editing.

- *Cover page.* The cover page should include information about both the applicant and the funding source, such as the organizational name, address, telephone and fax numbers, email address, and website address. The applicant and funding-source contact person should be specified. The cover page also should include the address to which the proposal should be mailed, along with the deadline date and time. Some funders may require a signature of the applicant's President or Chief Executive Officer stating that they agree to the conditions submitted in the proposal.

- *Table of contents.* As the proposal is developed, use clear topical headings to allow the reader to quickly find specific information. List the location of these headings in a table of contents.
- *Abstract.* A brief overview of the entire project allows the reader to quickly assess the broad purpose of the project. A clearly and concisely written abstract allows a proposal reviewer to easily compare the project with the competition.
- *Budget.* The budget basically tells the reader how much it will cost to fund the project and how the funds will be used. Be sure to allocate enough funds in the budget to operate the program well and to account for contingencies such as staff turnover and low referrals for services in the initial year of operation.
- *Organizational summary.* This tells the reader about the organization applying for the funding. Briefly describe the history of the organization, its mission, the administrative structure, physical facilities, staffing size and composition, current services provided, financial summary, and accreditation or affiliation. The proposal reviewer needs to know that this organization is worthy of the added funding and will manage the funds well.
- *Narrative.* The narrative describes the proposed project in sufficient detail that the reviewer clearly understands exactly how the project will work, and what the expected outcome of the project will be. In short, the narrative describes what the funder will get for the money. Many proposals also include statements about how spending this money will save money in the long run—sort of a return on investment.
- *Résumés of key staff.* If the staff for the project is already hired, attach the résumés. If not, include a detailed description of the job, including the minimum qualifications of the person targeted for each position.
- *Timetable.* The timetable includes the key components or milestones of the project and the start and completion times for each component.
- *Appendices.* Most proposals include a required set of appendices. Below are typical examples.

  - *Letters of support.* Often, the support of several agencies and organizations is needed for the funded project to succeed. Identify those and ask the key contacts in these organizations to write letters demonstrating that they strongly support the project.
  - *Memoranda of agreement.* When there is need for close collaboration with a given agency or organization (e.g., they will refer clients), often a memorandum is developed to articulate the specific relationship and communication planned.

Hint: Have someone not directly associated with the development of the proposal review the finished product to make sure that all of the needed components are present. Incomplete proposals are often rejected with little regard to the potential merit of the project.

The Step-By-Step Process to Funding a Project

So far, sources of funding and common elements in proposals have been discussed. Here, the steps needed to assemble a winning proposal are delineated. Common tasks include the following:

- Assembling the planning team
- Determining the organizational structure needed to gain funding
- Contacting key stakeholders
- Determining community need—target population
- Determining the methodology for client identification, prioritization, and referral
- Determining desired project outcomes
- Determining the methodology for program evaluation
- Writing a narrative of the overall project
- Developing a timeline
- Determining personnel needs
- Determining needs for equipment and office space
- Determining needs for operating expenses
- Determining needs for training and technical assistance
- Determining a detailed program budget with notes
- Reviewing and approving a draft proposal
- Assembling the final proposal and printing copies
- Submitting the proposal to the funding source
- Following up

Assembling the Planning Team

Project development teams contain members with skills and interests relating to the purpose of the project. Members generally fall into one of two categories, champions and stakeholders. The term "champion" refers to those individuals who have the vision of what the project will accomplish, and the time and interest to directly participate in the development and ongoing support of the project. "Stakeholders," on the other hand, refer to those individuals who are directly impacted by the purpose and intended outcome of the project, but may not play an active role in the development process. Champions are often persons in the community who initiate the "grassroots" efforts, such as parents, community leaders (formal and informal), business people, and residents of the neighborhood or community. Stakeholders might include persons representing funding organizations, public agencies, schools, health care, potential referral agencies, politicians, and leaders in other organizations operating within the neighborhood or community. Although stakeholders might take less direct roles in the project development, they stand to benefit directly from the results, and thus, their support is essential.

Start by identifying the champions within the community. Assemble a team with defined roles and responsibilities. For example, one person might assume the lead role in managing the project while another focuses on the written proposal. Another champion might target the engagement of one or more stakeholders. Someone else might handle the logistics of the meeting place, and so on.

Determining the Organizational Structure Needed to Gain Funding

Often funding sources for MST programs require that the funds be given to a chartered, not-for-profit 501(c)(3) corporation. The planning team will determine if actual incorporation is needed, or if there is a chartered corporation that might serve as the intended provider agency when the funds are received. If the organization that is the intended provider is not a chartered corporation, the team will need to determine if an existing 501(c)(3) can serve as the fiscal agent.

Contacting Key Stakeholders

Develop a list of the systems, agencies, and organizations that are essential for the success of the project. Within each identified system, identify the best available contact or liaison to serve as a guide when interacting with that system. This liaison will assist with engagement, collaboration, and problem-solving efforts later on. Visit with each contact person and explain the project. Inquire about the needs of that stakeholder and organization and discuss how this project might provide benefit. Discuss how to best define the relationship between the project and the stakeholder's system and determine if a formal Memorandum of Agreement is needed. Seek a letter of support detailing how the project would provide benefit and the role the stakeholder's agency or system will play in the project. Finally, ask the stakeholder to define the desired outcomes in measurable terms. These will be needed later when program goals and evaluation plans are developed.

Determining Community Need—Target Population

Most project definitions start with a statement of community need. For MST programs, the statements of community need often include the following:

- Too many youth in our community get in trouble with the law.
- Too many youth in our community do poorly in school and often drop out.

- Too many youth in our community become involved with drugs and alcohol.
- There are too few positive activities for youth in our community.
- The crime rate is too high in our community.
- Parents in our community find it difficult to get help when experiencing problems with their children.

Articulating the problems provides the basic structure to develop a mission statement. Mission statements provide a clear articulation of the purpose of the project so that all who read it immediately understand why the project is needed. The preceding need statements might generate a mission statement such as the following:

> The mission of this project is to make our community a safer place by providing alternate activities for our youth that reduce their involvement in crime and drug or alcohol abuse and increase their success in school and positive activities while supporting the families of these youth to better manage the task of parenting.

Moving from the general to the specific, the final definition of the target population will describe the specific characteristics that would qualify a youth and family for participation. In addition, all exclusion criteria are listed that would disqualify a youth or family from participation.

Determining the Methodology for Client Identification, Prioritization, and Referral

When the target population is defined, a specific process is developed to assure that the program will operate at or near maximum efficiency. More MST programs fall below expected performance due to underutilization than for any other reason. The referral process needs to include a step-by-step guide, starting with how the youth will be first identified, who will make key decisions regarding prioritization, qualification, funding availability (when funding is tied to the client, as with Medicaid), and program availability. When and how the family will be recruited is articulated in a manner respectful of the family's needs and mindful of the need for engagement, even when the family might show initial reluctance. Often, a flowchart is developed to depict the steps and key contact persons along the way.

Determining Desired Project Outcomes

The next task is to define the scope of work, in order to focus the funding search. The scope may vary somewhat, depending on the source of funding and the type of projects they promote. For MST, the scope of work typically includes the development of a treatment team to implement intensive interventions with youth having the most serious behavioral difficulties and their families. The MST treatment model provides many resources to assist with the articulation of the project through the publications and Web resources currently available (i.e., *www.mstservices.com*).

The next stage of refinement is to develop program-level goals. Development of these goals often requires the input and full support of the stakeholder agencies and organizations. For example, developing a goal regarding crime reduction should include input from the police, the courts, probation, the prosecutor, the public defender, and victim advocacy groups. Although it may seem a daunting task to include all of these groups, doing so at the initial stage of the project will ensure greater collaboration later. In setting goals and objectives:

• Decide who will benefit, both directly (e.g., courts with lower number of cases) and indirectly (e.g., schools that might experience fewer behavior problems if the youth decrease involvement in crime).
• Draft the expected project outcomes in measurable terms. For example, "Youth receiving MST will increase school attendance as measured by a reduction in absenteeism during treatment compared with attendance records of the year prior to treatment, and outcomes will be sustained at least 12 months following treatment."

Determining the Methodology for Program Evaluation

When the desired outcomes are clear, translate these into concrete goals. Determine the data needed to accurately measure these goals, and articulate a specific method for data collection and analysis. While this may sound like a highly complicated procedure, actually the most effective proposals include a very simple evaluation method. Often only three or four indicators are tracked for demonstration of long-term outcomes. For example, to evaluate the impact of the program on future criminal activity, the method might simply be to ask parents every 6 months for 18 months posttreatment if their child has been rearrested. Although more objective data might be available, this simple question to the parent might prove much less expensive to collect and still meet the criterion of reasonable reliability for the purpose of program evaluation. The key issue here is that the more complicated the evaluation process, the more expensive. Most communities rate direct service a higher priority over program evaluation. Find the best balance for the project. Program evaluations must address the following questions:

• Will the selected measures sufficiently track the program's performance and meet the reliability requirements of the key stakeholders?
• Is it possible to conduct the evaluation with the resources allocated for this purpose?

- When the outcomes are published, will the funding agencies continue funding, will the referral agencies continue referring, and will the collaborating systems still collaborate?
- Will the evaluation make a difference to the end users of the program, the youth and family, in terms of the quality and effectiveness of services received?

Writing a Narrative of the Overall Project

A large amount of information will be collected during the development of a project. Many persons might contribute to the narrative description of the project, but one person must edit and compile the final product. This will avoid the appearance of seemingly unrelated items attached using widely varying writing styles. Some organizations employ a professional writer to assemble the final product. Do not assume, however, that a professional grant writer should do the whole job. The process of engaging key persons will prove more important than the final product, even if the professional writer can "make it look good." Having said that, the professional writer presents the final outcome of the development process in a single, well-organized form that will increase the likelihood of funding. First look to the assembled development team, but be realistic about the need for a professional product and the talents of the development team. Few persons have the experience *and* inclination to do this well.

Developing a Timeline

Two separate timelines should be developed. The first, the proposal development timeline, provides guidance and deadlines for the development of the proposal. This timeline is used only by the organization, and is not part of the final proposal. The second, the project timeline, includes the steps and deadlines to implement the project. This timeline is submitted with the final proposal.

The proposal development timeline includes all critical proposal development steps listed in this chapter, including the funding cycle of the intended funding organization (e.g., the budget development cycle for public budgets or the grant cycles for foundations). The submission deadline dictates when the program developer must have all components complete and ready for submission. Working backward, the developer then determines the final date when each stage of development must be completed based on the necessary sequence of steps and the time allotted for each step. Plan to submit the proposal 1 week before the due date and schedule accordingly. If the timeline works well, the job will be done ahead of time. If something takes more time than planned, the extra week provides some buffer. Keep in mind that most grant proposals must be submitted with several copies, one for each person in the review process. Allow time for preparing the materials and making all copies prior to submission.

The project timeline includes all of the critical tasks involved with implementing the project when funding is granted. For example, securing facilities and equipment, recruiting staff, initiating referral processes, and starting services to referred clients are all included on the project timeline. Each task has time allocated. For example, staff recruitment includes developing job descriptions, advertising, interviewing, selecting staff, allowing the staff to give notice at the old job, and finally, training the new personnel. A well-constructed project timeline communicates to the funder that if granted, this organization will effectively and efficiently implement the program, making the most of the funds allocated.

Hint: Factor in plenty of time to write and edit multiple drafts of the proposal.

Determining Personnel Needs

Many projects may differ regarding personnel requirements. The common factors are the talents, education, and experience needed to do the job. MST, for example, requires that a program manager have the ability to operate the business end of the program and maintain the needed collaboration with the key stakeholders. The MST supervisor must have superior clinical training and experience plus the talent to effectively lead the program. The therapists must have clinical training and experience to work with families experiencing multiple challenges and the talent to engage persons who may show reluctance to participate. A program administrative assistant must be able to communicate effectively with clients by telephone, and be able to organize the business tasks that might include billing, office management, outcome data collection, and conducting adherence interviews with clients. The number of each type of staff will vary with the scope of the project.

Determining Needs for Equipment and Office Space

Physical facilities represent a large fixed cost for most programs. Many organizations can make space available in existing facilities for minimal costs, but some programs must seek out new office space at considerable cost. The majority of the MST services are provided in the client's home and in the community. Still, space is needed for completing the necessary paperwork, planning treatment, and conducting supervision sessions. Secure file facilities must meet standards to safeguard confidentiality of the clients. Therapists need the use of cell telephones for safety as well as efficiency. When planning a project such as this, conduct a thorough evaluation of the needs of the program to assure adequate funding to cover everything needed.

Determining Needs for Operating Expenses

Operating expenses might include such items as travel costs, telephone bills, and even a client fund for special circumstances. As with the cost of office space and equipment, these expenses can be accurately estimated in a budget proposal.

Determining Needs for Training and Technical Assistance

A common feature in programs such as MST is the need for program development, staff training, and ongoing program support to assure the quality of services provided. For research-proven programs with specific implementation protocols, this expense might be similar to adding a part-time employee to the payroll. Do not consider this a temporary expense, but rather a cost of doing business. Improvements in the treatment technology, turnover of staff, changes in the stakeholder requirements for the program, and many other factors can affect the implementation of a program. Ongoing support through training and technical assistance will improve program stability, productivity, and outcomes.

Determining a Detailed Program Budget with Notes

Budgets are cost projections that provide information about how a project will be implemented and managed. Plan the budget carefully to assure it is realistic, fits within the guidelines of the funding agency, and is sufficient to conduct the program. Budgets typically include a note page explaining each budget area and justifying any unusual expenses. When reviewing budgets, funders often use the following criteria:

- Can the job be accomplished with this budget?
- Are costs reasonable for the market?
- Is there sufficient budget detail and explanation?
- Was the budget submitted in the required format? (Often a requirement to make comparison easier)
- Were matching or in-kind revenues listed? (sometimes required)
- Is there flexibility to allow for negotiation of costs?

Although most requests for proposals do not require a highly detailed budget, the program development team might still ask someone with accounting experience to assist with this portion of the proposal.

Reviewing and Approving a Draft Proposal

The primary writer will develop a draft of the final proposal. Each member of the development team should read the draft to assure that it makes sense, communicates the intentions of the team, and includes all the required information. Allow plenty of time for incorporation of edits and corrections.

Assembling the Final Proposal and Printing Copies

The final steps of assembling and reproducing the proposal should not be left to a committee. The principal program developer should be responsible for guiding the proposal through the final stages up to and including submitting the final document to the right location at (preferably before) the right time. Much hard work has been lost due to the final steps being poorly managed.

Submitting the Proposal to the Funding Source

Get it to the right place. Get it there on time (preferably early). Leave nothing to chance. A simple delay in the mail system could cost the program thousands of dollars in lost funding, not to mention the time spent. If the grant is sent via UPS or FedEx, the package can be tracked to assure that delivery has occurred simply by checking the website.

Following Up

Developing and submitting funding proposals does not guarantee funding. Follow up with the funding source about the status, evaluation, and outcome of the proposal. Request feedback about the proposal's strengths and weaknesses (although this information is often not available, especially where there are large volumes of submissions). Treat each proposal submission as a learning experience, and strive to improve each time a proposal is developed.

Funding and Sustaining Neighborhood-Based Programs

Building neighborhood-level programs primarily requires getting the people of a neighborhood to work together effectively, which is known as accessing social capital. Doing so involves determining the strengths and resources already available in the community with regard to people and routing those resources toward accomplishing the neighborhood's goals. As programs are built, a financial base will need to be established to pay for goods, running of the programs, and required overhead (e.g., phone bills, Internet). If a neighborhood is going to be in the business of running multiple programs, taking donations, and providing services for citizens that go above and beyond day-to-day support of a neighbor, then the neighborhood will need to act like a business. In particular, if the neighborhood is to sustain its programs, the neighborhood will need to become a business. In this section, steps that neighborhoods must take to become a business are discussed.

Grassroots Community Development

Before a community can become a business, the people must organize and determine their goals and how best to move forward. Grassroots organizations are those that are for the people and by the people, using local resources and assets. In some communities, such as Union Heights where the Neighborhood Solutions Project was implemented, a neighborhood council might already be formed. If a structured group is not yet formed, then the leaders conducting grassroots development need to decide what type of entity would best serve their purpose. Options include an organization that is either faith-based or community-based. Either of these organizations can become eligible to accept donations and grant funds.

Faith-Based Organizations

The newest and most controversial players in the world of grassroots change are those defined as faith-based. As the name denotes, the primary impetus for action with these groups is a very strong religious leaning. Neighborhoods might have a church or network of churches through which they wish to run their programs. If this is the case, leaders need to keep in mind that different churches have different beliefs and different priorities or goals related to their particular membership. That said, stakeholders will need to assure that the goals of a communitywide faith-based organization address the needs of all people in the community and are not specific to one faith or one church. A few key points regarding faith-based organizations and funding:

- No separate stacks of monies are available for exclusive use.
- The same short stack of funding is available, but now faith-based groups are to receive equal treatment in terms of accessing.
- The transfer of funds in no way nullifies the Establishment clause of the Constitution.
- Most religious organizations will need a separate nonprofit arm to

receive the funds, but occasionally there are exceptions. Section 1 of the Executive Order on the establishment of the White House Office of Faith-Based and Community Initiatives indicates the following:

> Policy. Faith-based and community organizations are indispensable in meeting the needs of poor Americans and distressed neighborhoods. Government cannot be replaced by such organizations, but it can and should welcome them as partners. The paramount goal is compassionate results, and private and charitable community groups, including religious ones, should have the fullest opportunity permitted by law to compete on a level playing field, so long as they achieve valid public purposes, such as curbing crime, conquering addiction, strengthening families and neighborhoods, and overcoming poverty. This delivery of social services must be results oriented and should value the bedrock principles of pluralism, nondiscrimination, evenhandedness and neutrality." (*www.whitehouse.gov*)

Since the inception of the Office of Faith-Based and Community Initiatives, many churches and religious organizations have begun filing the necessary paperwork to create nonprofit entities that will allow them to compete for federal dollars. In fiscal year 2003, Congress approved $30 million for the Compassion Capital Fund, the centerpiece for faith-based initiatives. The agency has weathered several storms since it came into being: the first director resigned (perhaps in the face of mounting criticism that the plan was not taking form); then the President's original funding request was whittled down by about $5 million. Throughout the nation, many people had, and some still do have, serious qualms about the government getting involved in church activities. On the other hand, many religious organizations argued that they were already doing the work and had been doing so for a long time—so show us the money!

Community-Based Organizations

If the neighborhood leaders determine that a community-based organization (e.g., a neighborhood council) is the best entity for them, they will need to begin the steps for building it. Many resources exist for gathering information to build a neighborhood group. For example, the City of Phoenix (2001) has an Internet-accessible Neighborhood Association Tool Kit that provides a guide for forming a neighborhood association. The steps typically include (1) forming a core group—a steering committee, (2) defining the neighborhood boundaries, (3) developing a mission statement, (4) applying for incorporation, (5) developing the bylaws, (6) establishing a Board of Directors, (7) obtaining an employer identification number (EIN), and (8) setting up financial records.

Forming a Core Group—A Steering Committee

Informal neighborhood leaders, those interested in organizing their community toward meeting certain goals, initially form the steering committee, which serves as a de facto board of directors until the organization is formalized. Several interested citizens of a neighborhood can start a core group by making personal contacts and holding community organizational meetings. These meetings might initially include 8–10 people and can be in a home. The point is that the meetings will need to be held in the neighborhood where there are no barriers to attending due to transportation problems. The initial core group should talk with the city government to seek their support and any information available on starting a neighborhood association. After an initial steering committee is formed, the decision is made regarding the bounds of the neighborhood association.

Defining the Neighborhood Boundaries

Some communities will have boundaries established by the city or county. In larger urban areas especially, neighborhoods might encompass such a large area that one association cannot serve an entire neighborhood. The steering committee should decide the boundaries of the Association. This does not mean that an individual not living on a defined street in the Neighborhood Association, who has a vested interest in the neighborhood, should be excluded. In fact, neighborhoods will likely want to keep an open policy and spirit of welcome to people who live outside the bounds of the neighborhood, but offer resources and interest in that neighborhood. For example, Mrs. Smith grew up on 10th Street, married and moved across the overpass to 30th Street, but is still highly involved in the 10th Street Children's Center. She is a volunteer there, and her children participate in the after-school program. The bounds of the Association are set from 1st Street to 25th Street. Whereas the Association will likely not want to take on organizing and solving the problems of the neighborhood beyond their bounds, they also will likely not want to exclude Mrs. Smith and the resources she can offer the neighborhood.

Developing a Mission Statement

Figuring out the mission and writing the mission statement are crucial steps for a Neighborhood Association. The central question that must be answered is What exactly does your group want to do for the community? The mission should be the Association's passion and their rallying cry. Similarly, the mission statement should be concise. Disregard lengthy and complex paragraphs with never-ending phrases. Statements of this type are seldom read, less often understand, and quickly forgotten. Consider FedEx: We deliver overnight. Thus, in writing the mission statement, simply describe the purpose of the organization.

- Why it exists
- Who it serves
- What it does

If the mission has several components, that's fine. Just break each down into bite-sized morsels. Visitors dropping in from Ulan Bator, Mongolia, should be able to understand what the group is all about and what it's striving to accomplish. An example of a mission statement is

> The mission of the Neighborhood Council is to make the 10th Street Neighborhood an attractive, safe place to live and where education and family are valued.

One more point: Make the mission statement visible to everyone. Consider hanging a large placard on a wall in the most visible spot. Some organizations also have a Vision Statement, which charts the direction of the organization's future, and Guiding Principles, which provide an ethical framework of how work will be accomplished.

Applying for Incorporation

The first legal step to starting a nonprofit organization is to form a corporation, which is regulated under the laws of the state in which they are formed. The steering committee should decide on a name for the corporation and develop the articles of incorporation. First, obtain the needed paperwork from the appropriate state office (i.e., usually the Secretary of State) and make sure the name chosen is not already in use. The articles name the corporation and delineate why the corporation exists. The articles for a nonprofit specify that it is not being formed to create profit for the Board of Directors. The location of the organization and the range of its operation are specified. The group's incorporators sign the document, have it notarized if needed, and send it to the Secretary of State's office if that is the entity that incorporates nonprofits in a particular state. Most states charge a filing fee that will need to be sent in with the application. Keep in mind that just because the organization has been incorporated as a nonprofit does not mean that it is tax exempt. Acquiring this status requires another process discussed later in this chapter.

Developing the By-Laws

After the mission statement is complete, the bylaws should be written by a Board of Directors or the steering committee. The bylaws are the rules for the organization. The purpose of bylaws is to (1) provide structure and govern the internal workings of the organization; (2) set the requirements for the operation of the board, including its size, tenure, number of meetings; (3) establish the offices and number of officers; (4) define committees and their functions; (5) specify legal and financial protocols; and (6) establish methods for resolving conflicts.

Depending upon the specific needs, bylaws might or might not need to be extensive. Prior to development of the organization's bylaws, those of other organizations should be reviewed to get a sense of format and provisions. The following questions, while not comprehensive, should be answered in the bylaws:

1. What is the purpose of the organization?
2. Where is the organization located?
3. Will the organization have any members?
4. What is the length of terms for the Board members?
5. How many members will be on the Board?
6. What are the duties of officers?
7. How many committees will be formed?
8. What are the provisions for amending the bylaws?
   and so on . . .

Once the bylaws have been drafted, it would be a good use of time to have an attorney or paralegal review them before they are formally adopted. The bylaws constitute a document that is available for perusal by any member of the neighborhood at any time.

Establishing a Board of Directors

The Board of Directors might be comprised of some or all steering committee members. However, others might be brought in as well. The Board is charged with governing and the members serve as fiduciaries of the nonprofit corporation. Fiduciaries stand in special relationship of legal trust to others. Some activities assumed by the Board include budget, finance, strategic and annual planning, fund raising, public relations, policy making, and human resources.

When recruiting Board members consider an individual's willingness to work, sincerity, availability, dependability, level of expertise, and qualifications. Also, make certain that the person can differentiate between governing and micromanaging day-to-day activities. Board members of a nonprofit organization must be able to adhere to the basic duties of care, loyalty, and obedience. Duty of care means that the Board member must pay attention and make decisions based on good information. Loyalty refers to putting the interest of the organization first and above other interests when making decisions. Obedience means acting in accordance with the nonprofit organizations' mission and goals (Hutton & Phillips, 2001).

Obtaining an Employer Identification Number (EIN)

After incorporation is complete, the organization should apply for an EIN through the Internal Revenue Service. The EIN is similar to an organization's Social Security number. No fee is required, but an SS-4 form must be completed. The EIN can be applied for through the mail, over the phone from the IRS (800-829-1040 can provide a correct phone number), or online (*www.irs.gov*). The date the business started (i.e., date on the incorporation papers) and how many employees are expected to be hired in the next year should be known. Even if the EIN number is assigned over the phone, the SS-4 form must be faxed to the IRS within 24 hours (Hutton & Phillips, 2001).

Setting Up Financial Records

When the organization is formally and legally established, the Board will need to set up financial records. Small organizations sometimes set up bank accounts with a member's Social Security number, but this places the member in a precarious position with regard to liability. The best route is to open an account under the business name using the EIN. Then, setting up a simple spreadsheet to record revenue and expenditures on a regular basis is the next step. Small organizations may start their records on paper. If at all possible, it is best to maintain computerized records to assure a greater level of accuracy.

From an Organization to a Viable Nonprofit Business

Many community groups desiring to expand their territory are getting to the next level by becoming 501(c)(3) nonprofit corporations. Why should an organization become a 501(c)(3)? Consider the following reasons:

1. Donations are tax deductible.
2. The corporation is considered a legal entity with rights, privileges, and liabilities separate from those managing it.
3. Tax-exempt status enables organizations to apply for potentially millions of dollars in grant funding.

With a good plan, an organization can become a nonprofit in as few as 3 months and not usually longer than 1 year. Building a neighborhood organization and establishing it formally and legally accomplishes half the battle. The final two steps to becoming a 501(c)(3) nonprofit corporation are (1) applying for 501(c)(3) status with the IRS and (2) registering as a charity.

Applying for 501(c)(3) Status with the IRS

Applying for tax exemption is an arduous process. Prior to tackling the application, it may be helpful to attend a workshop on applying for 501(c)(3) status. Having a consultant to answer questions can make a difficult process feel doable. Nonprofits must operate for specific purposes, such as being religious, educational, or charitable. It is crucial that the organization understand the IRS rules and regulations for nonprofits. Not following the laws can result in loss of 501(c)(3) status in the best-case scenario. Organizations should apply for tax-exempt status within 27 months of incorporation. To apply for tax-exempt status, the IRS form 1023 is completed. This form is available online at *www.irs.gov*; search under "Forms." Once the packet is complete, it may be helpful to have an attorney or certified public accountant review the application for accuracy before mailing. A filing fee must be included, and all forms should be photocopied to keep in the organization's records. Copies of the articles of incorporation and bylaws should be included with the application (Hummel, 2002). When the official notice, a determination letter from the IRS, arrives, celebrate! Guard this letter with your life, as copies of it will need to accompany every grant application submitted from here on.

Registering as a Charity

State law will likely require registration as a charity with the appropriate state office. In most states an annual fee accompanies the application. Call the Secretary of State or Attorney General's office to obtain the application and information on fees. Keep all application materials handy in a sturdy binder, in a very safe location, for public viewing if requested.

Managing and Growing the Neighborhood Business

Now that the organization is official, it is time to shift priorities to management and growth. Be advised that the original group, which started the process, may or may not continue, so this is a wonderful time to recruit "new blood." The recruitment phase provides a terrific opportunity to tell the organization's story all over again, which ties into the public relations plan. Now is the time to devise a strategy for getting the word out.

- Start networking with other nonprofit organizations.
- Create and disseminate flyers for local houses of worship
- Contact radio and television stations to inquire about public service announcements.
- Letters to the editors and op-ed pieces are useful in establishing expertise.
- If funding is available, consider launching a website.

Not-for-profit Boards must keep in mind that in addition to implementing strategies to grow the organization, annual housekeeping must be done to retain the nonprofit status:

1. On an annual basis, file a 990 form with the IRS. This form is considered the "return" for organizations with tax-exempt status. Form 990 will require an accounting of income, expenses, assets, and liabilities.

2. For states that collect a state income tax the 990 should also be submitted annually to the state Department of Revenue.

3. On an annual basis, the nonprofit organization must update its registration as a charity with the Secretary of State's office. Doing this requires an annual fee.

Some municipalities require nonprofit corporations that intend to solicit funds to file for a permit or solicitation license. These are required annually and must be accompanied by an annual report of expenses, income, and expenditures.

Sustainability through Grant Writing

Now that the organization has its 501(c)(3) status, doors that were formerly closed in the grant world can be opened. So what exactly is a grant? Generally, a grant is a specific amount of money made available by an individual or a local, regional, corporate, state, or federal funding source that allows the initiation and completion of a project, program, or activity that is consistent with the mission of the funding source.

That last part is very important—funders give money to organizations that are doing things in which the funding source is interested. Consider sponsoring a grant writing seminar and invite other nonprofits—they may have someone on staff who will lead the training for free or at a substantially reduced rate. Over the past few years, a trend has developed among some funders to use a standard grant application. Other funders require a response to their specific requests for information, and still others put out requests for proposals (RFPs). Grant money does not have to be repaid unless the applicant is unable to execute the plan or defaults on the original agreement. Grant funding can range from very small amounts to millions of dollars, depending on the funding source and purpose. Competition for grant funding can be fierce, but as noted earlier in this chapter, applicants who are in sync with the desires of the funding source and present a well-written, concise proposal tend to be rewarded for their efforts. It is worth repeating that

- The first step in the grant writing process should be research. Find out what funding sources share missions consistent with the organization. Rule out those who do not, but remember that what does not work for one organization might work for some other group. Share the information with them, and they will return the favor in the future.
- Once a preliminary list of potential funders is created, call the program officer or listed contact or send a query letter. Calling is bold but can pay off in terms of establishing rapport and tends to be better received with the small-to-medium foundations. Unknown to many, program officers at the federal level do not ignore their phones. Applicants should not be skittish about phoning to ask questions; program officers understand that applications are daunting. E-mail is also an efficient way to correspond at the federal level.
- Respond to everything on the application very carefully and follow all instructions to the letter. If the application specifies that every page must be stapled in the upper right-hand corner, do not staple on the left. Deviating from the instructions, even in the slightest, can cause even the best-written proposal to be discarded.
- After the entire application is complete, find several other fresh eyes to review it thoroughly. Small mistakes add up quickly.
- In general, completed grant applications (incompletes are considered nonresponsive and are not reviewed) that are received on time are reviewed by a panel, committee, or, in the case of a family foundation, by family members. Although the number of proposals usually outweighs the amount of available money, funders enjoy giving awards to organizations that have done their homework.
- The review process can be lengthy, so while waiting, continue research for the next project.

Do applications get funded every time? No, of course not, but persevere in providing the best application and success will follow more often than not. Do not forget that once funding is awarded, keep accurate records—a grants management course would be a good start.

Although proposal writing is a popular and effective way to fund nonprofits, it is only one way to increase revenues. Several other strategies can be used to raise funds, and success requires using the right strategy at the right time for the right purpose (Scott, 2003).

Sustainability through Fund Raising

If the organization is going to raise money, the first step is to develop a fund raising plan. This plan must (1) be written out, (2) be agreed to by everyone who cares about the organization (i.e., Board, leaders, staff), (3) have the names of the person responsible next to each "to do" item, and (4) have dates and deadlines (Quatmann, 2002). Fund raising is aimed at securing one-time or recurring donors who will provide cash. Although by no means comprehensive, some basic fund raising activities include putting on a concert, selling T-shirts, sponsoring a community fun-run, holding bake sales at various houses of worship, collecting items and holding a community garage sale, or working at concession stands at local sporting events. More sophisticated techniques include a capital campaign—raising money for your own building; an endowment fund—assets contributed by one or more wealthy individuals and/or a number of foundations and corporations; or planned giving—which involves a major gift that fits a particular donor's financial needs, that is, through a will, living trust, or life insurance (Hummel, 2002).

As with grant writing, careful research is the key and a smart investment for the organization. Whatever strategy is developed, make sure that it is consistent with the organization's mission and goals.

Keeping the Dream Alive

After the organization has received funding from an outside source, attention should turn to the issue of sustainability. Funding sources are also concerned with this issue, and many request a plan of action in the original application. Almost all grant applicants note that other grant funds will be sought to keep the program going, but is there another community group that might consider adopting the program? Also, check on the availability of discretionary and end-of-year funding. If the program is having a measurable effect on some societal ill, codify the results and share them with local politicians. Also send the results to the office of your U.S. senator and ask for his or her ideas and support. Identify other existing organizations that might be trying to address the problem. Perhaps there is an opportunity for partnership. If the original project had a human services leaning, contact local houses of worships or ministerial alliances to see if goals are compatible. Again, this presents another opportunity for partnership. But above all else, continue to research opportunities. New funding sources pop up on the radar screen regularly. Someone is interested in the organization's work because it is improving lives by focusing bright lights directly on the problems and calling attention to them. There is money out there waiting to be used for good purposes. Go for it—your community and neighbors need you!

CONCLUSION

Any neighborhood that wishes to implement a neighborhood-based project will need to start with a search for funding. The requirements of the funding process obviously overlap with the overall development of a program, be it a specific program such as MST or a broader program such as a communitywide organization. Done well, a financing strategy will permit the employees of the program or members of a community to focus on the targeted outcomes of the project in a stable, well-managed organizational environment. This will lead to staff stability, program stability, and the best opportunity for outcomes.

CHAPTER 12

Summary and Conclusions

This book details implementation of the Neighborhood Solutions Project, a neighborhood-based project that addressed youth violence, substance abuse, school behavior, health, and neighborhood crime. Conclusions are synthesized from the scientific literature, from the experiences of the professional staff, and from the life experiences of residents who changed their inner-city neighborhood. The goals of this final chapter are:

1. To summarize key points through a question-and-answer format
2. To provide an avenue for the neighborhood residents and others to make direct comments

QUESTIONS AND ANSWERS REGARDING DEVELOPING AND IMPLEMENTING A NEIGHBORHOOD-BASED PROGRAM

Question: Is it possible to implement a neighborhood-based project that includes MST in my community?

Answer: Yes. Although the master plan detailed in this book may seem overwhelming, every community has champions who are concerned about the welfare of residents and environmental integrity. These champions are likely already committing countless hours to their community. This existing level of energy and work can be channeled into starting a neighborhood project that integrates a variety of activities into a well-articulated theme and mission (e.g., decreasing juvenile crime). The experiences from the Neighborhood Solutions Project provide a guide for getting started.

Question: My neighborhood is different from Union Heights. How can I implement this project in my neighborhood if it is so different?

Answer: This project was specifically designed for and by the Union Heights neighborhood, and such a project in a different neighborhood would be tailored to that neighborhood. As shown in Chapter 11, residents can come together through grassroots efforts and organize a formal structure to start the important work of neighborhood development. The formal structure does not have to be large; it can be as small as a steering committee. Then, as shown in Chapter 4, the people of the community will lead the way regarding the aims and structure of the project. Even though the MST clinical model should be implemented with fidelity across sites (e.g., home-based, small caseloads, using empirically supported intervention techniques), the model is tailored to the individual strengths and needs of families, and thus, interventions are not the same for each family. Similarly, neighborhood projects will share characteristics in their basic structure, but the content of services will be specific to the neighborhood.

Question: How can I convince someone that this project is needed in my community? What might be the benefits?

Answer: As shown in Chapter 1, community violence is very high in urban areas, and boys and minority youth are particularly at risk. The problem of community violence carries serious consequences for youth, their families, and their neighbors. Youth who witness and directly experience violence are at increased risk of problems with mental health, physical health, and school performance. Of particular concern is that experiencing violence is a risk factor for substance abuse, which then carries further risk for committing crimes and violence. To reduce the risk of these serious problems in high-crime areas, intervening at the neighborhood level is essential. Neighborhood environments can produce negative or positive influences on youth. Factors that increase risk are found in low institutional resources (e.g., absence of medical services, child care), low social support and warmth in relationships, and low cohesion and trust among neighbors (i.e., collective efficacy). The most important thing a neighborhood can do for its children is to pull together and increase collective efficacy—that is, empower caregivers and youth with indigenous social support and increase accessibility of formal institutional resources. Further, youth participating in serious criminal behavior are prime candidates for intensive community-based interventions. As with the Neighborhood Solutions Project, the benefits might be reductions in criminal activity, substance abuse, and school problems (see Chapters 5, 6, and 7).

Question: From which stakeholders should I seek buy-in for a neighborhood-based project?

Answer: In each chapter that discusses development of neighborhood-based services, the consistent thread is involvement of stakeholders across multiple organizational levels—city government, the neighborhood, and other professionals. For example, support from the officer on the beat through the mayor's office is needed for community policing to be successful.

Question: What kinds of problems should my community target?

Answer: The community must target problems that are important to that community. To discover the priorities, neighborhood leaders or professionals from outside the community can follow the suggestions provided in Chapter 4.

Question: Is funding available to conduct a neighborhood-based project that includes MST?

Answer: Yes. Most communities or agencies that want to conduct an MST project at the neighborhood level should be able to find funding. Chapter 11 shows ways to attain funding for MST clinical services and for neighborhood-based health and wellness activities. At the outset, MST program developers must evaluate the adequacy of start-up and long-term funding. Key stakeholders and local political representatives can start the process by meeting to brainstorm funding possibilities. Federal, state, and foundation funding possibilities that have goals consistent with the neighborhood's mission should be considered. After initial funding is secured, stakeholders can work to develop the community as a business.

Question: Why should my community consider MST or other evidence-based practices?

Answer: Chapter 2 presents consensus opinions from highly respected scientists and policy analysts about what works to reduce youth crime and substance abuse. Youth participating in serious criminal behavior or substance abuse are prime candidates for intensive family- and community-based interventions. Effective treatment models for youth engaging in criminal activity and/or substance abuse address risk factors comprehensively and build on known protective factors, use behavioral intervention techniques, have rigorous evaluation components, are well specified, use quality-assurance protocols to support program fidelity, and have devoted significant efforts to quality dissemination.

Question: How can I get regular citizens involved?

Answer: Chapters 4, 8, and 11 address community involvement. Chapter 11 discusses community grassroots development and suggests steps to starting a neighborhood or faith-based organization to address neighborhood problems. Chapter 4 describes how to bring stakeholders together and determine priorities for setting goals. Chapter 8 shows how to involve citizens through violence-free activities that are designed to capture the interest of neighborhood residents and build cohesion. Outreach strategies are needed in the beginning of a project to attract adults and children to activities.

Question: As a professional I would like to start an MST project in an inner-city troubled neighborhood. Where do I start, and what are important factors to consider?

Answer: Go to Chapter 4. Intensive groundwork is needed to gain access to a neighborhood and get to know its residents. Keep in mind that the people who live in a neighborhood know their youth and neighbors best. Outsiders must appreciate the aims of the residents, and the project should reflect these desires. Furthermore, professionals from outside the neighborhood will need advice from a neighborhood leader on how to fit in, gain trust, engage with families, and remain safe. The neighborhood residents will teach, and the project staff must always remain open to learning. Over time, conducting a successful project in a neighborhood requires becoming a part of the family of that neighborhood.

Question: How can I, as a professional, conduct competent interventions that consider the neighborhood culture if that culture is unfamiliar to me?

Answer: To learn the culture of a neighborhood, professionals must become "students" and never pretend they understand something they do not understand. One or more cultural guides can be recruited to help. Also, professionals can watch neighborhood leaders and follow their rules of etiquette. Doing so shows respect. Professionals must not dismiss input from anyone, even law violators. Furthermore, rather than assuming people are resistant to treatment, professionals need to understand that many people do not engage in counseling because of a lack of trust in the system and in the effectiveness of counseling. To combat stigmatization, sessions can be held in nontraditional ways and nontraditional places. The religious and spiritual values of a neighborhood or ethnic group must be learned and kept in mind, as these values can help in times of difficulty. Finally, for professionals who are conducting research, understanding the history of research for disenfranchised participants is essential to successful implementation. The practical purpose of the research must be clear to the residents of the neighborhood.

Question: As a professional, how can I feel comfortable with my safety in a troubled neighborhood?

Answer: Chapter 4 describes how safety was addressed in the Neighborhood Solutions Project. Mainly, safety requires the outsider to become a "known factor" and relies on the guidance of neighborhood stakeholders. Working in a "high crime" neighborhood requires special interactions with the police. A balance must be achieved between being sufficiently involved with the police to collaborate toward the good of youth, but not so involved that the youth view the professional as an informant. Overall, reasonable precautions and good common sense go a long way toward ensuring safety.

Question: How can my neighborhood build and sustain violence-free, prosocial activities?

Answer: Chapter 8 illustrates ways a neighborhood can build and implement health and wellness activities. Activities must fit the culture and interests of a neighborhood, but should also introduce youth to new opportunities. Activities can be forms of entertainment or forums for teaching skills and values. Engaging youth in neighborhood activities might require outreach efforts. Children might not try certain activities because they feel foreign or because the child has little understanding of how to participate. Therefore, the child must slowly be taught skills that will facilitate participation. Holding "weekly activity rounds" can help a community keep organized, assure that goals are being met, and provide an avenue for inviting additional help. The activities a community can implement are restricted only by the creativity and effort from the community. The best way to sustain funding for such activities is for the neighborhood to become a business and pursue dollars through grants and fund raising.

Question: I am a therapist and have some great ideas that I would like to implement in a high-crime neighborhood. How can I make people listen to me and carry out my ideas?

Answer: The approach of making people listen to your ideas will not get very far. Instead, when going into a neighborhood, maintain an open mind and a willingness to listen to what the people want. As stated in Chapter 4, canned programs are unlikely to be accepted.

Question: Many people in my neighborhood are high risk for hypertension, but most do not seek medical services because they are too hard to access. How can I bring those services to us?

Answer: As shown in Chapter 9, preventive care is essential to reducing risk and slowing the disease process in a neighborhood with a high prevalence of serious diseases such as diabetes and hypertension. Neighborhood champions are needed to develop neighborhood-based primary care and to partner with professionals who can provide the resources. When developing neighborhood-based health services, sustainability should be addressed at the outset. Similar to introducing MST services in a community, health service providers coming into a community should carry out adequate groundwork, provide services that meet the community's needs and desires, and work to develop trust.

Question: People in my neighborhood often have negative interactions with the police. Crime is pervasive, and the residents feel untrusting of the police. What can we do to change this?

Answer: Crime in even the most troubled neighborhoods can be reduced with the help of a community-policing team. As with other services, community-policing programs should also carry out the preliminary groundwork, establish trust, and consider the needs and priorities of a community. Trust is established through the ways people are treated and through the quality of the work provided by the professionals. Implementation of a community-policing program also requires buy-in from city officials, the police chief, and officers.

CONCLUSION

Any neighborhood that is concerned about its youth and has a few leaders willing to put in a lot of sweat equity can implement a neighborhood-based project such as the Neighborhood Solutions Project. This book outlined a master plan for developing and implementing such a project. The reader must keep in mind that all neighborhood-based projects will not look alike. In keeping with the MST model, a neighborhood-based project should be tailored to the strengths, needs, characteristics, and culture of a given neighborhood.

In conclusion, this book ends with the voice of the people who started this project and made it possible, the people of the Union Heights neighborhood and people who are affiliated with these residents through regular involvement.

"Having my therapist work with me has helped me cope with some of the problems I'm dealing with, and I believe that if she had not been there when she was, I would have taken my life by now. All I need is someone to talk to me, and tell me it's all right—someone I don't know. She came at the right time."

—*Le'Rone White*

"The Neighborhood Solutions Project helped me to deal with my anger and stay drug free, off the streets, and on to a job."

—*Brandon Grant*

"The Neighborhood Solutions Project has helped me a lot. It's a good program that has helped a lot of children off the Hike. The therapist helped us with compassion, like they wanted to be there, not as if they were forced. Each therapist took a special effort to help us, and I am very thankful because I know I need that extra push."

—*Bridgette Neely*

"This project has been helpful. Thanks for all the support we received through the project."

—*Parent*

"The Neighborhood Solutions Project has helped my family with our problems and has helped with problems in the community. They provided therapy for anger management, and have been there through the worst of times."

—*Eva Grant, Parent*

"The Neighborhood Solutions Project in the Union Heights community has done more than any other project for the young children that have problems with drugs, crime, and school. I am proud to be working with the people who run this program."

—*Neighborhood Leader*

"Neighborhood Solutions has been an asset to our school. We have worked with team members to facilitate students' educational and emotional needs. On many occasions, we have been able to review and use their psychological reports to initiate special education services for students. Team members have served as "shadows" for students with behavior problems, as well as following up on medication and counseling needs. All of the team members that I have met seem to genuinely care about their clients and try to help them set realistic goals. Team

members help clients 'map out' paths to reach these goals. Our association has been beneficial even though the clients have varied needs."
                                                            —Ruth Harkleroad, Teacher

"I have had two young juveniles whom I have supervised on parole involved in the Neighborhood Solutions Project in the past 2 years. I have been very favorably impressed with the support these young juveniles have received, with the array of activities they have been involved in and with the sincerity and professionalism demonstrated by their therapists."
                                                    —Charles Agee, Probation Officer

"As principal of a local elementary school and as a concerned citizen, I can say, without fear of contradiction, the Neighborhood Solutions Project has been invaluable in assisting my students and parents in helping children to stay in school and to focus on their education."
                                                        —Dr. Don Butler, Principal

"With their interest for MST fueled by Dr. Henggeler's presentation in Norway, a group of 11 Norwegian professionals and officials arrived in Charleston in January 1999. As a part of the introduction to MST they were taken to the Neighborhood Solutions Project in North Charleston to see for themselves how the treatment model might be implemented in regular practice. They were received at the Gethsemani Community Center by the local representatives of the project. The local project staff was genuinely devoted to doing something positive for the young people at risk in the community, and informed the Norwegian visitors about a number of activities organized to keep them off the streets and away from crime and drugs. The Norwegian group was taken for a walk through the neighborhood and introduced to its social and cultural characteristics.

"Afterwards additional information about the aims, contents, and experiences about the project was given at a meeting in the community house. Two MST therapists were present, and they described in practical detail their roles and how they were operating in the community. The Norwegian guests were also served a delicious meal prepared by women from the neighborhood.

"During the meeting one of the MST therapists was called on the cell phone. An 11-year-old kid in the MST program who was living with his grandmother refused to go to school. He would not even get out of bed, and his grandmother couldn't make him change his mind. The therapist promptly picked up his mother, and together they drove to the Grandma's house. While the MST therapist waited downstairs, the kid's mother got him out of bed, disregarding all protests from the young man. The MST therapist drove them both to school, and while the therapist was waiting in the car, the mother delivered the boy to his teacher and apologized for him being late to school. She also told her son that the procedure would be repeated if he refused to go to school. Then the MST therapist drove the mother back to where she had been before. The therapist then rejoined the Norwegian visitors and told us about the principles of 'on call' and parent empowerment.

"The Norwegian group was impressed by how well the project was integrated into the local community and by the hospitality of the participants. A number of informal talks and discussions were taking place during the meal. One of the visitors made an improvised and sincere thank you speech before the Norwegian group returned to the Family Services Research Center for more information about MST. Ultimately, the Charleston visit resulted in the decision of implementing MST nationwide in Norway."

—*Professor Terje Ogden, University of Oslo*

"Our community is very fortunate to have MUSC and its Family Services Research Center as an integral part of our community. Working with them to provide health care otherwise not available to a segment of our community has been a most rewarding experience for all involved, especially the youth of Union Heights and their families."

—*R. Keith Summey, Mayor, City of North Charleston*

"The Neighborhood Solutions Project that was implemented in the Union Heights neighborhood in North Charleston, South Carolina, is an incredible program. I have referenced this program over the years as a model for other communities to follow. The data speaks for itself—less crime, better school performance for children, better community–police relations, etc. This project has truly tapped into a comprehensive methodology that makes for a healthier community—a community in which people of all ages feel safe, loved, and cared for."

—*David Mack, III, South Carolina House of Representatives*

References

Adams, R. E., Rohe, W. M., & Arcury, T. A. (2002). Implementing community-oriented policing: Organizational change and street officer attitudes. *Crime and Delinquency, 48,* 399–430.

Alexander, J. F., & Parsons, B. V. (1982). *Functional Family Therapy: Principles and procedures.* Carmel, CA: Brooks & Cole.

Alexander, J. F., & Sexton, T. L. (2002). Functional Family Therapy (FFT) as an integrative, mature clinical model for treating high risk, acting out youth. In J. Lebow (Ed.), *Comprehensive handbook of psychotherapy: Vol. 4. Integrative/eclectic* (pp. 111–132). New York: John Wiley.

American Diabetes Association. (2003). Clinical practice recommendations 2003. *Diabetes Care, 26*(Suppl. 1), S1–S156.

American Public Health Association. (1998). *Community-oriented primary care: Health care for the 21st century.* Washington, DC: Author.

Amini, F., Zilberg, N. J., Burke, E. L., & Salasnek, S. (1982). A controlled study of inpatient vs. outpatient treatment of delinquent drug abusing adolescents: One year results. *Comprehensive Psychiatry, 23,* 436–444.

Anderson, E. T., & McFarlane, J. M. (1996). *Community as partner: Theory and practice in nursing.* Philadelphia: Lippincott-Raven.

Aos, S., Phipps, P., Barnoski, R., & Lieb, R. (2001). *The comparative costs and benefits of programs to reduce crime* (Document 01–05–1201). Olympia: Washington State Institute for Public Policy.

Attar, B. K., Guerra, N. G., & Tolan, P. H. (1994). Neighborhood disadvantage, stressful life events, and adjustment in urban elementary school children. *Journal of Clinical Child Psychology, 23,* 391–400.

Bell, C. (1995, January). Exposure to violence distresses children and may lead to their becoming violent. *Psychiatric News, 15,* 6–8.

Bell, C. C., & Jenkins, E. J. (1993). Community violence and children on Chicago's Southside. *Psychiatry, Interpersonal and Biological Processes, 56,* 47–54.

Borduin, C. M., Henggeler, S. W., Blaske, D. M., & Stein, R. J. (1990). Multisystemic treatment of adolescent sexual offenders. *International Journal of Offender Therapy and Comparative Criminology, 34,* 105–113.

Borduin, C. M., Mann, B. J., Cone, L. T., Henggeler, S. W., Fucci, B. R., Blaske, D. M., & Williams, R. A. (1995). Multisystemic treatment of serious juvenile offenders: Long-term prevention of criminality and violence. *Journal of Consulting and Clinical Psychology, 63,* 569–578.

Borrero, M. (2001). The widening mistrust between youth and police. *Families in Society, 82,* 399–408.

Boydstun, J. E., & Sherry, M. E. (1975). *San Diego community profile: Final report.* Washington, DC: Police Foundation.

Bronfenbrenner, U. (1979). *The ecology of human development: Experiments by design and nature.* Cambridge, MA: Harvard University Press.

Brown, L. P. (2002). Community policing: A practical guide for police officials. In S. L. Gabbidon, H. T. Greene, & V. D. Young (Eds.), *African American classics in criminology and criminal justice* (pp. 215–226). Thousand Oaks, CA: Sage.

Brown, T. L., Henggeler, S. W., Schoenwald, S. K., Brondino, M. J., & Pickrel, S. G. (1999). Multisystemic treatment of substance abusing and dependent juvenile delinquents: Effects on school attendance at posttreatment and 6–month follow-up. *Children's Services: Social Policy, Research, and Practice, 2,* 81–93.

Budney, A. J., & Higgins, S. T. (1998). *A community reinforcement plus vouchers approach: Treating cocaine addiction.* Rockville, MD: U.S. Department of Health and Human Services, National Institutes of Health, National Institute on Drug Abuse.

Buka, S. L., Stichick, T. L., Birdthistle, I., & Earls, F. J. (2000). Youth exposure to violence: Prevalence, risks, and consequences. *American Journal of Orthopsychiatry, 71,* 298–310.

Bukstein, O. G. (2000). Disruptive behavior disorders and substance use disorders in adolescents. *Journal of Psychoactive Drugs, 32,* 67–79.

Bureau of Justice Assistance. (1994). *Understanding community policing: A framework for action.* Washington, DC: Bureau of Justice Assistance Response Center.

Carroll, K. M. (1998). *A cognitive-behavioral approach: Treating cocaine addiction* (Publication No. NIH 98–4308). Washington, DC: U.S. Department of Health and Human Services, National Institutes of Health.

Carroll, K. M., & Nuro, K. F. (2002). One size cannot fit all: A stage model for psychotherapy manual development. *Clinical Psychology: Science and Practice, 9,* 396–406.

Catalano, R. F., Arthur, M. W., Hawkins, J. D., Berglund, L., & Olson, J. J. (1998). Comprehensive community- and school-based interventions to prevent antisocial behavior. In R. Loeber & D. Farrington (Eds.), *Serious and violent juvenile offenders* (pp. 248–283). Thousand Oaks, CA: Sage.

Center for Substance Abuse Prevention. (2001). *Strengthening America's families: Model family programs for substance abuse and delinquency prevention.* Salt Lake City: Department of Health Promotion and Education, University of Utah.

Center for Substance Abuse Treatment. (1999). Treatment of substance use disorders among adolescents (Treatment Improvement Protocol [TIP] Series 3, K. C. Winters, Ed.). Rockville, MD: Author.

Centers for Disease Control and Prevention. (1994). Homicide among 15–19 year old males: United States 1963–1991. *Morbidity and Mortality Weekly Report, 43,* 725–727.

Chamberlain, P. (1998). *Family Connections: A treatment foster care model for adolescents with delinquency.* Eugene, OR: Castalia.

Clark, L. (1985). *SOS! Help for parents.* Bowling Green, KY: Parents Press.

Cooley-Quille, M. R., Boyd, R. C., Frantz, E., & Walsh, J. (2001). Emotional and behavioral impact of exposure to community violence in inner-city adolescents. *Journal of Clinical Child Psychology, 30,* 199–206.

Cooley-Quille, M. R., Turner, S. M., & Beidel, D. C. (1995). The emotional impact of children's exposure to community violence: A preliminary study. *Journal of the American Academy of Child and Adolescent Psychiatry, 34,* 1362–1368.

Crimmins, S. M., Cleary, S. D., Brownstein, H. H., Spunt, B. J., & Warley, R. M. (2000). Trauma, drugs and violence among juvenile offenders. *Journal of Psychoactive Drugs, 32,* 43–54.

Cunningham, P. B., Donohue, B., Randall, J., Swenson, C. C., Rowland, M. D., Henggeler, S. W., & Schoenwald, S. K. (2003). *Integrating contingency management into multisystemic therapy.* Charleston, SC: Family Services Research Center

Cunningham, P. B., & Henggeler, S. W. (1999). Engaging multiproblem families in treatment: Lessons learned throughout the development of multisystemic therapy. *Family Process, 38,* 265–281.

Dawkins, M. P. (1997). Drug use and violent crime among adolescents. *Adolescence, 32,* 395–405.

Decker, S. H. (1981). Citizen attitudes toward the police: A review of the past findings and suggestions for future policy. *Journal of Police Science and Administration, 9,* 80–87.

Derogatis, L. R. (1993). *Brief Symptom Inventory: Administration, scoring, and procedural manual.* Minneapolis, MN: National Computer Systems.

Dicker, T. J. (1998). Tension on the thin blue line: Police officer resistance to community-oriented policing. *American Journal of Criminal Justice, 23,* 59–82.

Dishion, T. J., McCord, J., & Poulin, F. (1999). When interventions harm: Peer groups and problem behavior. *American Psychologist, 54,* 755–764.

Donohue, B., & Azrin, N. H. (2001). Family behavior therapy. In E. F. Wagner & H. B. Waldron (Eds.), *Innovations in adolescent substance abuse* (pp. 205–227). New York: Pergamon.

Earls, F., McGuire, J., & Shay, S. (1994). Evaluating a community intervention to reduce the risk of child abuse: Methodological strategies in conducting neighborhood surveys. *Child Abuse and Neglect, 18,* 473–485.

Eck, J. E., & Spelman, W. (1987). *Problem solving: Problem-oriented policing in Newport News.* Washington, DC: Police Executive Research Forum.

Elliott, D. S. (1994). *Youth violence: An overview.* Boulder: University of Colorado, Center for the Study and Prevention of Violence, Institute for Behavioral Sciences.

Elliott, D. S. (Series Ed.). (1998). *Blueprints for violence prevention* (University of Colorado, Center for the Study and Prevention of Violence). Boulder, CO: Blueprints Publications.

Elliott, D. S., Huizinga, D., & Ageton, S. S. (1985). *Explaining delinquency and drug use.* Beverly Hills, CA: Sage.

Elliott, D, Wilson, W. J., Huizinga, D., Sampson, R., Elliott, A., & Rankin, B. (1996).

The effects of neighborhood disadvantage on adolescent development. *Journal of Research in Crime and Delinquency, 33,* 389–426.

Ellis, D. A., Naar-King, S., Frey, M., Rowland, M. D., & Greger, N. (2003). Case study: Feasibility of multisystemic therapy as a treatment for urban adolescents with poorly controlled Type 1 diabetes. *Journal of Pediatric Psychology, 28,* 287–293.

Ericson, N. (May, 2001). *Substance abuse: The nation's number one health problem* (OJJDP Fact Sheet #17). Washington, DC: Office of Juvenile Justice and Delinquency Prevention.

Farnworth, L. (1999). Time use and leisure occupations of young offenders. *American Journal of Occupational Therapy, 54,* 315–325.

Farrell, A. D., & Bruce, S. E. (1997). Impact of exposure to community violence on violent behavior and emotional distress among urban adolescents. *Journal of Clinical Child Psychology, 26,* 2–14.

Farrington, D. P., & Welsh, B. C. (1999). Delinquency prevention using family-based interventions. *Children and Society, 13,* 287–303.

Feindler, E. L., Ecton, R. B., Kingsley, D., & Dubey, D. R. (1986). Group anger-control training for institutionalized psychiatric male adolescents. *Behavior Therapy, 17,* 109–123.

Fitzpatrick, K. M. (1993). Exposure to violence and presence of depression among low income, African-American youth. *Journal of Consulting and Clinical Psychology, 61,* 528–531.

Fitzpatrick, K. M., & Boldizar, J. P. (1993). The prevalence and consequences of exposure to violence among African- American youth. *Journal of the American Academy of Child and Adolescent Psychiatry, 32,* 424–430.

Flannery, D. J., Singer, M. I., & Wester, K. (2001). Violence exposure, psychological trauma, and suicide risk in a community sample of dangerously violent adolescents. *Journal of the American Academy of Child and Adolescent Psychiatry, 40,* 435–442.

Fo, W. S., & O'Donnell, C. R. (1975). The buddy system: Effect of community intervention on delinquent offenses. *Behavior Therapy, 6,* 522–524.

Foa, E. B., Rothbaum, B. O., Riggs, D. S., & Murdock, T. B. (1991). Treatment of posttraumatic stress disorder in rape victims: A comparison between cognitive-behavioral procedures and counseling. *Journal of Consulting and Clinical Psychology, 59,* 715–723.

Follette, V. M., Ruzek, J. I., & Abueg, F. R. (1998). *Cognitive-behavioral therapies for trauma.* New York: Guilford Press.

Freeman, L. N., Mokros, H., & Poznanski, E. O. (1993). Violent events reported by normal urban school-aged children: Characteristics and depression correlates. *Journal of the American Academy of Child and Adolescent Psychiatry, 32,* 419–423.

Furstenburg, F. F., Jr. (1993). How families manage risk and opportunity in dangerous neighborhoods. In W. J. Wilson (Ed.), *Sociology and the public agenda* (pp. 231–238). Newbury Park, CA: Sage.

Garbarino, J., Dubrow, N., Kostelny, K., & Pardo, C. (1992). *Children in danger: Coping with the consequences of community violence.* San Francisco: Jossey-Bass.

Garbarino, J., Kostelny, K., & Barry, F. (1998). Neighborhood-based programs. In P. K. Trickett & C. J. Schellenbach (Eds.), *Violence against children in the family and the community* (pp. 287–314). Washington, DC: American Psychological Association.

Gendreau, P. (1996). Offender rehabilitation: What we know and what needs to be done. *Criminal Justice and Behavior, 23,* 144–161.

Gladstein, J., Rusonis, E. J. S., & Heald, F. P. (1992). A comparison of inner city and upper-middle class youths' exposure to violence. *Journal of Adolescent Health, 12,* 275–280.

Goldstein, H. (1990). *Problem-oriented policing.* New York: McGraw-Hill.

Guide to Community Preventive Services. Retrieved September 9, 2003, from *http://www.thecommunityguide.org/social.*

Hahn, P. H. (1998). *Emerging criminal justice: Three pillars for a proactive justice system.* Thousand Oaks, CA: Sage.

Haley, J. (1976). *Problem solving therapy.* San Francisco: Jossey-Bass.

Halpern, R. (1995). Neighborhood-based services in low-income neighborhoods: A brief history. In P. Adams & K. Nelson (Eds.), *Reinventing human services* (pp. 19–39). New York: Aldine De Gruyter.

Hawkins, J. D., Catalano, R. F., & Miller, J. Y. (1992). Risk and protective factors for alcohol and other drug problems in adolescence and early adulthood: Implications for substance abuse prevention. *Psychological Bulletin, 112,* 64–105.

Health and Urban Development. (2003). Retrieved December 1, 2003, from *http://www.huduser.org/publications/econdev/ezecexecsum.h*tml#newtop

Health Research and Educational Trust. (2002). *Community care notebook: A practical guide to health partnerships.* Chicago: Author.

Henggeler, S. W. (1991). Multidimensional causal models of delinquent behavior. In R. Cohen & A. Siegel (Eds.), *Context and development* (pp. 211–231). Hillsdale, NJ: Erlbaum.

Henggeler, S. W., & Borduin, C. M. (1990). *Family therapy and beyond: A multisystemic approach to treating the behavior problems of children and adolescents.* Pacific Grove, CA: Brooks/Cole.

Henggeler, S. W., & Borduin, C. M. (1992). *Multisystemic Therapy Adherence Scales.* Unpublished instrument. Department of Psychiatry and Behavioral Sciences, Medical University of South Carolina.

Henggeler, S. W., Borduin, C. M., Melton, G. B., Mann, B. J., Smith, L., Hall, J. A., Cone, L., & Fucci, B. R. (1991). Effects of multisystemic therapy on drug use and abuse in serious juvenile offenders: A progress report from two outcome studies. *Family Dynamics of Addiction Quarterly, 1,* 40–51.

Henggeler, S. W., Clingempeel, W. G., Brondino, M. J., & Pickrel, S. G. (2002). Four-year follow-up of multisystemic therapy with substance abusing and dependent juvenile offenders. *Journal of the American Academy of Child and Adolescent Psychiatry, 41,* 868–874.

Henggeler, S. W., Melton, G. B., Brondino, M. J., Scherer, D. G., & Hanley, J. H. (1997). Multisystemic therapy with violent and chronic juvenile offenders and their families: The role of treatment fidelity in successful dissemination. *Journal of Consulting and Clinical Psychology, 65,* 821–833.

Henggeler, S. W., Melton, G. B., & Smith, L. A. (1992). Family preservation using multisystemic therapy: An effective alternative to incarcerating serious juvenile offenders. *Journal of Consulting and Clinical Psychology, 60,* 953–961.

Henggeler, S. W., Melton, G. B., Smith, L. A., Schoenwald, S. K., & Hanley, J. H. (1993). Family preservation using multisystemic treatment: Long-term follow-up to a clinical trial with serious juvenile offenders. *Journal of Child and Family Studies, 2,* 283–293.

Henggeler, S. W., Pickrel, S. G., & Brondino, M. J. (1999). Multisystemic treatment of substance abusing and dependent delinquents: Outcomes, treatment fidelity, and transportability. *Mental Health Services Research, 1,* 171–184.

Henggeler, S. W., Pickrel, S. G., Brondino, M. J., & Crouch, J. L. (1996). Eliminating (almost) treatment dropout of substance abusing or dependent delinquents through home-based multisystemic therapy. *American Journal of Psychiatry, 153,* 427–428.

Henggeler, S. W., Rodick, J. D., Borduin, C. M., Hanson, C. L., Watson, S. M., & Urey, J. R. (1986). Multisystemic treatment of juvenile offenders: Effects on adolescent behavior and family interaction. *Developmental Psychology, 22,* 132–141.

Henggeler, S. W., Rowland, M. D., Randall, J., Ward, D. M., Pickrel, S. G., Cunningham, P. B., Miller, S. L., Edwards, J., Zealberg, J. J., Hand, L. D., & Santos, A. B. (1999). Home-based multisystemic therapy as an alternative to the hospitalization of youths in psychiatric crisis: Clinical outcomes. *Journal of the American Academy of Child and Adolescent Psychiatry, 38,* 1331–1339.

Henggeler, S. W., & Schoenwald, S. K. (1998). *The MST supervisory manual: Promoting quality assurance at the clinical level.* Charleston, SC: MST Institute.

Henggeler, S. W., Schoenwald, S. K., Borduin, C. M., Rowland, M. D., & Cunningham, P. B. (1998). *Multisystemic treatment of antisocial behavior in children and adolescents.* New York: Guilford Press.

Henggler, S. W., Schoenwald, S. K., Rowland, M. D., & Cunningham, P. B. (2002). *Serious emotional disturbance in children and adolescents: Multisystemic therapy.* New York: Guilford Press

Henggler, S. W., & Sheidow, A. J. (2002). Conduct disorder and delinquency. In D. H. Sprenkle (Ed.), *Effectiveness research in marriage and family therapy* (pp. 27–51). Alexandria, VA: American Association for Marriage and Family Therapy.

Hill, H. M., Levermore, M., Twaite, J., & Jones, L. (1996). Exposure to community violence and social support as predictors of anxiety and social and emotional behavior among African-American children. *Journal of Child and Family Studies, 5,* 399–414.

Hollon, S. D., & Beck, A. T. (1994). Cognitive and cognitive-behavioral therapies. In A. E. Bergin, & S. L. Garfield (Eds.), *Handbook of psychotherapy and behavior change* (4th ed., pp. 428–466). New York: John Wiley and Sons.

Horowitz, K., Weine, S., & Jekel, J. (1995). PTSD symptoms in urban adolescent girls: Compounded community trauma. *Journal of the American Academy of Child and Adolescent Psychiatry, 34,* 1353–1361.

Howard, D. E. (1996). Searching for resilience among African-American youth exposed to community violence: Theoretical issues. *Journal of Adolescent Health, 18,* 254–262.

Howell, J. C. (2003). *Preventing and reducing juvenile delinquency: A comprehensive framework.* Thousand Oaks, CA: Sage.

Huey, S. J., Henggeler, S. W., Brondino, M. J., & Pickrel, S. G. (2000). Mechanisms of change in multisystemic therapy: Reducing delinquent behavior through therapist adherence and improved family and peer functioning. *Journal of Consulting and Clinical Psychology, 68,* 451–467.

Hummel, J. (2002). *Starting and running a nonprofit organization.* Minneapolis: University of Minnesota Press.

Hutton, S., & Phillips, F. (2001). *Nonprofit kit for dummies.* New York: Hungry Minds.

Institute of Medicine (1990). *Treating drug problems: Vol. 1. A study of the evolution, effectiveness, and financing of public and private drug treatment systems.* Washington, DC: National Academy Press.

Institute of Medicine, Committee on Communication for Behavior Change in the 21st Century: Improving the Health of Diverse Populations. (2002). *Speaking of health: Assessing health communication strategies for diverse populations.* Washington, DC: National Academies Press.

James, S. A., & Kleinbaum, D. G. (1976). Socioecological stress and hypertension-related mortality rates in North Carolina. *Journal of Public Health, 66,* 354–358.

Jarrett, R. L. (1997). Bringing families back in: Neighborhoods' effects on child development. In J. Brooks-Gunn, G. J. Duncan, & J. L. Aber (Eds.), *Neighborhood poverty: Vol. 2. Policy implications in studying neighborhoods* (pp. 48–64). New York: Russell Sage Foundation.

Jenkins, E. J., & Bell, C. C. (1994). Violence among inner city high school students and post-traumatic stress disorder. In S. Friedman (Ed.), *Anxiety disorders in African Americans* (pp. 76–88). New York: Springer.

Jenkins, P., Seydlitz, R., Osofsky, J. D., & Fick, A. C. (1997). Cops and kids: Issues for community policing. In J. D. Osofsky (Ed.), *Children in a violent society* (pp. 300–322). New York: Guilford Press.

Johnson, S. B. (1995). Insulin-dependent diabetes mellitus in childhood. In M. C. Roberts (Ed.), *Handbook of pediatric psychology* (2nd ed., pp. 263–285). New York: Guilford Press.

Jones, M. B., & Offord, D. R. (1989). Reduction of antisocial behavior in poor children by nonschool skill development. *Journal of Child Psychology and Psychiatry and Allied Disciplines, 30,* 737–750.

Joshi, P. T., & Kaschak, D. G. (1998). Exposure to violence and trauma: Questionnaire for adolescents. *International Review of Psychiatry, 10,* 208–215.

Kazdin, A. E. (1987). Treatment of antisocial behavior in children: Current status and future directions. *Psychological Bulletin, 102,* 187–203.

Kazdin, A. E., & Weisz, J. R. (1998). Identifying and developing empirically supported child and adolescent treatments. *Journal of Consulting and Clinical Psychology, 66*(1), 19–36.

Kelling, G. L. (1981). Conclusions. *The Newark foot patrol experiment.* Washington, DC: Police Foundation.

Kelling, G. L. (1988). Police and communities: The quiet revolution. *Perspectives on Policing, 1,* 1–8.

Kelling, G. L., & Moore, M. H. (1988). The evolving strategy of policing. *Perspectives on Policing, 4,* 1–16.

Kelling, G. L., Pate, A., Dieckman, D., & Brown, C. E. (1974). *The Kansas City preventive patrol experiment: A technical report.* Washington, DC: Police Foundation.

Kilpatrick, D. G., Acierno, R., Saunders, B., Resnick, H., Best, C., & Schnurr, P. P. (2000). Risk factors for adolescent substance abuse and dependence: Data from a national sample. *Journal of Consulting and Clinical Psychology, 68,* 19–30.

Kolbe, L. J., Kann, L., & Collins, J. L. (1993). Overview of the Youth Risk Behavior Surveillance System. *Public Health Report, 108*(suppl. 1), 2–10.

Kolko, D. J., & Swenson, C. C. (2002). *Assessing and treating physically abused children and their families: A cognitive behavioral approach.* Thousand Oaks, CA: Sage.

Kovaks, M. (1981). Rating scales to assess depression in school aged children. *Acta Paedopsychiatrica, 46,* 305–315.

Kretzmann, J. P., & McKnight, J. L. (1993). *Building communities from the inside out: A path toward finding and mobilizing a community's assets.* Chicago: ACTA.

Leahy, R. L., & Holland, S. J. (2000). *Treatment plans and interventions for depression and anxiety disorders.* New York: Guilford Press.

Lemanek, K. L., Kamps, J., & Chung, N. B. (2001). Empirically supported treatments in pediatric psychology: Regimen adherence. *Journal of Pediatric Psychology, 26,* 253–275.

Leventhal, T., & Brooks-Gunn, J. (2000). The neighborhoods they live in: The effects of neighborhood residence on child and adolescent outcomes. *Psychological Bulletin, 126,* 309–337.

Lewinsohn, P. M., & Gotlib, I. H. (1995). Behavioral theory and treatment of depression. In E. E. Beckham, & W. R. Leber (Eds.), *Handbook of depression* (2nd ed., pp. 352–375). New York: Guilford Press.

Liddle, H. A. (1999). *Multidimensional family therapy treatment manual.* Miami, FL: University of Miami School of Medicine.

Liddle, H. A., & Dakof, G. A. (1995). Efficacy of family therapy for drug abuse: Promising but not definitive. *Journal of Marital and Family Therapy, 21,* 511–543.

Liddle, H. A., Dakof, G. A., Parker, K., Diamond, G. S., Barrett, K., & Tejeda, M. (2001). Multidimensional family therapy for adolescent drug abuse: Results of a randomized clinical trial. *American Journal on Drug and Alcohol Abuse, 27,* 651–687.

Lochman, J. E., Burch, P. R., Curry, J. F., & Lampron, L. B. (1984). Treatment and generalization effects of cognitive-behavioral and goal setting interventions with aggressive boys. *Journal of Consulting and Clinical Psychology, 52,* 915–916.

Loeber, R., & Farrington, D. P. (Eds.). (1998). *Serious and violent juvenile offenders: Risk factors and successful interventions.* Thousand Oaks, CA: Sage.

Lovell, R., & Pope, C. E. (1993). Recreational interventions. In *The gang intervention handbook* (pp. 319–332). Champaign, IL: Research Press.

Lurigio, A. J., & Rosenbaum, D. P. (1994). The impact of community policing on police personnel. In D. P. Rosenbaum (Ed.), *The challenge of community policing: Testing the promises* (pp. 147–163). Thousand Oaks, CA: Sage.

Lurigio, A. J., & Skogan, W. G. (1994). Winning the hearts and minds of police officers: An assessment of staff perceptions of community policing in Chicago. *Crime and Delinquency, 40,* 315–330.

Maher, L., & Curtis, R. (1995). In search of the female urban "gangsta": Change culture, and crack cocaine. In B. R. Price & N. J. Sokoloff (Eds.), *The criminal justice system and women: Offenders, victims, and workers* (2nd ed., pp. 147–166). New York: McGraw-Hill.

McBride, D. C., VanderWaal, C. J., Terry, Y. M., & VanBuren, H. (1999). *Breaking the cycle of drug use among juvenile offenders* (Publication No. NCJ 179273). Washington, DC: National Institute of Justice.

McElroy, J., Cosgrove, C., & Sadd, S. (1993). *Community policing: CPOP in New York.* Newbury Park, CA: Sage.

McGoldrick, M., & Gerson, R., (1985). *Genograms in family assessment.* New York: Norton.

McMahon, R. J., & Wells, K. C. (1989). Conduct disorders. In E. J. Mash & R. A. Barkley (Eds.), *Treatment of childhood disorders* (pp. 73–132). New York: Guilford Press.

Meadows, E. A., & Foa, E. B. (1998). Intrusion, arousal, and avoidance: Sexual trauma survivors. In V. M. Follette, J. I. Ruzek, & F. R. Abueg (Eds.), *Cognitive-behavioral therapies for trauma* (pp. 100–123). New York: Guilford Press.

Meichenbaum, D. (1994). *A clinical handbook/practical* therapist manual for assessing and treating adults with post-traumatic stress disorder (PTSD). Waterloo, Ont.: Institute Press.

Meredith, C., & Paquette, C. (1992). Crime prevention in high-rise rental apartments: Findings of a demonstration project. *Security Journal, 3,* 161–169.

Minuchin, S. (1974). *Families and family therapy.* Cambridge, MA: Harvard University Press.

Munger, R. L. (1993). *Changing children's behavior quickly.* Lanham, MD: Madison Books.

National Institute on Drug Abuse. (1999). *Principles of drug addiction treatment: A research-based guide* (NIH Publication No. 99-4180). Bethesda, MD: Author.

Newcomb, M. D., & Bentler, P. M. (1988). *Consequences of adolescent drug use: Impact on the lives of young adults.* Newbury Park, CA: Sage.

O'Donnell, L., Stueve, A., San Doval, A., Duran, R., Atnafou, R., Haber, D., Johnson, N., Murray, H., Grant, U., Juhn, G., Tang, J., Bass, J., & Piessens, P. (1999). Violence prevention and youth adolescents' participation in community youth service. *Journal of Adolescent Health, 24,* 28–37.

Office of Technology Assessment, U.S. Congress. (1991). *Adolescent health: Volume 2. Background and the effectiveness of selected prevention and treatment services* (Publication No. OTA-H-466, pp. 499–578). Washington, DC: U.S. Government Printing Office.

Ogden, T., & Halliday-Boykins, C. A. (2004). Multisystemic treatment of antisocial adolescents in Norway: Replication of clinical outcomes outside of the U.S. *Child and Adolescent Mental Health, 9,* 76–82.

Ollendick, T. H., & Cerny, J. A. (1981). *Clinical behavior therapy with children.* New York: Plenum.

Olson, D. (1986). Circumplex Model VII: Validation studies and FACES III. *Family Process, 25,* 337–351.

O'Neil, E. H., & the Pew Health Professions Commission. (1998). *Recreating health professional practice for a new century.* San Francisco: Pew Health Professions Commission.

Osofsky, J. D., & Thompson, D. (2000). Adaptive and maladaptive parenting: Perspectives on risk and protective factors. In J. P. Shonkoff & S. J. Meisels (Eds.), *Handbook of early childhood intervention* (2nd ed., pp. 54–75). Cambridge, UK: Cambridge University Press.

Osofsky, J., Wewers, S., Hann, D. M., & Fick, A. C. (1993). Chronic community violence: What is happening to our children? *Psychiatry, Interpersonal and Biological Processes, 56,* 36–45.

Overstreet, S., & Braun, S. (2000). Exposure to community violence and posttraumatic stress symptoms: Mediating factors. *American Journal of Orthopsychiatry, 70,* 263–271.

Palinkas, L. A., Atkins, C. J., Miller, C., & Ferreira, D. (1996). Social skills training for drug prevention in high-risk female adolescents. *Preventive Medicine, 25,* 692–701.

Passmore, A. (1998). *The relationship between leisure and mental health in adolescence.* Unpublished doctoral dissertation, University of Western Australia, Perth.

Patterson, G. R. (1976). *Living with children: New methods for parents and teachers.* Champaign, IL: Research Press.

Phoenix, City of. (2001). *Neighborhood association tool kit: A guide for neighborhood associations.* Phoenix, AZ: Author.

Poulin, F., Dishion, T. J., & Burraston, B. (2001). Three-year iatrogenic effects associated with aggregating high-risk adolescents in cognitive-behavioral preventive interventions. *Applied Developmental Science, 5,* 214–224.

Pynoos, R. S., Frederick, C., Nader, K., Arroyo, E., Steinberg, A., Eth, S., Nuez, F., & Fairbanks, L. (1987). Life threat and posttraumatic stress disorder in school-age children. *Archives of General Psychiatry, 44,* 1057–1063.

Pynoos, R. S., & Nader, K. (1988). Psychological first aid and treatment approach to children exposed to community violence: Research implications. *Journal of Traumatic Stress, 1,* 445–473.

Quatmann, V. (2002). *You can do it: A volunteer's guide to raising money for your group in words and pictures.* Maryville, TN: Southern Empowerment Project.

Randall, J., Halliday-Boykins, C. A., Cunningham, P. B., & Henggeler, S. W. (2001). Integrating evidence-based substance abuse treatment into juvenile drug courts: Implications for outcomes. *National Drug Court Institute Review, 3,* 89–115.

Randall, J., Henggeler, S. W., Cunningham, P. B., Rowland, M. D., & Swenson, C. C. (2001). Adapting multisystemic therapy to treat adolescent substance abuse more effectively. *Cognitive and Behavioral Practice, 8,* 359–366.

Resick, P. A., & Schnicke, M. K. (1992). Cognitive processing therapy for sexual assault victims. *Journal of Consulting and Clinical Psychology, 60,* 748–756.

Resick, P. A., & Schnicke, M. K. (1993). *Cognitive processing therapy for rape victims.* Newbury Park, CA: Sage.

Rice, D. P., Kelman, S., Miller, L. S., & Dunmeyer, S. (1990). *The economic costs of alcohol and drug abuse and mental illness: 1985* (DHHS Pub. No. [ADM] 90–1694). Rockville, MD: National Institute on Drug Abuse.

Richters, J. E., & Martinez, P. (1993). The NIMH Community Violence Project I: Children as victims and witnesses to violence. *Psychiatry, Interpersonal and Biological Processes, 56,* 7–21.

Robin, A. L., Bedway, M., & Gilroy, M. (1994). Problem solving communication training. In C. W. LeCroy (Ed.), *Handbook of child and adolescent treatment manuals* (pp. 92–125). New York: Lexington Books.

Rodick, J. D., & Henggeler, S. W. (1980). The short-term and long-term amelioration of academic and motivational deficiencies among low-achieving inner-city adolescents. *Child Development, 51,* 1126–1132.

Rosenbaum, D. P., & Lurigio, A. J. (1994). An inside look at community policing reform: Definitions, organizational changes, and evaluation findings. *Crime and Delinquency, 40,* 299–314.

Rothman, D. J. (1982). Were Tuskegee and Willowbrook "studies in nature"? *Hastings Center Report, 40,* 5–7.

Rovet, J., & Fernandes, C. (1999). Insulin-dependent diabetes mellitus. In R. T. Brown (Ed.), *Cognitive aspects of chronic illness in children* (pp. 142–171). New York: Guilford Press.

Sampson, R. J., Raudenbush, S. W., & Earls, F. (1997). Neighborhoods and violent crime: A multilevel study of collective efficacy. *Science, 277,* 918–924.

Santisteban, D. A., Coatsworth, J. D., Perez-Vidal, A., Kurtines, W. M., Schwartz, S. J., LaPerriere, A., & Szapocznik, J. (2003). Efficacy of brief strategic family therapy in modifying Hispanic adolescent behavior problems and substance use. *Journal of Family Psychology, 17,* 121–133.

Scarpa, A. (2001). Community violence exposure in a young adult sample. *Journal of Interpersonal Violence, 16,* 36–53.

Schinke, S., Brounstein, P., & Gardner, S. (2002). *Science-based prevention programs and principles* (DHHS Pub. No. [SMA] 03-3764). Rockville, MD: Center for Substance Abuse Prevention, Substance Abuse and Mental Health Services Administration.

Schoenwald, S. K. (1998). *Multisystemic therapy consultation guidelines.* Charleston, SC: MST Institute.

Schoenwald, S. K., Henggeler, S. W., Brondino, M. J., & Rowland, M. D. (2000). Multisystemic therapy: Monitoring treatment fidelity. *Family Process, 39,* 83–103.

Schoenwald, S. K., Henggeler, S. W., & Edwards, D. (1998). *MST Supervisor Adherence Measure.* Charleston, SC: MST Institute.

Schoenwald, S. K., Sheidow, A. J., Letourneau, E. J., & Liao, J. G. (2003). Transportability of multisystemic therapy: Evidence for multilevel influences. *Mental Health Services Research, 5,* 223–239.

Schoenwald, S. K., Ward, D. M., Henggeler, S. W., Pickrel, S. G., & Patel, H. (1996). MST treatment of substance abusing or dependent adolescent offenders: Costs of reducing incarceration, inpatient, and residential placement. *Journal of Child and Family Studies, 5,* 431–444.

Schwab-Stone, M. E., Ayers, T. S., Kasprow, W., Voyce, C., Barone, C., Shriver, T., & Weissberg, R. P. (1995). No safe haven: A study of violence exposure in an urban community. *Journal of the American Academy of Child and Adolescent Psychiatry, 34,* 1343–1352.

Schwartz, D., & Proctor, L. J. (2000). Community violence exposure and children's social adjustment in the school peer group: The mediating roles of emotional regulation and social cognition. *Journal of Consulting and Clinical Psychology, 68,* 670–683.

Scott, G. (2003). *Receiving grants.* Jacksonville, FL: Connecting the Dots.

Selner-O'Hagan, M. B., Kindlon, D. J., Buka, S. L., Raudenbush, S. W., & Earls, F. J. (1998). Assessing exposure to violence in urban youth. *Journal of Child Psychology and Psychiatry and Allied Disciplines, 39,* 215–224.

Shahinfar, A., Fox, N. A., & Leavitt, L. A. (2000). Preschool children's exposure to violence: Relation of behavior problems to parent and child reports. *American Journal of Orthopsychiatry, 70,* 115–125.

Shakoor, B. H., & Chalmers, D. (1991). Co-victimization of African-American children who witness violence: Effects on cognitive, emotional, and behavioral development. *Journal of the National Medical Association, 83,* 233–238.

Sherman, L. (1992). Attacking crime: Police and crime control. *Crime and justice: A review of research* (pp. 159–230). Chicago: University of Chicago.

Sherman, L., & Weisburd, D. (1995). General deterrent effects of police patrol in crime "hot spots": A randomized controlled trial. *Justice Quarterly, 12,* 625–648.

Simcha-Fagan, O., & Schwartz, J. E. (1986). Neighborhood and delinquency: An assessment of contextual effects. *Criminology, 24,* 667–703.

Singer, M. I., Anglin, T. M., Song, L. Y., & Lunghofer, L. (1995). Adolescents' exposure to violence and associated symptoms of psychological trauma. *Journal of the American Medical Association, 273,* 477–482.

Smith, P. E., & Hawkins, R. O. (1973). Victimization, types of citizen–police contacts and attitudes toward the police. *Law and Society Review, 8,* 135–152.

Snyder, H. N., & Sickmund, M. (1999). *Juvenile offenders and victims: 1999 national report* (Publication No. NCJ 178257). Pittsburgh, PA: U.S. Department of Justice, Office of Justice Programs, Office of Juvenile Justice and Delinquency Prevention, National Center for Juvenile Justice.

Song, L., Singer, M. I., & Anglin, T. M. (1998). Violence exposure and emotional trauma as contributors to adolescent's violent behaviors. *Archives of Pediatric and Adolescent Medicine, 152,* 531–536.

Springer, C., & Padgett, D. K. (2000). Gender differences in young adolescents' exposure to violence and rates of PTSD symptomatology. *American Journal of Orthopsychiatry, 70,* 370–379.

Stanton, M. D., & Shadish, W. R. (1997). Outcome, attrition, and family-couples treatment for drug abuse: A meta-analysis and review of the controlled, comparative studies. *Psychological Bulletin, 122,* 170–191.

Stark, M. J. (1992). Dropping out of substance abuse treatment: A clinically oriented review. *Clinical Psychology Review, 12,* 93–116.

Swenson, C. C., & Brown, E. J. (2000). Cognitive-behavioral group treatment for physically-abused children. *Cognitive and Behavioral Practice, 6,* 212–220.

Szapocznik, J., & Williams, R. A. (2000). Brief strategic family therapy: Twenty-five years of interplay among theory, research and practice in adolescent behavior problems and drug abuse. *Clinical Child and Family Psychology Review, 3,* 117–134.

Taylor, I. S., & Swenson, C. C. (2001). *H-Town youth co-op: Preparing H-Town today for the world tomorrow.* Unpublished membership manual, North Charleston, South Carolina.

Teplin, L. A., Abram, K. M., McClelland, G. M., Dulcan, M. K., & Mericle, A. A. (2002). Psychiatric disorders in youth in juvenile detention. *Archives of General Psychiatry, 59,* 1133–1143.

Thompson, G. J., & Jenkins, J. B. (1994). *Verbal judo.* New York: Quill.

Thornberry, T. P., Huizinga, D., & Loeber, R. (1995). The prevention of serious delinquency and violence: Implications from the program of research on the causes and correlates of delinquency. In J. C. Howell, B. Krisberg, J. D. Hawkins, & J. J. Wilson (Eds.), *A sourcebook: Serious, violent, and chronic juvenile offenders* (pp. 213–237). Newbury Park, CA: Sage.

Thurman, Q. C., Giacomazzi, A., & Bogen, P. (1993). Research note: Cops, kids, and community policing—an assessment of a community policing demonstration project. *Crime and Delinquency, 39,* 554–564.

U.S. Department of Health and Human Services. (2000, November). *Healthy people 2010: Understanding and improving health* (2nd ed.). Washington, DC: U.S. Government Printing Office.

U.S. Preventive Services Task Force (1996). *Guide to clinical preventive services, 2nd ed.* Baltimore: Williams & Wilkins.

U.S. Public Health Service. (1999). *Mental health: A report of the Surgeon General.* Rockville, MD: U.S. Department of Health and Human Services, National Institutes of Health, National Institute of Mental Health.

U.S. Public Health Service. (2001). *Youth violence: A report of the Surgeon General.* Washington, DC: Author.

Waldron, H. B. (1997). Adolescent substance abuse and family therapy outcome: A review of randomized trials. In T. H. Ollendick & R. J. Prinz (Eds.), *Advances in Clinical Child Psychology, 19,* 199–234.

Waldron, H. B., Slesnick, N., Brody, J. L., Turner, C. W., & Peterson, T. R. (2001). Treatment outcomes for adolescent substance abuse at 4– and 7–month assessments. *Journal of Consulting and Clinical Psychology, 69,* 802–813.

Weinberg, N. Z., Rahdert, E., Colliver, J. D., & Glantz, M. D. (1998). Adolescent substance abuse: A review of the past 10 years. *Journal of the American Academy of Child and Adolescent Psychiatry, 37,* 252–261.

Wilkinson, G. S. (1993). *The Wide Range Achievement Test III.* Austin, TX: PRO-ED.

Williams, J. S. (2003). Grouping high-risk youths for prevention may harm more than help. *NIDA Notes, 17*(5), 1, 6.

Williams, R. J., & Chang, S. Y. (2000). A comprehensive and comparative review of adolescent substance abuse treatment outcome. *Clinical Psychology: Science and Practice, 7,* 138–166.

Wilson, D. K., Kliewer, W., Plybon, L., Zacharias, J., Teasley, N., & Sica, D. A. (1998). Violence exposure and ambulatory blood pressure in African-American adolescents. *International Journal of Rehabilitation and Health, 4,* 223–232.

Wilson, J. Q., & Kelling, G. (1982). Broken windows. *The Atlantic Monthly, 249,* 29–38.

Winters, K. C., & Henly, G. A. (1989). *Personal Experience Inventory: Professional manual.* Los Angeles, CA: Western Psychological Services.

Winters, K. C., Latimer, W. W., & Stinchfield, R. (2001). Assessing adolescent substance use. In E. F. Wagner & H. B. Waldron (Eds.), *Innovations in adolescent substance abuse interventions* (pp. 1–29). New York: Pergamon.

Wisby, G. (1995, January 6). Cops fail youth "respect" test. *Chicago Sun Times*, p. 3.

Woodbury, R. (1972). Delinquent attitudes toward the juvenile justice system. *Psychological Reports, 32*, 1119–1124.

World Health Organization. (1978). *Primary health care: Report of the International Conference on Primary Health Care, Alma Ata* (Health for All Series, p. 1). Geneva, Switzerland: Author.

World Health Organization. (1995). *World health statistics annual, 1994*. Geneva, Switzerland: Author.

Wycoff, M. A. (1988). The benefits of community policing: Evidence and conjecture. In J. R. Greene & S. D. Mastrofski (Eds.), *Community policing: Rhetoric or reality* (pp. 103–120). New York: Praeger.

Zeanah, C. Z., & Scheeringa, M. (1996). Evaluation of posttraumatic symptomatology in infants and young children exposed to violence. *Zero to three, 16*, 9–14.

Index